THE BIG
SMALL CHURCH BOOK

THE BIG
SMALL CHURCH BOOK

David R. Ray

The Pilgrim Press
Cleveland, Ohio

The Pilgrim Press, Cleveland, Ohio 44115
© 1992 by The Pilgrim Press

Printed in the United States of America
The paper used in this publication is acid free and meets the minimum requirements of American National Standard for Information Sciences-Permanence of Paper for Printed Library Materials, ANSI Z39.48-1984

02   01   00   99   98   97   7   6   5   4   3

Library of Congress Cataloging-in-Publication Data

Ray, David R., 1942–
    The big small church book / David R. Ray.
      p.   cm.
    Includes bibliographical references and index.
    ISBN 0-8298-0936-8 (alk. paper)
    1. Small churches.   I. Title.
BV637.8.R387   1992
254—dc20
                                          92-30774
                                          CIP

Contents

Preface

"Not by might, nor by power, but by my spirit," says the Lord of hosts. . . . For whoever has despised the day of small things shall rejoice."

—Zechariah 4:6, 10

From the first century through the twentieth century, most churches have been small. Sixty percent of the churches in America have fewer than seventy-five people in Sunday worship. Many more think and act like small churches. Small churches are the norm, primarily because many, many people still find them to be the right size in which to love God and their neighbor. I expect they will continue to be the norm.

This book is for the pastors and lay people of these churches, for the students who are preparing for ministry with them, and for the denominational and seminary leaders who work with these churches and students. Rather than dealing with one aspect of small church life, this comprehensive book covers all aspects of small churches. It offers a theological and biblical foundation to undergird small churches, a theoretical understanding to interpret why they are as they are, and several chapters to guide the reader in helping them be as faithful and effective as possible.

I've been in the crucible of small church ministry for twenty years, serving three very different small churches, while studying, writing, teaching, speaking, and consulting about small church matters. Now, while serving a small church in Emmetsburg, Iowa, I'm also working with fifty-two mostly small and rural churches as a United Church of Christ area conference minister in northwest Iowa. I know from experience that both sin and grace, problems and possibilities, abound in small churches. I know from experience that although many of these churches are barely surviving, many others are striving to be faithful, and many are, indeed, thriving. This is a book of possibilities for all small churches, whether they are simply surviving, striving, or thriving.

I have two fundamental convictions about small churches. First, they are the *right size* to be all that God calls a church to be. They are not premature, illegitimate, malnourished, or incomplete versions of "real" churches. Second, they are a *different* breed of church. A small church is as different from a large church as a Pekingese is from a Saint Bernard. They look, feel, think, and act differently. Differences in size yield crucial differences in form and function. Ministry not in tune with and tailored to these differences in size is doomed to failure.

In 1980–81, after nine remarkable years as part-time pastor of the Trinitarian Congregational Church of Warwick, Massachusetts, I wrote *Small Churches Are the Right Size,* expressing my understanding of and belief in small churches. The book was well received and resulted in many opportunities to learn from and speak with pastors, lay people, seminarians, and church leaders from several denominations around the country. After fourteen years in Warwick, I was called as full-time pastor of the Shrewsbury Community Church in Shrewsbury, Vermont. The personality, style, and expectations of the Shrewsbury church and community were very different from those in Warwick. In both settings, the church was the only active church in a steadily growing rural community.

Then in 1989, the Iowa Conference of the United Church of Christ and the United Church of Christ of Emmetsburg, Iowa, called me as a half-time area conference minister and half-time pastor. Rather than being pastor of the only church in a growing community, I was now in a declining community of four thousand people with a strong Irish Catholic presence, two strong Lutheran churches, a big Methodist church, two conservative churches, a small Episcopal church, and the struggling

UCC church. I'm a different person than I was when I wrote the first book—both wiser and humbler.

The small church situation has changed in the last ten years. There are more of them. As costs have gone up, more churches are less able to pay a full-time salary and support a building. As farms have failed in the Midwest and East and people—especially younger people—have migrated to urban and Sun Belt areas, many stable and vital churches have become smaller and their membership older. With the decline of mainline denominations, many churches, now small, have been left on the sidelines. With the coming of refugees from Latin America, Asia, and elsewhere, there are many new, small, ethnic churches.

Many small churches have closed, merged, federated, yoked, or gone to part-time ministries in an effort to deal with economic realities. More is now known about small churches because people like Carl Dudley, Doug Walrath, Lyle Schaller, Steve Burt, Tony Pappas, and others have contributed both theory and methodology. Theological education and denominations have sought to be more relevant and helpful to small churches.

In addition, the world has changed. It's more urban, and rural areas exercise less influence. It's more cosmopolitan, and small church kinds of people often feel left out. It's more high tech and expensive, leaving many people and churches less able to cope and compete. The world is more dangerous as doom-portending issues like various environmental crises, health-care issues, a changing world order, and a teetering world economy compete for space on the evening news, causing most of us to experience some level of impotence and irrelevance.

Because I, small churches, and the world are different, this book is NOT a warmed-over rehash of *Small Churches Are the Right Size*. Informed by what I've learned from others and my own experience over the last decade, I have written three totally new chapters. One is a "small theology," a theological and biblical understanding of small churches and their place in the realm of God. Even a small boat needs a rudder, and without that theological, biblical rudder, many smaller churches have been lost at sea or foundered on the rocks. Second, although this book is relevant for both urban and rural churches, more of my experience is rural and more small churches are rural, so there is a chapter on the rural setting. Third, small churches are not going to save themselves. They are dependent on seminaries to prepare pastoral leadership for them and on denominations to help connect, enable, and equip them. So there is a chapter on how these helpers can be more helpful.

Chapters 3 through 10 bear some resemblance to chapters in *Small Churches Are the Right Size*, but each is significantly different. Chapter 3, which offers wide-ranging theory about small churches, is deeper and broader and reflects what I and others have learned in the last decade. Chapter 4, rather than just describing my ministry in one small church, compares and contrasts my three different ministries in three different places.

The next five chapters discuss the five basic areas of church life—worship, Christian education, caring for one another, mission in the outside world, and the maintenance tasks of the church. The emphasis in each chapter is on how each task needs to be done in size-appropriate ways, ways different from how they are done in larger churches. Each chapter is grounded in theology and theory and offers an abundance of experience, ideas, and resources. Chapter 10 explores the unique nature of small church ministry.

This book can be used as an introduction to the big world of small churches, a textbook, a discussion guide, a planning tool, and a treasure chest of illustrations and ideas. It deals with prevalent problems but stresses possibilities. It offers and illustrates basic principles that enable small churches to be more effective and faithful. From beginning to end, I hope readers will be able to relate to the affection and respect I have for small churches and those who labor in these small vineyards.

I could not have written this book by myself. It has been a cooperative effort of many people, but only some knew they were helping. Not only has my wife, Lucinda, urged me to keep writing, but as a professional editor she was very helpful in editing the first draft. She has the gift of knowing when and how to affirm, suggest, and correct. And special thanks to my special adolescents, Noelle and Aaron, who both shared me with this project and who keep me humble and love me just the same.

The Emmetsburg church had the wisdom to hire Jeanie Murphy as church secretary before they called me as pastor. She is most helpful in picking up the details that slip past me, and her proofreading of the manuscript and her suggestions from the point of view of the intelligent layperson were integral to the process of this book.

I am profoundly thankful to the people of the Trinitarian Congregational Church of Warwick, Massachusetts; the Shrewsbury Community Church of Shrewsbury, Vermont; and the United Church of Christ Congregational church of Emmetsburg, Iowa, for teaching me so much about small churches. Without them, I would have had little to say. I pray they were helped by what I learned in their midst. And thanks to all those students, laypeople, and pastors who have questioned and affirmed what I've written and said in the past. It is for them and those like them that this book is written.

1. ◆ *Introduction*

A lack of understanding and appreciation for things small is at the root of the problems of small churches. Overlooking the incredible information-carrying capacity of the tiny computer chip, the herculean powers of the little ant, the incredible potential for good or bad found in the atom, our culture is enamored and obsessed with bigness. The biggest pumpkin, hamburger, skyscraper, fish, Gross National Product, sex organs, salary, muscle, and church are the measure of excellence.

Our language illustrates the "sizism" prevalent among us. In a thesaurus you will find that typical synonyms for *big* are: great, grand, considerable, substantial, generous, ample, comprehensive, imposing, tremendous, stupendous, mighty, heroic, and full-grown. Typical synonyms for *small* are: runt, shrimp, peewee, small fry, poky, piddling, dinky, one-horse, pint-sized, undersized, limited, narrow-minded, meager, unimportant, niggardly, petty, and puny. Our language reveals our values.

In the world of the church, the pastors with the most members, the biggest buildings, the largest salaries, and the fastest-growing Sunday schools are the ones who brag the loudest. The churches with the most mission giving, the fastest church growth, and the largest budgets get the

1

recognition. In both culture and church, bigness is synonymous with best and quantity with quality.

As a result, it is tough for small churches to compete or hold their heads high in a size-obsessed world. It is hard for them to hang on and hang in when they're not the size and stature that others respect and honor. It is difficult to expend energy seeking to live, when others see you as expendable.

On Monday, 1 January 1990, the *Des Moines Register* (Iowa) reported on the "Last Day in the Life of a 132-Year-Old Albia Church." The United Presbyterian Church of Albia closed its doors after 132 years. Its membership had declined in numbers and climbed in age. With only 35 members and a Sunday attendance of about ten, the congregation held its last service 31 December 1989.

Sixty-six-year-old Virginia Overturf said after the service: "I have mixed emotions. I hate to see the church closed, but we couldn't go on the way it was." Tearful Mildred Schroeder lamented, "I've been a member 30 years, and our six children grew up in this church. It just seemed like the older members passed away and no younger ones came in." Marvin Kness summed up the church members' feelings: "We tried everything we knew to help the church grow, but nothing seemed to work. The changing times just caught up with us."[1]

There are thousands of churches like the Albia church, churches that aren't considered viable according to current standards. Thousands of churches have been and will be closed. Churches short on "bodies or bucks" have been considered expendable. But I'm not convinced that church euthanasia or existence dependent upon denominational life-support systems are the only choices for churches like the Albia church. Could one of its own people have been trained as a lay pastor so that its ministry could continue? Could it have joined in a shared ministry with a neighboring church? I have pastored two churches that considered closing. Both were restored to vibrant and vital life.

All too often, the plug has been pulled on churches that failed the tests of economic viability and administrative efficiency. Those by themselves are not the valid tests of church viability. The proper test has three questions—a theological question, a spiritual question, and a practical question. The theological question is, What is the will of God and does the church still have or could it have a genuine ministry? The spiritual question is, Does the church, or significant parts of it, have the will to live? The practical question, if the first two questions are answered in the affirmative, is, How can we find a way for the church to live? If those three questions had been lovingly, faithfully, and creatively explored, many churches that are now only a brief notation in a historian's book would still be doing redemptive ministry. If we don't ask the right questions, we pursue the wrong answers.

In addition to those struggling churches that still have a vital ministry, there are others who could have such a ministry someday. Many churches in Iowa and other places cling to life by the slenderest of threads simply because the population around them moved to greener pastures and brighter lights. But 1989 was the first year in several decades that more people moved to Iowa than left it. In an era of spiraling costs, rampant crime and drug abuse, gridlocked traffic, and schools out of control, places like Iowa, which are inexpensive to live in and offer room to breathe and air worth breathing, are attracting many immigrants. In the era of computers, sophisticated communication systems, and rapid transportation, increasing numbers of people no longer have to live where they work. Many people are moving and will move to places where there are churches in need of new people. In increasingly impersonal urban areas, people are looking for places where they feel at home and cared about. Churches with those characteristics have a precious commodity to offer.

Not all small churches are struggling to survive. Many are surviving quite nicely. Perhaps their people understand stewardship and are generous stewards. Perhaps a benefactor left them a sizable bequest and they have learned how to use it without leaning on it as a crutch. Perhaps they have found that a bivocational or part-time pastor or a lay pastor can give them quality leadership. Perhaps they have retrofitted or abandoned a costly building that was draining their resources. Most importantly, perhaps they have learned that it is okay to be small in a big world and found the emotional muscle and spiritual power to put flesh on their possibilities for ministry and mission.

Then there are those small churches who find their diminutive size an advantage. They thrive with their intimate worship, their exploring and experiential style of education, their intense caring for one another, their passionate outreach to a world in pain. They know how to manage any financial and personnel dilemmas.

This book is for those small churches that are barely surviving, those that are striving to be faithful and effective, and those that are already thriving as they live out a life of discipleship. It is also for larger churches that would like be small. By that I mean churches that want to recapture the small church qualities of immediacy, intimacy, caring, involvement, and simplicity. When as an adjunct professor at Andover Newton Theological School I was meeting my "Ministry in Small Churches" course for the first time, a pastor of one of our larger UCC churches in Massachusetts entered the classroom. I asked, "Paul, what are you doing here?" He responded thoughtfully, "I'm here to learn how to help my church be smaller by having the qualities of intimacy and involvement that characterize small churches." Wise larger churches will seek some of the qualities of smallness.

Last summer our family was vacationing at our island farmhouse in Maine. As we were preparing for a large family to visit, our plumbing failed and we finally located a young plumber who said he would come the next morning. Sure enough, he did. I was impressed as I watched him solve our plumbing problems, and as he finished I asked him, "Did you learn to do this by experience or by studying plumbing in school?"

The plumber thought and then said, "Well, my two brothers are plumbers, my father was a plumber, and my grandfather was a plumber. So, I've been doing this all my life." Then, very seriously, he put his hand to his chest and said: "But you have to have a *fire in your heart* for it!"

If all pastors and people in small churches had a fire in their heart for their church, what a difference it would make! I have a fire in my heart for small churches because God has called me to be there, I am at home there, and they have been very good to me. At their best, they provide an antidote to the isolation and individualism described by T. S. Eliot in his poem "Choruses from 'The Rock'":

> *What life have you if you have not life together?*
> *There is no life that is not in community,*
> *And no community not lived in praise of God.*
>
> *. . . . .*
>
> *And now you live dispersed on ribbon roads,*
> *And no man knows or cares who is his neighbor*
> *Unless his neighbor makes too much disturbance,*
> *But all dash to and fro in motor cars,*
> *Familiar with the roads and settled nowhere.* [2]

"What life have you, if you have not life together?" The Creation story tells us we were made for community with God and one another. In a world where few care or know who is their neighbor, small churches have the potential—often realized—to be an oasis of caring in a desert of isolated individuals. The fire burns in my heart for small churches, not as much for what they are but for the redemptive caring communities they can be—which is the true nature of the Body of Christ.

Carl Dudley beautifully expresses this essential nature of small churches at their best:

> In small churches, more people know more people, and know more about more people, than in most larger congregations. . . . When compared to other kinds of caring groups, the small church is much larger than it "ought to be." When church size is measured by human relationships, the small church is the largest expression of the Christian faith![3]

When small churches work as they could, not only do people have life together, but through that togetherness, they live in praise of God.

Despite their Christian nature, small churches have a problem. They don't do things "right." Students are taught in seminary and pastors and lay people are encouraged by denominations to do things in conventional ways. Church people have been taught and encouraged to worship correctly, to provide Christian education correctly, to support the mission of the wider church correctly, to fill out forms correctly, to do things by the manual. Without realizing it, all these correct procedures were determined with a certain size and style church in mind—larger churches.

In *Small Churches Are the Right Size* I wrote of a certain duck hunter who ordered a fully trained retriever from a breeder in the Midwest. The dog was shipped by air freight and the hunter picked him up at the regional airport. On the way home, he stopped at a pond to see what the dog could do. The hunter threw a stick across the pond and commanded, "Fetch!" The pup leaped for the water, *ran across the water* to the stick, plucked it from the water, and *ran back across the water.* Astounded, the hunter repeatedly threw the stick, and the dog repeatedly retrieved it in the same unorthodox fashion.

Wanting to show off this remarkable dog, the hunter took his hunting partner, George, out for a demonstration. With a knowing smile, the hunter threw a stick, gave the command, and the dog ran across the water and retrieved the stick. The hunter looked at George, who returned a noncommittal look. The stick was again thrown and retrieved, but still there was no response from George. With some disappointment and irritation, the hunter demanded, "What do you think of my new dog?" After a long, disinterested pause, George answered, "Dog can't swim very well, can he?"

So it is with our most faithful and effective smaller churches. With either intellectual or intuitive understanding, they do things differently, knowing that size makes all the difference in the world in how organizations and groups function. Many small churches are busy running pell-mell *across* ponds and lakes, while their "superiors" are dismissing them because they can't swim.

It's not my desire to help small churches achieve success by learning to do things the way their larger cousins do them. It is my aim to offer whatever wisdom, experience, and direction I can to help the various breeds of small churches get to their holy goal any way they can, whether by running, riding, flying, or even swimming. And, I hope to help you, the reader, put God's loving fire for small churches in your heart.

2. A Small Theology

Theology is about the ultimate, the essential meaning and nature of things. In Walker Percy's novel *The Moviegoer*, Binx Bolling cogitates about the importance of searching for ultimate things:

> What is the nature of the search? you ask. Really it is very simple, at least for a fellow like me; so simple that it is easily overlooked. The search is what anyone would undertake if he were not sunk in the everydayness of his own life. . . . To become aware of the possibility of the search is to be on to something. *Not to be on to something is to be in despair.*[1]

There is great despair among many, many small churches. They are "sunk in the everydayness" of not enough money to pay the bills, not enough people to pay the money that pays the bills, not enough happening to attract the people who pay the money that pays the bills. Rather than being "on to something," they despair in futility. They struggle to survive without the conviction of why they are surviving. The primary problem of most small churches is theological; it is *not* the lack of people and resources.

There are two primary theological questions for small churches: What is their essential nature? and What is their essential purpose? A church who knows *who* it is and *why* it is can figure out *how* to be who and why it is. The intent of this chapter is the search for a "small theology" that will answer the who and why questions of a small church. A church with answers to these questions is then free to seek out what it has to know in order to fulfill its nature and accomplish its purpose.

The abstract and ethereal nature of much theologizing may tempt some readers to skip or skim this chapter in order to get to the meaty material ahead. Too often attempts at theology have been devoid of life rather than lively interpretations of life. Theologian John Macquarrie stresses: "Theology is indispensable to the Church, and where theology fails, we must take this as a demand for better theology and certainly not as an excuse for turning away from it or for imagining that the Church can get along without it."[2] Small theology must be flesh, blood, and marrow-filled bone, unlike Ezekiel's valley of dry bones.

A reader may yet ask, Why a "small" theology? The simple reason is that much generic theology doesn't speak to the peculiar nature and needs of those who labor in small vineyards. We need a small theology in the same ways that blacks need a black theology, women need a feminist theology, Third World Christians need a liberation theology, and those who care about our environment need a theology of creation. These particular theologies, although running the risk of missing the whole forest while focusing on a particular tree, can amplify and bring clarity to the small voices of those not part of or heard by dominant cultures and viewpoints.

There are two other reasons for developing a small theology. First, just as we easily overlook the tasty mushrooms growing on the forest floor, the ingredients of a small theology are all around us in scripture and historical theology—we've just missed them. Second, and most important, small churches will be at the mercy of wind and tide unless they find and learn to use the rudder of theology, which can keep them on course and responsive to the winds of the Holy Spirit.

In the last dozen years, there have been several books about small church culture, style, methodology, worship, evangelism, education, and so on. What have been largely ignored are the biblical and theological underpinnings necessary to withstand the onslaught of cultural forces and to undergird the faithful and effective day-to-day, nuts-and-bolts life of small churches.

Small Theology Begins in Poetry

In e. e. cummings's book *95 poems* is this little poem:

i am a little church(no great cathedral)
far from the splendor and squalor of hurrying cities
—i do not worry if briefer days grow briefest,
i am not sorry when sun and rain make april

my life is the life of the reaper and the sower;
my prayers are prayers of earth's own clumsily striving
(finding and losing and laughing and crying)children
whose any sadness or joy is my grief or my gladness

around me surges a miracle of unceasing
birth and glory and death and resurrection:
over my sleeping self float flaming symbols
of hope,and i wake to a perfect patience of mountains

i am a little church(far from the frantic
world with its rapture and anguish)at peace with nature
—i do not worry if longer nights grow longest;
i am not sorry when silence becomes singing

winter by spring,i lift my diminutive spire to
merciful Him Whose only now is forever:
standing erect in the deathless truth of His presence
(welcoming humbly His light and proudly His darkness)[3]

Cummings knew the difference between large and small churches. He was born in Cambridge, Massachusetts, and his father was minister of the Old South Church in Boston, a large, prestigious church. The poet spent his later years in Madison, New Hampshire, a white-clapboarded New England village clustered around a village church. The poem can be the basis for a provocative sermon about small churches and an effective tool for helping groups begin to work with the ethos, style, and nature of small churches—rural or urban.

The poem also offers a helpful, poetic doorway into a small theology. I find in it the unique soul of a healthy small church. William Carlos Williams wrote: "cummings is the living presence of the drive to make all our convictions evident by penetrating through their costumes to the living flesh of the matter."[4] In this poem, cummings penetrates to the living flesh of healthy small churches.

In cummings's poem the little church knows who it is and who it isn't. Even an urban small church can be in, but not of, the "splendor and squalor" of the hurrying city around it. It accepts, even affirms, itself as is rather than seeking to be what it is too small to be. The little church lives in its own rhythm; its life is seasonal. It knows that when life grows dark ("briefer days grow briefest"), sun and rain will bring light and life—in due season.

The church's life is wholistic, with death and rebirth part of the same garden. Life there is organic, not synthetic. It is acutely communal, yet compassionate toward the wider world. Prayers (and its efforts) are not just for itself but also for all "of earth's own clumsily striving / (finding and losing and laughing and crying)children." Enduring and generous empathy mean anyone's sadness or joy is the church's sadness or joy.

The little church's everyday life is infused and surrounded by divine "birth and glory and death and resurrection." The baptism of a baby, the joining of hands at the altar, the prodigal who comes home, the resolution of a church fight, the elderly who have weathered the vicissitudes of life, the faithful pillar being buried from her church are all "flaming symbols of hope" that make the little church as solid and enduring as the mountains.

The observer is reminded that the little church is apart from the frenzied, ecstatic, despairing larger world. It doesn't fret when life becomes difficult and is happily content when song pierces its solitude.

In every season, the little church faithfully lifts its spire—its head—to the good and gracious God whose imminent presence is the doorway into eternity. The healthy, faithful little church lives humbly in God's refracted light and proudly in God's dark world.

This little church feels like an anachronism in the gluttony and glamor of contemporary culture. It has much more in common with the "poor in spirit," "those who mourn," the "meek," "those who hunger and thirst for righteousness," the "merciful," and the "pure in heart" named by Jesus in the Beatitudes. It doesn't expect to bring in the Realm of God in a day by its own power. Neither does it shrink from affirming who it is and doing what it can. Cummings has penetrated the idyllic stereotype and revealed the qualities of the healthy, faithful little church.

Certainly small churches can be valid, but does size matter in matters of faithfulness? Is the right size of a church merely an issue of personal preference or sociological determination? Is there a size below which or beyond which a church ceases being a "church" and becomes something else?

Around the turn of the last century, German social scientist Georg Simmel posed the question this way: "How many people make a crowd? . . . How many grains of wheat make a heap? Since one, two, three or four grains do not, while a thousand certainly do, there must be a limit after which the addition of a single grain transforms the existing single grains into a 'heap.'"[5] I believe church size is not just a matter of personal preference or sociological determination, but that it is also a matter of theological relevance. I have a hunch God cares about church size and that churches can be too small or too big.

How many are needed for a church? How many are too many? Jesus said: "Where two or three are gathered in my name, I am there among them" (Matt. 18:20). (Did Jesus mean he was *even* there or *especially* there?) So two plus Christ must be the minimum for a church. But can there be too many? There are a growing number of megachurches with as many as twenty thousand members. Theologically, are these churches, religious conglomerates, or simply large crowds?

The Bible's Small Theology

A thoughtful reading of the Bible can find a small theology. There is bias in the Bible. One doesn't have to read far in the law, the prophets, the gospels, and the epistles to find a bias or preference for the poor, the dispossessed, the disadvantaged, the righteous, the young—and *the small*. In Genesis alone, God found it necessary to start over three times with smaller communities—with Noah and his family, when all the people tried to settle in one large urban conglomerate around the tower of Babel, and when Jacob divided Israel into twelve small tribes.

Israel's history is a cyclic saga of God's people growing large and prosperous, then unfaithful and self-destructive, with a small, faithful remnant emerging—only to repeat the tragic cycle. Deuteronomy 7:7–8 documents God's bias for small Israel: "It was not because you were more numerous than any other people that the Lord set his heart on you and chose you—for you were the fewest of all peoples. It was because the Lord loved you and kept the oath that he swore to your ancestors." It wasn't because of their small size that God loved Israel. But their smallness contributed to the qualities of dependence and devotion that made them candidates for being God's chosen cadre.

Another illustration of God's bias for smallness is the story of Gideon and the Midianites in Judges 6–7. As a consequence of Israel's great sinfulness, the nation was occupied and oppressed by the Midianites. After they were "greatly impoverished," Israel cried to God for help. The angel of the Lord appeared to Joash's son, Gideon. In an example of biblical satire, God's angel addressed young Gideon, who was surreptitiously threshing wheat in a wine press out of fear the Midianites might see him: "The Lord is with you, you mighty warrior." Gideon whined: "But Sir, why is this happening to us?" God, now speaking instead of the angel, countered: "Use your might to deliver Israel from the hand of Midian." Gideon fearfully begged off: "But sir, how can I deliver Israel? My clan is the weakest in Manasseh, and I am the least in my family." Never one to entertain excuses, God cut him short: "But I will be with you."

Cowardly but not stupid, Gideon proceeded to test God three times. God passed the test, so Gideon recruited an army of thirty-two thousand. Recalling Israel's past behavior, God knew that if Israel prevailed over Midian with thirty-two thousand soldiers, they would (as the King James Version says) "vaunt themselves" against God, saying, "My own hand has delivered me." So God winnowed the thirty-two thousand down to a piddling three hundred soldiers. This remnant army, using outrageously creative tactics, prevailed over the Midianites, who were "as thick as locusts; and their camels were without number, countless as the sand on the seashore."

Part of God's bias for the small is a result of the temptation for the big to believe they are the masters of their own destiny and to become a god unto themselves. The small, with no alternative, must rely on God's grace rather than on their own clout.

The Old Testament, particularly the prophets, repeatedly speaks lovingly of and to the faithful *remnant* among the faithless masses. These overlooked but plentiful remnant texts speak a word of hope and courage to our own dispirited remnant churches. The sensitive preacher who understands the potential power of the Word can use power-laden passages to empower people who feel powerless. Here are samples of some pregnant remnant texts, how they might be used:

Genesis 45:7–8b. (Joseph) "God sent me before you to preserve for you a remnant on earth, and to keep alive for you many survivors. So it was not you who sent me here, but God." A pastor or outside helper can say to a dwindling flock that God has sent her or him to stabilize and revive those who are left—God's remnant.

2 Kings 19:30–31. "The surviving remnant of the house of Judah shall again take root downward, and bear fruit upward; for from Jerusalem a remnant shall go out, and from Mount Zion a band of survivors. The zeal of the Lord of hosts will do this." Beyond merely surviving, the remnant is expected to become firmly rooted in their faith and to bear the kind of life-giving fruit that Jesus and Paul expect. God is zealous in seeking their renewal.

Jeremiah 23:3–4. "Then I myself will gather the remnant of my flock . . . and they shall be fruitful and multiply. I will raise up shepherds over them who will shepherd them, and they shall not fear any longer, or be dismayed, nor shall any be missing, says the Lord." Again the remnant is expected to bear fruit. The task of the pastor/shepherd is to minister to its fear, despair, and feeling of insignificance.

Romans 11:5–6. "So too at the present time there is a remnant, chosen by grace. But if it is by grace, it is no longer on the basis of works, otherwise grace would no longer be grace." The remnant church is neither an accident nor failure. This remnant is validated, not by its merit or works, but by God's gracious love and loving grace.

Among other promising remnant passages are: 2 Kings 19:3–4, 2 Chronicles 30:6b–7a, Ezra 9:8, Isaiah 10:20–22, Jeremiah 31:7–8, Amos 5:15, and Micah 4:7. These texts remind us that, whenever possible, our remnant churches should be affirmed for their resoluteness, rather than criticized for lack of faith, stewardship, or evangelical zeal. Also, these texts remind all churches that no community of faith is too little to be loved by God or big enough to succeed or earn God's love by its own effort.

Repeatedly throughout scripture God affirms the few, the small, and the insignificant who live by faithfulness rather than forcefulness. With few exceptions biblical faithfulness does not come from, or result in, large numbers. God is willing to spare Sodom and Gomorrah if only ten righteous people can be found. Christ is present where two or three gather in his name. The widow's mite is the largest gift. The boy with a few loaves and fish provides food for thousands. Jesus fed five thousand but only shared the Lord's Supper with the Twelve and was revealed to the two in Emmaus as they broke bread. The mustard seed, the pearl of great price, the leaven in the loaf, the lost sheep and coin, the sparrows, and the numbered hairs on a person's head are all powerful signs that small can be theologically mighty.

Even the incarnation gives witness to God's bias for the small and seemingly insignificant. For centuries the messianic expectation of the people of God had been for a royal, mighty supreme being who would liberate, judge, and rule forever. The actual incarnation was something else. Scripture tells us Jesus was born in a borrowed stable and buried in a borrowed tomb. In between, he grew up in a peasant family in an infamous backwater village. Anonymous until about the age of thirty, Jesus practiced an unassuming itinerant town-and-country ministry with the aid of a dozen nondescript followers. Whenever possible, he deflected attention from himself and depended on others to house and feed him. Up until the tragic end, he studiously avoided Jerusalem, the capital of his faith, and more often than not retreated from the large groups who pursued him.

The gospel Jesus preached and practiced stressed intimacy, disciplined discipleship, personal and communal relationships, attention to individual gifts and needs, and compassionate response to the oppressed and dispossessed. Jesus did not create organizations, build institutions, or encourage mass movements. He spent an inordinate amount of time training and nurturing his motley little crew of twelve followers. His person-to-person ministry ended in an ignoble death, with his closest friends hiding in the crowd. Jesus the Christ, God's messiah, came and went as a commoner. I can more easily picture him as a circuit-riding pastor than as a televangelist or senior minister of a great church.

Even Christ's resurrection appearances were not the extravaganzas one might expect. Instead, they were encounters in a garden, on a road, behind locked doors, and on a quiet seashore. The Savior of the world was most at home in small groups, friends' homes, on remote hillsides, by the lakeshore, and in small towns. He had a special affinity for the simple, the young, people in need, and those shut out by the dominant culture: women, lepers, the mentally ill, prostitutes, and tax collectors. Those he picked to continue his ministry were not the movers and shakers, the religious leadership, but the common people who answered his call.

We can learn much about his priorities and our discipleship by looking at those he paid attention to. I think particularly of the hemorrhaging woman, whose touch he felt in the pressing crowd, and Bartimaeus, the blind, loud-mouthed beggar whose voice Jesus heard in the midst of the clamor of those going to market. Jesus cared about individual needs, not mass markets. His image of the Messiah was of a servant who washed feet.

The Nature of the Church

This theme of individual needs is also evident in the biblical model of the church, the church we find in Acts and the Epistles, the church out of which and for whom the Gospels were written. Although three thousand people joined the church on the day of Pentecost, *"all the believers continued together in close fellowship and shared their belongings with one another . . . and they had their meals together in their homes"* (Acts 2:44–46).

The early churches were house churches. Apparently the first church growth strategy was to divide the three thousand into small house churches where mentoring, caring, sharing, discipleship, and dinner-table communion were practiced. It appears their evangelistic zeal led the early Christians to create more churches, rather than large churches. This was the primary church growth strategy until the latter part of this century.

1 Corinthians 14:26–33 describes a highly participatory style of worship in the early church. The weekly worship included a love feast, or agape meal. Offerings were taken for those among them who were in need. The little, intimate churches depended on every member using his or her spiritual gifts for the welfare of all. Paul stressed that the various members were integral parts of the one Body of Christ.

In 1 Corinthians 11, Paul chastises the Corinthian church for losing the corporate intimacy and concern for one another, which often happens when a church grows large and impersonal. As a result of the church's burgeoning size, the members had fragmented into cliques and lost sight of each other's needs. The biblical model of what a church is supposed to be is what a church of small numbers can *naturally* be—if it remembers and chooses to be.

The assumption in that culture, as in ours, was that validity comes in large numbers and that might makes right. The Apostle Paul knew this was not God's assumption:

> Consider your call, brothers and sisters: not many of you were wise by human standards, not many were powerful, not many were of noble birth. But God chose what is foolish in the world to shame the wise; God chose what is weak in the world to the shame the strong; God chose what is low and despised in the world, things that are not, to reduce to nothing things that are, so that no one might boast in the presence of God (1 Cor. 1:26–29).

Society measures success by the size of response and equates faithfulness with success. That is not the biblical way. Success is a relative term. Faithfulness is more concerned with intent and fidelity than with numerical results.

The biblical marks or expectations of the church are quite clear. The Word is to be heard and the sacraments or ordinances are to be observed. Love and justice are to be practiced. The Christ is to be incarnated in word and deed. The body is to expend itself in redemptive action. There is nothing radically new in these requirements, and numerical size might seem irrelevant. But when one asks what kind of religious community can best fulfill these expectations, small size has a potentially large advantage.

Jesus had clear expectations of what should happen in Christian communities. In the area of *worship* he was quite explicit. We are to preach the Gospel to the whole creation, to pray "in this way," to celebrate the Lord's Supper "in remembrance of me," and to baptize in the name of the "Father, the Son, and the Holy Spirit." In the twentieth-century church, particularly most larger ones, these events occur in a passive manner. The spectators observe while the paid players perform for the audience.

It is possible for small churches, fulfilling the potential of their size, to make worship highly participatory. Preaching can directly and personally engage the lives of the people, as Jesus' preaching did. Prayer can be very inclusive, personal, and intercessory. The Lord's Supper can be truly a family meal. Baptism can be an active adoption into the family of faith in which the whole church participates. The small church can worship the way the early church did in its vital and small beginnings. The word *liturgy* means "the work of the people," and in small churches *all* the people can do the work of worship together.

Another task or mark of the church is *education*. Jesus said, "make disciples" and teach "them to obey everything that I have commanded you." Perhaps we can give moral instruction and institutional orientation with some effectiveness in large numbers. Perhaps we can instruct *about* the Bible, Christianity, and church history. But Jesus commanded much more than this. He commanded disciple making. And that is best done experientially and face-to-face. Remember Jesus' own powerful encounter with the elders in the Jerusalem temple when he was twelve. Remember how he taught: with everyday stories drawn from the experience of his followers, by modeling with his own life, with spirited dialogue with critics and inquirers, by sending disciples out two-by-two to practice what they had been taught and debriefing them when they returned, and by going on retreat with two or three at a time.

The goals of Christian education—which are inclusion in the faith community, personal transformation, and equipping for discipleship—

are best met by involvement with the whole community, by providing role models or mentors, and by *praxis*—applying what has been taught in real life experiences. It is logical that the more learners there are, the more difficult it is for each to participate in active, meaningful, and personally appropriate ways. Large-group learning is passive, assembly-line learning. Large groups can subdivide into smaller groups, but these tend to be homogeneous collections of people of the same age, gender, or interest. It is easier being with people like ourselves, but more important things are probably learned when we are with people different from ourselves.

A third mark or requirement of the church is to *care for each other.* Jesus said, "Love one another." John said, "Let us love one another, because love is from God." Tertullian said of the second-century church, "Look how they love one another." But you can't love someone you don't know. You can't know or love fifty or a hundred pews full of people you at best barely recognize. It is hard to care for the children who have been segregated off into the education wing of the church. It is hard to care for people when there is no opportunity to share one another's deep joys and concerns. Often the church's best effort at caring is the coffee hour before or after worship, yet that is often infrequent, superficial, and intimidating.

Small churches are best known for their caring. Sadly, this isn't always the case. They can be hard for newcomers to break into. Some are riddled with conflict and feuds. Some are small because they have shut out people or driven them away. But they are the right size to care. In larger churches, caring is likely to be superficial, hit-or-miss, restricted to crisis time, and the job of the professional care-giver. But the church that is small enough for everyone to know everyone is small enough for everyone to care deeply and effectively for everyone.

A final mark or task of the church, the *raison d'être* of the Christian church, is to be a *people on a mission,* a people sent to save and transform the world (or at least real parts of it). Jesus said, "Love your neighbor as yourself" and "go into the whole world" to preach, feed, heal, clothe, visit, free the oppressed, make peace. Jesus sent his followers out two-by-two and was never too busy to attend to someone in need.

Large churches tend to do mission work by sending money, researching the community and developing strategies, hiring it done, or allowing a few like-minded zealots to perform missionary work in the name of the church. Small churches are often thinking more of survival than service. But when motivated, they can respond as a committee of the whole to a felt need and will commit muscle as well as money. Small churches are the right size to have the service begin when the worship ends.

This small theology assumes that a Christian church, by definition, is *not* a religious institution. Rather it is a community of faith, called by Christ, in which all members are "members one of another" (Eph. 4:25), living out their faith by building up their community and offering it in love to the world. Theologically, small churches are the right size to be and do *all* that God calls a church to be and do.

Tragically, most of them haven't lived up to that call. Their sin is that they have been captivated by our "bigger-is-better" culture and used their small size as an excuse for weak faith and little action. They have often focused on what they *can't* do, rather than doing what they *can* do. They have often felt sorry for themselves rather than empathy for one another. Some have moaned "poor us" and turned a deaf ear to the poor among and around them. Rather than enjoying the camaraderie of corporate worship, they have often worshiped dutifully as isolated individuals.

Too many small churches have failed to do their theological homework. They've missed the fact that God has historically chosen to work through small remnant groups. They weren't paying attention when Martin Buber taught us that the I-Thou relationships found in intimate, caring groups of people are the kind of relationships prized by God and characteristic of many small churches. They didn't understand Reinhold Niebuhr's premise in *Moral Man and Immoral Society* that the larger the grouping the more immoral and self-serving its attitudes and behavior tend to be. Paul Tillich taught us that the essence of sin is separation, yet we fail to recognize that life in larger groups tends to be more impersonal and fragmented.

Community and Place

We've missed a primary point of the Creation story. God created humankind for community, not for private autonomy or massive anonymity. Psalm 133 reminds us: "How very good and pleasant it is when kindred live together in unity!" Dietrich Bonhoeffer affirms that Christianity is synonymous with community: "Christianity means community through Jesus Christ and in Jesus Christ. No Christian community is more or less than this."[6] Elizabeth O'Connor, chronicler of the amazing story of the Church of the Savior in Washington, D.C., calls building community

> . . . the most creative and difficult work to which any of us will ever be called. There is no higher achievement in all the world than to be a

person in community, and this is the call of every Christian. We are to be builders of liberating communities that free love in us and free love in others. [7]

Paul Hanson, in his exhaustive study of the development of community in the Bible, *The People Called*, identifies this theme of community as the common thread that weaves through scripture from Genesis to Revelation:

> The entire history of the biblical notion of community points to the same transcendent referent—the God who creates out of nothing, delivers the enslaved, defends the vulnerable, nurtures the weak, and enlists in a universal purpose of salom all those responsive to the divine call. The biblical notion of community therefore finds its final unity and focus in worship of the one true God. From that center alone, it derives its understanding of what is true, just, and good, along with the courage and power to stand on the side of truth and justice, whatever the cost.
>
> The notion of community thus arising from our biblical heritage has a potentially profound contribution to make to a threatened world groping for direction. [8]

The small church is the suitable size to explore how to be community in this frenzied world, to practice being community, and then to model it for the larger church and the wider culture. It has enough people to be more than an isolated, insulated nuclear family. It does not have so many people that they can't know one another, care for one another, involve one another, and band together in mutual ministry and mission. Since biblical churches were small churches, today's small churches have the good fortune of having a model after which to pattern themselves.

One other theological theme contributes to my understanding of small churches: *place*. Walter Brueggemann, in his landmark book of biblical theology *The Land*, begins:

> The sense of being lost, displaced, and homeless is pervasive in contemporary culture. The yearning to belong somewhere, to have a home, to be in a safe place, is a deep and moving pursuit. Loss of place and yearning for place are dominant images. [9]

The poor who live in our urban parks, on our subway grates, in cars, and under bridges are *not* the only homeless. The term *refugee* applies to more than the millions who are uprooted and on the move across every continent because of famine, oppression, and war. In this nation where people move an average of once every four years and change jobs more frequently, where few feel rooted to land they love and work, where houses and condominiums are seen more as investments than the place where one belongs, we live in a time when increasing numbers are displaced and "homeless."

Yet at the same time, the urban and rural landscape is dotted with churches like the one in e. e. cummings's poem, where people have found and offer to others belonging, place, and home. In our high-tech world, the small church offers high touch. Being able to offer a place to those who are displaced is its most unique and valuable gift. The primary difference between big churches and small churches is that big churches offer programs in which to participate whereas small churches offer a place in which to belong. God, through Moses, offered slaves in Egypt a promised land. God, through small churches, offers rootless and homeless people a promised place.

Most small churches believe their biggest issue is fiscal viability—how to pay for everything they think they need. In fact their biggest issue is theological—how to be the kind of church God is calling them to be. A subplot may be how to pay the costs of being that kind of church. But any church that knows who it is and why it is will be able to figure out how to be that kind of church. That is, it will be able to figure out how to pay the costs of being that kind of church.

In our "bigger-is-better" and "might-makes-right" world, it may be time for another reformation. It is just possible small churches could lead a new reshaping of the Body of Christ. Small size is no excuse. Theologically and biblically small churches are the right size to be all that God calls the church to be. Upon this small but firm biblical and theological foundation we can now begin building, renovating, or restoring the small-church in the divine image, in order to meet the current need and possibility.

If that seems beyond reach as you reflect on your small church experience, remember that Martin Luther is supposed to have said: "God can ride the lame horse and carve rotten wood." I find much reassurance in that truth.

For Thought and Discussion

1. How do you define *theology?*
2. Refer to the quotation from Walker Percy that opens chapter 2. What is your church "on to?" Or is it in despair?
3. How is your church like the little church in e. e. cummings's poem quoted in this chapter? How is it different?

4. Thinking theologically, can a church be too small or too large?
5. Can you think of other examples of the Bible's "bias" for smallness?
6. How do you feel about the author's belief that on theological and biblical grounds, small churches are the right size to be all that God calls a church to be?

3. Theory: The Right Size and Different

A rose is a rose is a rose is a rose? Maybe. But not so with churches. Each is different from all others. Each requires different approaches, different ministry, different intentions. A Maine seafaring story gives the framework for the most important thing to know about small churches.

An old salty captain had spent forty years at the helm of an old cargo-carrying schooner. Each morning, after dressing, he conducted an almost religious ritual. He retrieved an old captain's chest from under his bed; fished out the key from his desk drawer; opened the chest; took out an aged scrap of paper; read it carefully, sometimes two or three times; put it back in the chest; locked it; and returned chest and key to their respective places.

One day at sea, he died of a heart attack. The first mate took command of the ship, conducted a proper sea burial, and moved into the captain's quarters. He knew of the old captain's unusual morning ritual and believed that in that chest, on that tattered slip of paper, was the secret for effectively commanding the fine ship.

Opening the chest the first mate found the yellowed slip of paper, held it to the light, and read it over and over. In the old captain's crude

23

handwriting was this sparse message: *"Left is port; right is starboard."* All other seafaring knowledge is of little value if the one at the helm doesn't know port from starboard.

One cannot begin to understand small churches without appreciating their port and starboard realities. The port reality is that *small churches are the right size* to be all that a church is meant to be. The starboard reality is that *small churches are different* from their ecclesiastical cousins.

Building on these fundamental claims, this chapter provides the handles by which the reader can grasp what makes a small church the right size and different and thereby how to provide the most appropriate leadership. To know it, love it, care for it, pastor it, and change it, you must understand it—who it is, where it is, how it works, what makes it tick. As a Baptist pastor in New York wrote to me,

> It is vital to our small churches that those of us coming to live within their communties and seeking to be in ministry with them understand what it is that we are doing! . . . It is an often bewildering and baffling existence until we slowly begin to figure out the dynamics, the primary importance of history versus the impulse toward "something new," the primary importance of tradition versus the tug towards innovation.

Historically and statistically the small church is the typical church. The Christian church began as small house churches, and up until the middle of the twentieth century, almost all churches were relatively small. According to Carl Dudley,

> History is on the side of the small church. Bigness is the new kid on the block. Historically, Protestant denominations in the United States have been comparatively small. At the time of the Civil War, the size of the average Protestant church was less than one hundred members. A few large churches were in the center of the city, or at the center of the ethnic community. By the turn of the century, the average congregation still had less than one hundred fifty members. [1]

Today the situation appears to have changed. The 1984 *Yearbook of American and Canadian Churches* recorded 341,000 local churches in the United States, totaling 135 million members and an average weekly attendance of over 65 million adults. [2] The average church, then, has about 395 members and 190 people in worship (not counting children and visitors). The relatively few megachurches inflate the statistics that give us this "average" size. A majority of Protestant churches are still small and have less than two hundred members. In 1982 Lyle Schaller wrote that one-fourth of North American Protestant churches have fewer than thirty-five in worship and one-half have fewer than seventy-five.[3] In 1988 Schaller observed that 70 percent of United Methodist and Nazarene churches average less than one hundred in worship, while 60 percent of American Baptist churches and 55 percent of United Church of Christ churches average less than one hundred.[4] The *1992 Year Book and Directory of the Christian Church* (Disciples of Christ) reports that nearly half their four thousand congregations have one hundred or fewer participating members.[5]

It is clear that most American Protestant churches are small but that most people are in large churches. The largest 15 percent of churches reach 50 percent of the American church members, and the smallest 50 percent of churches serve 15 percent of church members.[6]

Toward the middle of the twentieth century, there was a shift from more churches to larger churches. Toward the end of the century, when many churches declined in membership, the pressure accelerated to grow larger. The denominational goal and the model for success in the church is the large, multiprogrammed church. At least six trends in church and society account for this emphasis on bigness.

Trends Toward Bigness

1. In the twentieth century *we became an urban, centralized nation.* In 1790, 95 percent of America was rural. The 1920 census marked the transition of the United States from a rural to an urban nation—54.3 million people lived in urban areas, 51.8 million in rural areas. The trend continued for another fifty years before leveling off in the 1970s. In many places, however, the trend continues. For example, Iowa lost 5 percent of its population between 1980 and 1990. Forty-three of the fifty mostly rural communities in northwestern Iowa, where I work, lost population. The only significant growth in Iowa is in the Des Moines area and around the university cities.

With the centralization of population came the centralization of institutions—government, business, education, and religion. Centralized institutions are larger than decentralized ones. Urbanization meant that many rural churches declined and new suburban and urban churches thrived.

2. A second trend was the *revolution in transportation.* Thanks to Henry Ford and the Wright brothers, Americans became much more mobile. The horsedrawn carriage gave way to the horseless carriage, trucks, trol-

leys, buses, and subways. With better transportation, supermarkets replaced the corner grocery; regional schools replaced neighborhood schools; regional government overshadowed home rule; and the new, larger centralized church drew people from the old, smaller neighborhood and family church.

3. The *communications revolution changed institutions.* The development of sound amplification meant that more people could hear the preacher and sanctuaries could be larger. The print, audio, and visual revolutions changed the dominant concept of communication from active interpersonal exchange to passive individual reception. The small church's face-to-face style of communication seemed old- fashioned.

One result of the transportation and communicatons revolutions was a transition from high commitment to low commitment on the part of participants. Economist E. F. Schumacher notes that a "highly developed transport and communications system has one immensely powerful effect: it makes people footloose."[7] Involvement and commitment suffer as the church competes with the attraction of weekends away and the entertainment of the PC, CD, TV, and VCR.

4. Related to the growth of churches was the *growth of denominations.* Historian Winthrop Hudson has noted: "By 1900 most of the denominations had begun to assume direct responsibility for many activities previously carried on by voluntary societies."[8] The large, corporate denominational structure is a twentieth century phenomena. It has not always had the task of doing mission for the local church, of publishing the local church's materials, of overtly or covertly managing the affairs of the local church, of speaking for the local church to the wider world.

The denominational tail now wags the local church dog. Whether the denomination has assumed or been given its greater responsibilities and whether or not a corporate structure is the best means to accomplish the tasks of God's Realm, it takes larger churches and more money to fulfill the denomination's program and financial expectations. For the denomination to do all that it feels called to do, it needs large and generous local churches. One reason contemporary denominations seek to grow large churches is to pay for the denominational superstructure.

5. *Local churches need many people to pay for their own superstructures.* In the late 1970s Episcopal Church guidelines suggested, "For a parish to be economically healthy, it must have a budget of $60,000 with two hundred active communicants."[9] Allowing for inflation, imagine what the figure would be today? Lyle Schaller says that in the 1930s, a church that

averaged 30 or 40 in worship could afford a full-time pastor. In the 1980s, 120 to 140 worshipers were needed in order to afford the same full-time pastor. What about today?

Local church people aren't stupid. Pastors know a church of five hundred can more easily pay the bills and a larger salary than can a church of one hundred. Lay people assume that members of a church of five hundred won't need to contribute as much as members of a hundred member church. Everyone believes that a church of five hundred can afford more building, more staff, more resources, and more niceties than smaller churches. Cost effectiveness now rivals mission and discipleship as church goals. Smaller churches are competing in an ecclesiastical version of an arms race, which they can rarely win.

6. Perhaps most importantly, in our culture *size has become synonymous with success.* Kirkpatrick Sale, in *Human Scale,* writes:

> It has become part of the American character not only to accept bigness but actually to admire, respect, love, at times even worship bigness. Size is the measure of excellence. . . . Or as one nineteenth-century German summed it up: "To say that something is large, massive, gigantic, is in America not a mere statement of fact but the highest commendation."[10]

If our culture worships bigness and is embarrassed by smallness, it is only logical that our churches will do the same. Like the adolescent in the magazine ad who kept getting sand kicked in his face by the big bully, many small churches are yearning to grow big enough to hold their own on the beach of life. When churches feel big enough, they tend to stop seeking growth. Small churches may still be the typical church—simply because there are so many of them, but it is clear why they've been dwarfed by the more populous, popular, and powerful larger churches.

Small Churches are Different

Actually there is no typical small church. They come in a variety of shapes, colors, styles, and environments—as well as sizes. Small churches are different from large churches and from each other.

I've come to believe *size is the most important variable* in determining the nature of any organization. As I've traveled speaking and consulting about small church issues, I've discovered more similarity between small UCC churches in New England, small Southern Baptist churches in Alabama, and small Weslyan Methodist churches in Canada, than I find between small churches and large churches of the same denomination in the same region.

A mathematical equation that identifies how many relationships are in a group illustrates why size is crucial. It looks like this:

$$\text{Number of relationships} = \frac{\text{Number}^2 - \text{Number}}{2}$$

Here's how it works. Take the number of people in a group or organization and multiply the number by itself. Take that answer and subtract the original number from it. Then divide that answer by two. This answer will be the number of relationships or potential relationships in the group or organization. For example, let us determine the number of real or potential relationships in four churches where there are thirty-five, seventy-five, two hundred, and one thousand in worship:

1. $35 \times 35 = 1225 - 35 = 1190 \div 2 = 595$ relationships
2. $75 \times 75 = 5625 - 75 = 5550 \div 2 = 2775$ relationships
3. $200 \times 200 = 40,000 - 200 = 39,800 \div 2 = 19,900$ relationships
4. $1,000 \times 1,000 = 1,000,000 - 1,000 = 999,000 \div 2 = 499,500$ relationships

People in a fellowship group of thirty-five with 595 possible relationships will know each other, will know how most of the others know each other, and will care about all those relationships—not just their own. Seventy-five people worshiping together will know almost everyone else but will have little sense of the relationships that exist between many or most of the others, and they will primarily care only about their own relationships with the other seventy-four. Individuals in a large gathering of two hundred will vary in the amount of mutual knowledge that exists of each other, but they will really only care about some of the others and care little or not at all about the relationships that exist between the others. Those in a mass gathering of one thousand will know only a few or some of the others, and the only relationships that matter to them will be those they have with a select few.

Groups of thirty-five, seventy-five, two hundred, and one thousand are as different from one another as an ant is from an eagle is from a cow is from a whale. If Christian community is intrinsic to the nature of the Christian church, then the ant and perhaps the eagle are more the right size for being the Body of Christ.

Small churches are different. Kirkpatrick Sale is profoundly correct:

As we all know, a big mansion is not simply a bungalow with more rooms, a big party is not simply an intimate dinner with more people, a big metropolitan hospital is not simply a clinic with more beds and more doctors, a big corporation is not simply a family firm with more employees and products, a big government is not simply a town council with more branches.[11]

Small churches are not only different from other sizes of churches but different from each other. Their history, composition, locale, experience, theology, and expectations are factors that determine differentness. Following are examples of different kinds of small churches.

There's the *always small church*. The churches I served in Massacusetts and Vermont were always small churches. They've always been small and probably always will be. This kind knows how to act like a small church because they have plenty of experience. Self-esteem is less of a problem in these churches.

The *once large* or *remnant small church* is often a troubled church. The church I serve in Iowa, which once had three times as many members as it now has, is one of these. These churches remember or have heard of the good old days under Rev. Goodfellow when the pews, offering plates, and Sunday school overflowed. They are more likly to wither and die because they don't know how to be small.

The *not-yet-large small church* is the new church in the mushrooming suburb or the stable church with a new charismatic pastor. Often this church has key lay leaders with large church experience and expectations. This church behaves more like the large church it isn't yet.

The *schismatic small church* uses conflict to practice cell division and remain small. Every so often, perhaps when the church reaches its maximum size, an issue or maverick leader emerges, and a splinter group breaks off.

The *intentionally small church* comes in a couple of varieties. There are churches with people so jealous of their power that they exclude others. And there is the highly disciplined small church (like Church of the Savior in Washington, D.C.), often a house church, that has such demanding or particular expectations that most prospects won't make the stiff commitment.

The *clan small church* is made up almost entirely of one or two large extended families who believe blood is thicker than baptismal water. Normally the only route into full citizenship in these churches is by marriage or birth.

There are an increasing number of *ethnic small churches*—Hispanic, Vietnamese, Arabic, Lithuanian, and so on. Sometimes it is language, sometimes cultural customs, and sometimes racism that keeps these churches exclusive.

A small church is not small by accident. Among other things, it is a product of its environment or context. A church's nature, successes, and failures have much to do with the particular turf in which it is planted. Douglas Walrath, a sociologist and director of the Small Church Leadership Program at Bangor Seminary, has been particularly helpful in defining the dynamic relationship between small churches and their context. His chapter "Types of Congregations and Their Implications for Planning" in *Small Churches Are Beautiful* and the chapter "How Change Is Challenging Small Churches" in *Developing Your Small Church's Potential* are worth finding, studying, and applying.

Walrath says small churches are located in local contexts in three areas: rural, fringe, and city neighborhoods. The rural area includes open country and small settlements, villages, small towns, and independent cities. The fringe area includes exurbs where suburban growth is blossoming and fringe suburbs where suburban development is well established. City neighborhoods include ethnic and minority neighborhoods and redeveloping neighborhoods. Small churches are vulnerable to changing trends and tides around them, and in each of these areas, there are forces at work that influence and help shape the churches within them.

As populations have migrated, rural areas and city neighborhood areas have lost population to the fringe areas around the cities. Although change has meant loss and adjustment in many rural and inner-city areas, change has meant growth and accomodation in urban fringe areas. Contextual change in each of these areas affects the churches within them differently.

For example, the churches in towns and small cities that have been service centers for rural areas have often been hit hard by the losses around them. Many of the people who left have been those best able to move—younger people with enough education and skills to be most employable elsewhere. When the population and economic bases shrink, churches that once functioned independently now find it difficult to cooperate as they compete for the remaining people and dollars.

Open country and village-crossroads churches may find it easier to maintain themselves because they've always been the only church around or only church like themselves. They may find it more natural to make do, cooperate, and share resources and leadership with a church down the road because they've been sharing and cooperating for a long time and that style is more natural for agrarian people.[12]

In *Small Churches Are Beautiful*, Walrath distinguishes three kinds of social positions churches occupy within a community and how that social position impacts the identity and life of a church. The *Dominant church* is the prestige church, usually larger, richer, more historic, and located in the center of the community. The *Subordinate church* is the "other" church, in the middle of the block or on the edge of town. It's less affluent, perhaps less attractive, smaller, and attracts people one or two rungs down the social ladder. The *Exclusive church* accomodates a specific group. It might be the Catholic church in a Protestant community, the Swedish church in an otherwise homogenous community, or the fundamentalist church in a mainline community.

Life and ministry in a church in each of these social positions will be different. A small dominant church, if it can no longer afford a full-time pastor, will likely be happier with its own bivocational pastor than if it tries to yoke or share a pastor with another church. A small subordinate church might do better sharing a pastor with another subordinate church, even one of a different denomination, than to try sharing with a dominant church that is used to being independent. The small exclusive church will need to forge its own way, because it won't have enough in common to work well with a nonexclusive church.[13]

In *Developing Your Small Church's Potential*, Dudley and Walrath differentiate between three kinds of "cultural appeal" in churches: "newcomer" churches, "indigenous" churches, and "culturally mixed" churches. *Newcomer churches* are in communities where the population is increasing. The newcomers have become church leaders and often control the church. Native people often no longer feel comfortable in these churches. The Shrewsbury, Vermont, church is a newcomer church.

Indigenous churches are made up primarily of people native to the area. These churches have often decreased in size and find it difficult to attract and assimilate new people. Many pastors find these churches hard to understand and serve.

In between newcomer and indigenous churches are *culturally mixed churches,* which include both new and old people. These different people often have differing values, styles, and expectations. Sometimes they discover enough in common that they can overlook their differences. They are particularly susceptible to conflict and can be particularly difficult to serve as pastor.[14]

Lyle Schaller identifies seven categories of churches by size using descriptive names and nicknames, summarized in the following discussion.[15] He calls a church of up to thirty-five or forty in worship a *Fellowship church* and nicknames it "The Cat." The pastor (probably part-time) feeds the cat, does things for the cat, but the cat—true to its nature—does not "belong" to the pastor and can manage without one. This church is independent, self-sufficient, and enjoys its own company. Like a cat it may resist or ignore outside offers of help or rescue. One-quarter of all churches are cats.

The *Small church* has between thirty-five and one hundred in worship and accounts for one-third of American churches. Schaller calls it "The Collie" and it is characterized by love. It wants to be loved and will respond to and love those who love it. A pastor who cares for it will be loved in return. It, like Lassie, is more capable than it appears.

The *Middle-Sized church* will have between 100 and 175 in worship and is known as "The Garden." Churches of varying sizes can have this many in worship. The work of the gardener is never done. Weeds grow quite quickly when the garden is not tended.

A church that averages between 175 and 225 in worship is an *Awkward church* and is nicknamed "The House." Like a house it needs a variety of specialized skills (plumber, electrician, carpenter, and so on) to keep it in shape. It is in constant need of repair, rearranging, and remodeling.

The *Large church* attracts 225–450 to worship and is called "The Mansion." There is never enough help to keep it going. It is not very efficient, close knit, or well acquainted. People come and go.

A church that attracts 450–700 for worship is a *Huge church* and is more like a "Ranch." The senior minister is the Rancher. The Rancher can't do it all, so several hired hands are employed to try to keep the ranch in shape.

A church with more than seven hundred in worship is really a *Mini-Denomination*, sometimes called "The Nation." This superchurch acts more like a denomination. It subdivides into states and counties; creates its own curriculum; and runs its own school, camping program, music school. Again, each of these is a different animal, requiring different kinds of leadership, having a different time frame, living in the world in different ways.

Another typology by size has been developed by Arlin Rothauge in his booklet *Sizing Up a Congregation for New Member Ministry*. He identifies four sizes of churches, described below, and believes that each should implement a different form of evangelism in order to be effective.[16]

The *Family church* has up to fifty active members. Rather than trying to do everything, he says this size church should concentrate on one special vocation and do that as well as it can. It tends to attract new members through their preexisting ties with family members and friends who are already part of the church. It is the Gatekeepers, more than a pastor, who prepare the way for new people. Becoming part of this church is a gradual process of adoption.

The *Pastoral church* has between 50 and 150 active members. This church tends to revolve around the pastor and leadership circle of the church. New people come to the church through attention from the pastor. Hospitality and assimilation strategies are crucial for churches of this size.

The *Program church* has 150–350 members. Democratic procedures and leadership by the laity are critical for the effectiveness of this church. Lay leaders need to be trained and equipped to lead a variety of programs for various ages and interests. Programs are the bait that attracts and holds new people.

The *Corporation church,* over 300 active members, is complex and diverse. A charismatic, visionary leader able to communicate and coordinate is required. Like a corporation, it is only as effective as its smaller units.

Three other analysts of the church offer three different and intriguing observations that are relevant to understanding small churches. Carl Dudley in *Making the Small Church Effective* describes a small church as a "single cell" and a "culture-carrying organism." Rather than an organization of several cells or groups, a small church is one whole cell in which "members can associate the name with the face, the face with the family, and the family with the place where each person sits in worship."[17] It is characterized by the caring that holds the body together. In a small, single-cell church where everyone knows everyone else, people are likely to know *more* people than if they were in a larger multicell church.

As a culture-carrying group of people, the small church is not known by its activities but by the identity that grows from its world of shared experience, generally rooted in the past but very much alive in the present. Like a turtle under its shell, a small church's building is often part of the culture and identity it brings from its past into its present and future. Like a turtle and its shell, the church may die if its building is removed.

Another helpful insight into the personality of the church is provided by Rabbi Edwin Friedman, author of *Generation to Generation: Family Process in Church and Synagogue.* He has pioneered in the field of family theory and family systems and believes that churches are families that "function as organic structures . . . according to the rules and models of family life."[18] What he says about churches in general is even more true of small churches because of the closer proximity and greater intensity of their life together.

Friedman demonstrates how churches live, function, and fight like families, even to the point of inheriting patterns and personalities from their ancestors. He observes that people behave in their church family in response to the dynamics going on in their individual families. As a result, when people are troubled at home, they are more likely to make trouble at church.

Tony Pappas is an American Baptist pastor on Block Island, Rhode Island, and editor of *The Five Stones,* a quarterly journal about small churches. In *Entering the World of the Small Church,* Pappas builds his understanding of small church ministry on the concept of a "folk society," as described by anthropologist Robert Redfield in an article in the *American Journal of Sociology* in 1947. Some characteristics of a folk society are:

- It has a small number of people
- People know each other well
- There is a strong sense of belonging
- There is a strong identification with the place they occupy
- Oral communication is more important than written
- Relationships are ends in themselves and not means to an end
- Stability is more valued than change
- Moral worth is attached to traditional ways of doing things[19]

Pappas believes these characteristics are descriptive of small churches and he interprets his ministry and the behavior of his Block Island church by them.

The negative images, symbols, and models of small churches are the least helpful. In 1975, Paul Madsen, a denominational official, asked "why churches are small." His answer was because of their inadequate program, inadequate field (not enough people from which to draw), inadequate evangelism, inadequate vision, and inadequate personalities.[20] The clear message is, if they weren't so inadequate, they would grow up and bulk up and become what, for him, is their right size.

Theodore Erickson wrote in 1977: "A small church can be defined as one in which the number of active members and the total annual budget is inadequate relative to organizational needs and expenses. It is a church struggling to pay its minister, heat its building, and find enough people to assume leadership responsibilities."[21] In other words, a small church is one that doesn't measure up to the organizational criteria one has for a "legitimate" (that is, large) church.

Small churches used to be defined simply by the numbers. Two hundred members was the favorite divider between small and not small. Lyle Schaller's focus on worship attendance was an improvement in the statistical search for a workable distinction. For many, the bottom line in identifying small churches has been financial viability. Churches that couldn't afford the recommended full-time pastor's salary, maintain an adequate building, and pay the rest of their bills were "small."

The denomination often designated a church small if there weren't enough people for a "full-time" workload. I shuddered when I heard a Methodist district superintendent say, "I don't know how a pastor can be challenged with less than two to three hundred members." I remembered how "challenged" I was and how hard I worked as the full-time pastor of the small, one-hundred-member Shrewsbury church. Others have labeled a church "small" when they've compared it to a larger one. A pastor who grew up in a thousand-member church thinks her four-hundred-member church is "small." The urban church that has dwindled from fifteen hundred to five hundred and is rattling around in a building that is now too large, thinks it is small.

I find these statistical and comparative definitions of small churches dry and discouraging. It is more helpful to define a small church by the characteristics and qualities that tend to be present in a church with a relatively small number of people. My ministry becomes more faithful and effective when I use these characteristics and qualities as the lenses through which I focus my ministry. Rather than focusing on what a small church can't do, I concentrate on what is possible when there aren't a lot of people.

Twenty-six Characteristics of a Small Church

Ten years ago I listed ten characteristics that define a small church. Out of my experience and the wisdom of others, the list has grown to twenty-six. Apply them to the church(es) you know and see if they fit. Use them as the basis for strategizing ways of helping a church be "smaller" and more faithful and effective.

1. *A small church is the common expectations of its members.* The expectations we have of an organization we're part of helps determine the

nature of that organization. People in small churches expect to know each other and play a part. People who want the qualities they expect in a small church will drive past large churches to find one. Those who don't want that kind of church will drive past small ones in search of a larger one. Unfortunately, if they expect poor leadership, a weak Sunday school, and shoddy worship, they will too readily accept these things.

2. Everyone knows everyone or almost everyone else. Sociologist A. Paul Hare observes: "A group is usually defined as 'small' if each member has the opportunity for face-to-face interaction with all others."[22] In a small church, people expect to know each other's business—and they usually do. They're not just being polite when they ask "How are you?" Knowledge of one another is important because people feel and act differently with those they know.

Sometimes this is more myth than reality. In the three small churches I've pastored, everyone did not know everyone. In each church we've used a variety of strategies to help people know each other. A church that works seriously at this knowing task can remain "small" as it grows larger.

3. Beyond knowing one another, there's a sense of "family." This is what Tony Pappas means when he writes about the folk society or tribe. An academic term for this is "primary group." Larger churches will likely have several primary groups or cells, usually differentiated by age, gender, interest, or responsibility. The small church family, clan, or tribe will be one brilliant mosaic of ages, interests, abilities, and outlooks.

The church that is like an extended family meets the human need to be known, secure, and cared for. People who are not familiar with how such a "family" works, should beware. One doesn't just walk in and join a family. Other than by birth, the only way into a family is by marriage or adoption—and neither happens overnight. Another cause for caution is that most families fight. Because there's a tough bond between them, they're free to fight. Healthy families are careful to fight cleanly and particularly enjoy kissing and making up.

4. In a small church almost everyone feels and is important and needed. It has been demonstrated that a higher percentage of small church members are present for worship, more generous in giving, and more willing to share in the work of the church. Larger churches, with full-time or multiple staffs, can hire people to do the work; small church people are more likely to do it themselves. Small churches often fulfill the New Testament criteria in which "the whole body, joined and knit together by every ligament with which it is equipped . . . promotes the body's growth in building itself up in love" (Eph. 4:16). One of our most-valued Warwick lay leaders recalled having been in a large New York church: "I never had a chance to find out what I could do. . . . You didn't get asked to do the jobs unless you joined the groups. . . . My place was on the fringe."

5. *Organizational functioning is simple rather than complex.* The larger the mechanism the more it takes to move it. The more people in an organization, the more complex their interactions will be. In small churches everyone can and should have a direct voice in decision making. Frequently decisions can be worked through to a consensus decision. Small churches make more decisions in the parking lot than in committee meetings. Committees can function more as task forces than as decision-making bodies. They can meet, talk, deliberate, and then come to the whole church for decision, support, and assistance.

6. *Communication is rapid.* People want to know and expect to know. Communication is horizontal, not hierarchal. There is a grapevine, but it can't be trusted to reach everyone. A few planned phone calls can get the word to everyone. Since people expect to know, leaders need to be serious about communicating well. Criticism, rumor, and pettiness also travel the grapevine, but such news surfaces sooner, making clarification possible.

7. *Small churches are known by their distinctive personalities, more than by their programs.* Unlike larger churches, Carl Dudley believes that small churches find their identity in their character.

> The larger congregation knows who it is because of what it does, and it must keep on doing in order to assure its existence. The small church has identity because of the experiences that it brings from the past. . . . They find identity in their character, not in their activities.[23]

Since it is too small to offer a varied music program or a multifaceted education ministry, the small church relies on being and offering who it is. It will be known as the friendly church, the hard-working church, the caring church, or the snobbish church. It is particularly important for a small church to identify its distinctiveness, so this unqiueness can be highlighted and celebrated.

8. *It is likely to be rooted in its history and nervous about its future.* Families share a family history that usually includes legends, skeletons, heroes, humor, pathos, tragedy, and conquest. In a small church,

many members will have personal ties with their characters and saints, the holy moments and symbolic episodes that are its remembered and formative history. One of a new pastor's first tasks is to hear the old, old stories and begin to understand how they have shaped this people. The new pastor ceases being new when he or she has been around long enough to become a cast member of the stories.

The next task for the new pastor is to help the church believe in itself and shape its future. Dudley understands that a church's history can be the foundation upon which to build its future. "To appreciate the past is not to be bound by it, but to build on it. . . . The small church will die if it loses touch with its history. . . . When the future is constructed from pride in the past, then the richest energy of the small church is released and activated."[24]

9. *A small church's theology is relational, horizontal, and historical.* A church that has struggled and survived wants a real and practical faith, not ethereal speculations. Since the people's church experience is more relational than personal, they are likely to experience God in one another, more than privately. Since they are rooted in their history, they can identify God as being active in that history. The God who wrestled with Jacob and led the Psalmist "through the valley of the shadow," the Christ who pastored along the road and healed beside the sickbed, is the Holy One they know or seek. The preacher's experience with God is of more interest than her or his systematic theology.

10. *Small churches understand mission in personal and immediate terms.* Since they don't think in organizational or systemic terms, it seems like just another tax when the denomination asks for undesignated mission money to support a diversified, unspecified mission effort. They seldom get excited about this. They do get excited about helping their neighbors. When they're helped to put a name and a face to a neighbor in need in Brazil or Zaire, they get excited about those distant neighbors. Many would rather lend a hand than write a check. Small churches exist to care. We can make it easier for them to do so—locally and globally.

11. *A small church wants its minister to be a pastor, friend, and generalist,* not a professional, specialist, administrator, or chief executive officer. It wants precisely what the seminary often doesn't prepare students to be. Carl Dudley says that what a small church wants is a "lover," someone who cares effectively and personally. A church with no pretensions or delusions will puncture any pretensions or delusions a pastor

brings. This is not to say they don't want or need competent or skilled leadership. But the pastor must be able to exercise his or her competence and skill on a personal level.

12. *The small church model is the biblical model.* The churches the gospels were written for and the churches we read about from Acts to Revelations were small churches. Small churches can't and shouldn't try to identify with contemporary corporate and organizational models. They *can* identify with the biblical models of faithfulness. They can read Acts or Ephesians or James and say, "Yes, that's us!"

13. *Small churches are people oriented.* They aren't goal oriented or future oriented. They aren't turned on by planning or processing. They don't come to worship for private meditation or to meetings to make decisions. If they wanted those things, they'd find a big church. They come to worship with and work with their friends. What others call gossip, they call caring. The deacons won't want to tend to their "business" until they talk about who they need to talk about. In fact, that's much of what they see their business to be.

14. *Small churches are more likely to laugh and cry* than large ones. Emotions are closer to the surface when we're with those we know and care about. The priority in small churches is attending to those things about which we feel emotion. And church members are more likely to express those emotions than to repress them.

15. *Worship is their primary activity.* Larger churches offer a full menu and their people pick and choose the entrees they want. Worship is a small church's "house specialty." Anything else that's offered is often seen as an appetizer or dessert. Much happens during worship in small churches (like caring, education, and business) that happens at other times in other churches.

16. *Small churches are more story than treatise, more mythology than methodology.* Their stories are crucial to who they are, what they believe, and how they behave. Therefore they are likely to be more intuitive than rational and more artistic than scientific in their approach to faith and life. Ministry is helping them write a new chapter to their story or a new act in their drama.

17. *They operate on fluid, "people" time.* They take their time in making decisions. Tomorrow is far enough ahead to plan for. They don't watch the clock as much as they watch their neighbor. It matters not so

much if worship was more than an hour than if it felt like it was too long. If they say "it seems like only yesterday," it probably seems like only yesterday. Two years with some pastors will seem like an eternity, and ten years with others will be like a split second. Therefore, agendas and schedules should be written in sand, not cement.

18. *Most small church people would rather give what is needed, when needed, and give it privately.* It is more businesslike and less anxiety producing to have every-member canvasses to underwrite the budget for the next year or more. We like to think it is more faithful. One reason small church people like small churches is that the smaller their budget, the less businesslike they have to be. They will give more to support special projects than to support a budget. Small churches often have their own traditional ways of dealing with money and resist new ways. Some pastors pull out their hair in July when half the needed money for the year isn't in, not understanding that their church is always in the black by December.

19. *Lay people are more important than the pastor.* Ouch! Seminary taught us that the church revolves around the pastor. Small churches who have waited long periods between pastors, whose pastors have been too green or too gray, or who have rarely had a pastor stay long enough to become part of the family have learned to be self-reliant and self-sufficient. Part of the knack of pastoring a small church is having the humility and wisdom to know when and how to lead and when and how to get out of the way.

20. *Small churches are often hard to get into and harder to get out of.* By getting in, I don't necessarily mean getting your name on the membership list. If the church acts like and is a family, a new person only becomes a family member by being adopted into it or grafted onto the family tree. Either way it takes time—time to learn the stories, time to learn how things are done and what is expected, time to become known. "We don't just take anybody, you know!" But once you're in, they're not going to let you out without a fight. As Robert Frost said in "The Death of the Hired Man": "'Home is the place where, when you have to go there / They have to take you in.'"

21. *Small churches are tough!* Remember the little kid in school who survived by being tough? Small churches have survived because they are survivors. They know how to make do. They know how to weather a storm. Don't underestimate their resilience.

22. *Small churches would rather do it "our way."* They are not impressed by the denomination's way, or the new book's way, or the pastor's experience in the last church. Rather than meekly being another franchise in the "McChurch" chain of churches, they're better at being a customized, one-of-a-kind church. Each has its own special spiritual gift. The wise pastor will be able to discern that gift and use it appropriately.

23. *They're more effective than efficient.* Perhaps it is more efficient to close the too-little church in the country and merge it with the bigger church in town. It might be more efficient, but it is unlikely to provide a more effective and faithful ministry with those people left in the country. Most of the little churches outsiders think should be closed would have closed a long time ago if they weren't effective. Often effectiveness is confused with efficiency. Don't expect to do ministry in small churches "by the book" or as organizational theory teaches.

24. *Small churches are better at events than programs.* Large churches operate with a program year. Small churches live in their own seasonal rhythm. A pastor who doesn't hear the church's indigenous rhythm is likely to throw it out of synch. Seasonal celebrations, special worship services, fund-raising events, special trips, service projects, parties, work days, and so on. are more attractive to more people than long-term study groups, open-ended mission projects, and programs requiring long-term commitment.

25. *They're better at meeting immediate needs than long-range planning.* This immediacy has to do with their sense of timing, their distrust of the future, and their nuts-and-bolts way of working. Don't ask a small church to envision how things should be in ten years. Ask what do you think we need to do this week, month, year. Ask what do you think Jesus would do if he were here now. Do what's in character for that particular church. For them, the time that is most real is yesterday and now and maybe tomorrow.

26. *Small churches are locally owned and operated.* To survive they have had to be independent. They've experienced more benign neglect than sensitive assistance. They believe they know what's best for them—and they probably do. They're not going to buy the notion of "covenant" with the wider church until they're convinced covenant isn't a code word for giving up control of their own destiny.

Small churches may be small, but they're not simple. There is more to understanding them than meets the eye. Most important, I hope you see that they are the *right size* to be all that God expects in a church, and that they're *different* from one another and from all other churches. Those are the port and starboard realities of small churches.

For Thought and Discussion

1. How do you experience your church to be the right size?
2. How do you experience it to be different from larger churches?
3. How have the trends toward biggness affected your church?
4. Recognizing that small churches are different from one another, what kind of small church is yours?
5. Of the theories presented, which one rings the loudest bells with you in your experience?
6. Of the author's twenty-six characteristics of small churches, which ones best describe your church? What other characteristics would you add?

4. ◆ Twenty Years in the Crucible

In 1971, the Trinitarian Congregational Church of Warwick, Massachusetts, called me as their very part-time pastor. After fourteen years in Warwick, I served for four years as the full-time pastor of the Shrewsbury Community Church in Shrewsbury, Vermont, and, since March 1989, I've been the half-time pastor of the United Church of Christ church in Emmetsburg, Iowa. Each of these churches, communities, and experiences has been very different from the others. In each, I've operated out of my basic premise that small churches are the right size to be all a church is called to be and different. And I've used the particular principles that I believe are appropriate for small churches.

I will always be grateful to the people of all three churches for what they've taught me, accomplished with me, and given to me and my family. They've enriched my life in many ways. I apologize if in any way I've misrepresented any of them or what happened in their midst. I pray that what I write here will be fair and helpful for them and helpful for the reader.

A decade ago, after my first nine years of ministry in Warwick, I wrote *Small Churches Are the Right Size*. Since its publication, additional grist for my mill has come from the rest of that ministry, from a very different ministry in Shrewsbury, from my dual ministry in Iowa of pastoring in Emmetsburg and being an area minister, and from ongoing reading, writing, teaching, and consulting. But it has been primarily in the crucible of small church ministry in Warwick, Shrewsbury, and Emmetsburg that I've experienced, learned, and developed the principles and approaches found in this book.

Warwick, Massachusetts

> Consider your own call, brothers and sisters: not many of you were wise by human standards, not many were powerful, not many were of noble birth. But God chose what is foolish in the world to shame the wise; God chose what is weak in the world to shame the strong (1 Cor. 1:26–27).

In the spring of 1971, I was finishing three years as director of an ecumenical youth ministry in Brattleboro, Vermont. One of the sponsoring churches needed money to replace its furnace, and the youth ministry was deemed dispensable. I was out of a job and thinking of leaving ministry to be an elementary school teacher. The crisis center I'd help start was ready to hire me as their part-time director; I was enrolled in a masters program at the University of Massachusetts; Cindy, my wife, still had her teaching position in Brattleboro; and we'd built a small log home in Warwick, twenty miles away.

Before the termination of the youth ministry position, I'd noticed a sign on an old colonial house in Warwick that said "Metcalf Memorial Church—Trinitarian Congregational Church." We attended worship there and found the people made up in warmth what they lacked in numbers. Not knowing the proper etiquette, I went to visit the church patriarch, Charles Morse, and asked if they might like a part-time pastor. He guessed they might.

This was definitely one of Schaller's tiny fellowship or "cat" churches. It was the kind of church many denominational officials and church members despair over and too frequently close. The church had fourteen active members—five men, nine women, no young people. Six were retired. One or two had some college education. They were not affluent nor particularly sophisticated. The other church in town was the Unitarian church, which had a nice building but seldom held services.

That spring I was added to their rotation of lay and retired worship leaders. In the summer I became their weekly worship leader. In August, the church voted to call me as their thirty-dollar-a-day, two-day-a-week pastor. The church building was an 1816 white colonial house. The second floor was unused. The main floor had two heated rooms—a front room for worship and a back room for their tiny Sunday school. Behind this room was a storage room, outhouse, and shed. There was no running water, the wiring was antiquated, the sills and floor joists were rotting.

Warwick is a beautiful, heavily wooded, out-of-the-way hill town nestled at the foot of Mount Grace in northwestern Massachusetts. The population of 492 in 1970 was a combination of retired people; factory, foundry, and paper mill workers and their families; young adults who had moved there as part of the rural, back-to-the-land movement; a few self-employed loggers, carpenters, and farmers; a handful of merchants and professionals; and a very large commune (which was the cause of much anxiety). The only businesses were the general store, the Warwick Inn (a tavern), and a sawmill.

Warwick is about twenty miles from four larger communities in four different directions. Therefore, Warwick people traveled outward in four directions to work, shop, play, and receive services, and seldom came together. There was a local three-room elementary school and grades seven through twelve were bused to a regional school. There was no single newspaper or radio station that served the town. The signal-blocking interference of Mount Grace meant people couldn't even get the same television stations. More divided the town than unified it.

Charles Morse, Warwick's historian, had written the church's history in 1969. It could be a description of any one of thousands of other tiny, tenacious churches. He describes it as: "a typical small rural church which has had a continuous struggle to exist from the day of its birth. It still struggles and it still exists. . . . We are proud of the difficulties we have overcome, and we hope our story will be an inspiration to our fellow churches."

On 8 August 1971, in my sermon before my call as their pastor, I issued a challenge and painted a vision. The challenge was to move beyond being a worshiping-only chapel and to become a working church that would share ministry with me:

> I have a dream for this church and for Warwick. My dream is that this church will choose to embark on a new adventure. My dream is that we discover that energy, ability, financial, and personal resources put to work will return to us and to the town far more than we originally expended. My dream is that Warwick will become a place that under-

stands its problems and knows how to solve them. That's my dream.
What's yours?

It was no small matter for the church to pay me sixty dollars a week.
That meant more than doubling their budget from $1,585 to $3,665.
The church had no endowment or affluent givers. Their sense of stewardship had been to give enough to pay the bills and to spend no more than
necessary. They decided to be more vigorous in urging increased and regular giving and using offering envelopes. Three men salvaged materials
and built a "paper shack" at the town dump for a money-raising paper recycling project. One Sunday, Carl and Rotha Nordstedt drove to Am-
herst and paid a surprise visit on the UCC area minister and came away
with a five-hundred-dollar grant. The Women's Christian Service Society, newly revived, made a donation to the church from their treasury
and worked with great vigor on their Christmas fair.

Inactive church members and community people were invited to
church to meet "our new pastor." I called in the community and on anyone from town who was hospitalized. A youth group was started. Interest
grew, participation increased, and there was enough money to pay the
bills.

As I look back, there were ten things I emphasized in the beginning of
my Warwick pastorate—either intuitively or intentionally—that were
crucial in the transformation of that struggling remnant chapel into a
small but dynamic church. I've used the same principles in Shrewsbury
and Emmetsburg with positive results.

1. *Listening.* I spent a lot of time visiting the Morses, the Andersons,
Arthur Francis, Marion Copeland, the Nordstedts, and others. I listened
to their stories so I could learn the story that would be the key to leading
them from past to present to future. I read the Warwick history. Each
morning, I eavesdropped on town gossip at the post office, until the government closed the only place in town where people regularly gathered. I
attended town events. I moved from being acquainted with to knowing
these people. As I listened, they learned that I cared about them and
took them seriously. As I've worked with pastors, I've come to believe
the biggest mistake of many is talking too much and listening too little.

2. *Worship.* Worship is the heart and soul of a small church. For this
church, it was their primary activity. It was an event they could invite
others to. Worship was Warwick's only regular gathering for all ages and
both genders. It provides the opportunity for God to change the collec-

tive heart of the worshiping community. Worship leadership is something I could do more effectively than they had been experiencing in their rotation of supply preachers. So, we worked hard at worship. I used the elementary school's spirit duplicator to print bulletins that would lead the people through a new order of worship. The choir grew from two to a half dozen and more. Family services were held once a month. We had special worship celebrations: a birthday party for Jesus during Advent, a live nativity scene (with animals) before the new Christmas Eve service, a Good Friday service and Easter sunrise service, an outdoor worship and picnic on Pentecost. When their worship came alive the church came alive.

3. *Innovation and Action.* The traditional advice—which I've never followed—is start slowly and don't make major changes for at least a year. Worship was changed to be more contemporary, participatory, personal, and appropriate for this particular people. It took two weeks to start a coffee hour. The Sunday school collected for UNICEF and sold light bulbs. The new youth group renovated an upstairs room.

It was crucial to demonstrate to the church and community that something new and special was happening. We wanted that spirit to be contagious. The changes made our life together more alive and more rewarding. Changes were introduced with statements like, "Let's try it for awhile and see if we like it." They weren't costly, carved in stone, or threatening. Key people were consulted first and members were asked to help with the changes. The ultimate compliment was: "I like it now because something is always different. We don't go to sleep anymore!"

4. *Success upon Success.* Loss is many small churches' only experience with change. It was vital for the Warwick church to experience that change could mean gain and that they could make good things happen. We started with easy, sure things. I knew a coffee hour would be easy and popular. There were young people and parents eager for local youth activity and I was a trained youth worker, so we started a youth group. I was confident a Christmas Eve candlelight service would kindle community support, so we began this tradition. The typical small church syndrome of inferiority and futility was transformed into the stated sentiment that "we can do what whatever we want to do." Within a year, the church conducted an auction, food sale, and public supper and netted $1,800 in one day—an unprecedented achievement for them.

5. *Become Intergenerational.* Children and youth bring vitality and

provide a future. We brought children and youth into our midst. Children in worship, a youth group, and family activities encouraged family participation and nurtured liveliness and hope. As a result, some of those children are now pillars in that church.

6. *Community Outreach.* From the beginning, we reached out to the community. We sent a letter to each home in town introducing me, inviting them to worship, and offering a pastoral call. I preached the idea that we had a membership of a couple dozen but a parish of 492 people. Our deacon's fund was used to assist anyone in the community in need. As time passed, the church was credited with making Warwick a stronger, healthier community.

7. *World-consciousness.* The Warwick church, like so many small churches, was isolated from the wider church and the outside world. That first fall we borrowed a projector and showed a film about our denomination's mission programs, children collected for UNICEF, we took a One-Great-Hour-of-Sharing offering, and insisted our treasurer send the mission money to our denomination, which he'd been withholding. The youth group collected for the American Heart Association and put on a breakfast for Heifer Project International. By connecting our church with the world out there, we became less isolated and insulated.

8. *Commendation and Recognition.* Church work is often a thankless activity. These people had kept their church alive through long, hard times. From the beginning, I was careful to appreciate, applaud, and affirm. I urged others to do the same. One of the first meals we shared was an appreciation luncheon put on by the newcomers for the veterans of the church. With no kitchen, refrigeration, or plumbing, this was an accomplishment!

9. *Vision.* As a goal-oriented person, I tried to keep a vision before the church and encouraged their own envisioning. My first four sermons were my visions for the church in its worship, Christian education, and responsibility to the community and world. There were such challenges as a larger budget, a significant mission project, a growth goal, a building addition. Always the goal was realistic enough to be achievable—if we stretched, worked together, and trusted.

10. *A Commitment to the People.* I couldn't ask more of our people than I would ask of myself. People assumed I would soon move to something bigger and better. I assured them Warwick was our home, we were

happy there, and I would stay as long as they were responsive to my leadership. As people began to believe my commitment to them, they became willing to dream bigger dreams and make their own larger commitments.

The years 1972 through 1974 saw a continuation of the directions and principles of that first dramatic year. The church grew steadily. Several people with a Catholic background and various breeds of Protestants joined, and we became a truly ecumenical and community church. Worship and Sunday school attendance tripled. The budget quadrupled. Morale, trust, and confidence were high. We were ready for new challenges and opportunities. Two projects emerged.

In our second year, Alice Anderson, a semiactive member, suffered a stroke, was cared for by the church, and died six months later. To our amazement, she willed $70,000 to the church. The two years it took to probate her will gave us time to plan its use.

We were outgrowing our worship and Sunday school space and some yearned for something a little more churchlike. We were worried about our sills, floors, and wiring, and we wished for plumbing. The Anderson money seemed like the means of fulfilling our dreams. Those dreams ranged from remodeling our Metcalf Chapel house to building a traditional white-spired New England church building. For two years, through informal conversation, sermons, and committee and church meetings, we talked, proposed, deliberated, planned, and decided.

At a church meeting on 27 April 1975, we unanimously voted to renovate and restore the chapel to nearly its original form; to raze the back wing; and to add an addition that would be a larger worship room over a dining room and kitchen. The project would include a well, plumbing, new wiring, full insulation, and central heat. We would use half of the money from the Anderson estate. It would be accomplished with volunteer labor, except for one paid carpenter/foreman and the excavation, electrical, and plumbing work. The first Sunday of June we went outside during worship and broke ground and communion bread.

While we were involved in planning the building, Steve Fellows, a young man in the church, decided to spend a year as a volunteer at the Heifer Project Ranch in Arkansas. Steve and I proposed that the church try to raise the $1,800 annual stipend that Heifer Project volunteers are paid. No one said "no" or "impossible." To accept the challenge meant we would be trying to raise $9,200 in 1975 in contrast to our 1974 budget of $6,400. And it meant we'd be raising this money while we were building our addition with volunteer labor.

In a memorable January worship service, we circulated a check from the Anderson estate, received ten new members, commissioned Steve as our ambassador to Heifer Project, and passed out $150 in one-, five-, and ten-dollar bills to people willing to reinvest the money in projects re-enacting Jesus' parable of the talents. People showed great initiative. One grew and sold peas. Another made and sold bread. Another bought sap buckets and made and sold maple syrup. Firewood was cut and sold. Our $150 grew into $800. Central American crafts, greeting cards, and Heifer Project T-shirts were sold. A double ten-mile walkathon beginning in opposite directions and ending at the town common was held. Over $3,000 was raised—almost twice our goal!

We worked on our building while we worked on our Heifer Project challenge. About fifty volunteers—all ages, sizes, abilities, genders—from both church and community helped. About a dozen did the bulk of the work. Two of our men worked almost full-time. Major decisions (like paint colors, carpet, sanctuary arrangement) came before the whole church for discussion and decision. Our decorating task force took a school bus to neighboring churches looking for ideas and to Boston to buy light fixtures.

One particularly good memory lingers. It was time to put the finish on the wainscoting in the new sanctuary. In a split decision, we decided to paint rather than varnish. Ted, one of our hardest working volunteers, painted the prime coat. Emma, drawing on her interior decorating experience, walked in as the paint was drying, and exclaimed in her refreshing candor: "That looks awful!" Her second comment was that if others agreed a natural finish would be better, she would help strip the new paint . . . since she had "opened her mouth." On stripping day, outspoken Emma and patient Ted, alongside others of both persuasions, stripped paint together. When all was said, done, and varnished, everyone agreed the second decision was the best decision.

By dedication day in April 1976, we were—like our building—restored, new, larger, and ready for new experiences and challenges. Heifer Project had connected us with the wider world and taught us our only real limitations were self-imposed. Our building project gave us that attractive, functional, custom-made-for-us space we needed. Most importantly, we learned again what a gracious God and hardworking people can do together. It was upon this firm foundation that the rest of our time together was built.

As we were putting the finishing touches on our renewed and new chapel, I sought to change our focus and direction. In a sermon early in 1976, I pointed in a new direction:

Over the last year we've grown in numbers and achievements. We've worked very hard. We're a hardworking, loyal, spirited church. Now we need to grow spiritually—in faith, trust, sensitivity, and knowledge; in a sense of mission and responsibility. We've grown wider; now let's grow deeper. . . . I'm calling you to grow toward a risking, adventurous faith. That's going to be the emphasis in my ministry this year.

After a "sabbath-time" of rest and celebration for church and pastor, I searched for the vehicle that might move us in a new direction and into a new dimension. I found it in the experimental Doctor of Ministry program at Hartford Seminary in Connecticut. The program I chose offered a congregation-focused doctoral program for pastors in conjunction with a parish component in which seminary faculty would come to work directly with the pastors' churches. We discussed, found the money, and enrolled together in the program. It was transforming for the church and me.

I traveled ninety miles to Hartford for advanced courses in preaching, worship, mission, parish dynamics, conflict, Bible study, Christian education, and spirituality. I translated each course into small church reality. I came home and pursued course-related projects in our church. Hartford faculty traveled to Warwick for weekend-long, lay-oriented courses in envisioning a new mutual ministry, worship, parish life, caring and community, and Bible study.

We grew in every way. Our shared life and ministry continued to flourish. The church sponsored a community-wide, monthly newsletter, which still exists as the only source of community-wide communication. The Glad Rags thrift shop was started in an upstairs Sunday school room. It is still serving the community. A Helping Hands ministry was created to provide emergency services to our community. Our Sunday school for children during worship became an education hour for all ages before worship. Not only did we reach out in service, but we worked at faith development and disciple making. It was a proud winter day in 1982 when the president of Hartford Seminary came to Warwick to conduct the graduation service for both pastor and church.

About this time I initiated two ventures around which we did not find a common mind. The first was a personal dream that I hoped others would come to share. Our church was given 175 acres of prime woodlands. Different uses were considered. I envisioned developing a retreat center on the property and the management of that facility becoming an outreach ministry of the whole church. Some shared the dream and some didn't. We got as far as building sketches but couldn't find the money or the common will to make the dream a reality.

Second, we had became a teaching parish for Andover Newton Theological School in Newton Centre, Massachusetts. After a very positive three-year relationship with one student pastor, we called another. Our new student pastor was a second-career student who had been part of the Church of the Savior in Washington. She, the church, and I seemed to be well matched. I conceived of the church having a full-time ministry with each of us as half-time co-pastor. We all carefully explored the idea. With a giant leap of faith, we began a one-year trial coministry.

It didn't work. A full-time co-ministry did not generate enough money to pay for itself. Our working styles were dissimilar. We sometimes got in each other's way. Some seemed to respond more to her leadership and some to mine. Questioning how much longer I could have an effective ministry in Warwick and longing for a new challenge, I chose to resign and look for that challenge. Leaving Warwick was extremely painful— like a death or divorce. Many more good things happened there than there is space to share here and such good memories remain. The little chapel became a solid and faithful small church and remains so, and I learned much about ministry.

Shrewsbury, Vermont

> Enlarge the site of your tent, and let the curtains of your habitations be stretched out; do not hold back; lengthen your cords and strengthen your stakes. (Isa. 54:2)

It was a church in the mountains of Vermont that captured my imagination. The community and landscape were beautiful, the search committee was impressive, the people were friendly, our articulated goals were compatible, and the interviews went very well. I saw great potential, and they seemed to want what I had to offer. I accepted their call to begin a full-time ministry in June 1985.

The Isaiah 54 verse was my chosen text for Shrewsbury. My goals seemed to match their wants and needs and to be realistic: to help the church to become a caring community, to strengthen the organizational workings of the church, to grow in size and faithfulness, and to become a mission-minded and community-oriented church. In four years considerable progress was made in each area and there were many significant achievements. Yet, as it turned out, we weren't able to shake the forces of the past or the negative dynamics of the community.

I missed or ignored some clues to which I should have paid attention.

For example, after my candidating sermon, Cindy and I were left seques-
tered in a back room for forty-five minutes while the church debated the
failures of the previous ministry and the idea of a pastoral relations committee, before finally voting to call me as their pastor. After a brief
honeymoon period, old tensions surfaced and personality conflicts reap-
peared, although progress was made—but not easily.

Together, we had a lot going for us. I came experienced and energetic,
anxious for this new opportunity. The people were very cordial, had a
rich and varied church experience, and a serious approach to the Christian faith. Among them were abundant abilities and personal resources.
This was the only church in a community of over eight hundred people.
Their large endowment provided more than an adequate financial base.
After their two previous unhappy pastorates and our pain in leaving Warwick, we all voiced a desire to make this a good and long shared ministry.

Doing the right things, we got off to good start. In order to get to know
the congregation and learn their stories, I intensively and strategically
called on people. Cindy and I hosted everyone in the church at a dozen
different parsonage potlucks, in order to get acquainted. A Genesis series
of eight, varied special events were held to get the attention of the community and build interest in the church. I preached a sermon series on
my vision for the church. A mission committee was formed, the Christian education and music committees were reactivated, and work was begun to create a pastoral relations committee to help nurture a healthy
pastor-church relationship. Responses were good.

My greatest learning from Shrewsbury is how important history, context, personalities, and expectations are to the life of a church. There
were a complex of issues at work in Shrewsbury that shaped and shad-
owed my ministry there.

Shrewsbury is a beautiful community—encompassing mountains, mea-
dows, woods, sparkling streams, ponds, a mountain lake, and breathtaking views from virtually every road. It is a three-tiered town with Cuttingsville in the valley, Shrewsbury Center half-way up the mountain,
and Northam higher up. The town is one of the largest in the state in
area. The population of 850 is spread throughout the town and people
easily remain remote from their neighbors. There is no single crossroads
or center of town where everyone passes or gathers. Only a small percentage of the town's inhabitants regularly go to either of the two general
stores for staples and gossip.

Despite its rural appearance, Shrewsbury is a bedroom community for
Rutland, the second largest city in Vermont. Most people go to Rutland

to work and shop, and for services, culture, and social life. Many go there for church. They retreat back to Shrewsbury for home life and solitude. Since a minority are involved in community life, town organizations compete for a small pool of community-minded people. Shrewsbury is a leisure-minded community that attracts skiers in the winter and vacationers in the summer.

One could not find a community of more interesting people. Although almost entirely Caucasian, Shrewsbury is diverse in every other way: very wealthy to very poor, highly educated to poorly educated, well traveled to very provincial, very liberal and very conservative, young families and retired people. Many have just arrived and some have been there for ever. These characteristics may describe many towns, but Shrewsbury's extremes seem more pronounced. The wealth is obvious, the poverty well hidden. The serene beauty hides many tarnished dreams.

The stereotype of a Vermont town is grizzled, taciturn natives, content with themselves and closed to outsiders. The reality in Shrewsbury is that most residents are outsiders, or "flatlanders," who have come within the last ten or fifteen years. Adults who have lived there all their lives are unusual. Second-, third-, or fourth-generation families are rare.

The three communities within Shrewsbury are geographically and socially well separated, though not as much as they once were. Clear memories exist of bitter rivalries between the three villages. Each even has its own road to Rutland and had its own school and church. Cuttingsville had a Methodist church, Shrewsbury Center a Universalist church, and Northam a Christian church. About 1950, the three churches officially merged their small congregations into one church.

Shrewsbury is preoccupied with issues and politics. One of Vermont's two senators lives there and there is an active Amnesty International chapter. A deep environmental awareness energizes Shrewsbury and many citizens are involved in various environmental lobbies. Residents have played a major role in successfully fighting development in Shrewsbury and in the ski towns across the mountain. School, town, state, and national politics are favorite Shrewsbury sports. Town meeting, the second Tuesday of March, is the favorite day of the year. Often there is a conflict brewing, if not boiling. Shrewsbury people tend to be independent, fiesty, and politically savvy.

Like the town, the church is fascinating. It is both land and dollar rich. It owns two-and-a-half church buildings and a parsonage on 175 acres. When the churches merged, they kept all their buildings. Summer worship is divided between the Cuttingsville and Northam buildings.

September through May, worship is in Shrewsbury Center at the Meetinghouse in which the church owns the upstairs and the town owns the downstairs. The Meetinghouse committee, made up of delegates from church and town, administer the building and assess church and town for expenses. A large endowment provides over half the church's budget.

When I arrived there were 104 members, but only about forty-five were active. Like the town, the church is a diverse lot. Almost all the active members moved to Shrewsbury from somewhere else and from a wide variety of religious backgrounds. They brought with them their own denominational, suburban, large-church expectations of what a church should be and do. The church, like the community, had a history of conflict. There are many in the community who at one time or another left the church, for one reason or another. This pattern continues. As I got to know people, I became aware that an unusually large percentage were facing personal, family, vocational, or economic stresses in their lives, all of which have a way of spilling over into their church life.

Much was accomplished in those four years. The church's organizational life was in chaos. The trustees, with strong personalities and a clear mandate to manage the church's money and properties, were independent and dominant. The deacons had too many people (a dozen) and too few jobs (serving communion). The Christian education and music committees were inactive. No individual would agree to be the church's chairperson. Very little was brought to the church for church-wide decisions.

Over time, the trustees became a cohesive, thoughtful, and effective group. The group of deacons was pared to a manageable size, their job description was enlarged, and they became very effective. The Christian education committee and music committee were activated. A mission committee formed and became active and effective. The level of giving increased significantly, so that it exceeded the church's endowment income. After seven drafts of a descriptive document were written, the church voted—after heated debate—to create a Pastor-Parish Relations Committee. An effective chairperson for the church was recruited. The number of people actively involved in church leadership almost doubled. Communication improved and the church worked more faithfully and effectively.

The church became more of a caring community than it had been, though not what I had hoped for. Through community-building events, sharing of joys and concerns in worship, news through the new newsletter, my effort in caring and counseling, and the work of the deacons, we became more aware of one another, some healing took place, and people felt more cared for. Despite the loss of some who left, membership grew by about 10 percent.

The Shrewsbury church became less of an insulated church in the community and more of an outreaching church in the world. I became chaplain of the fire department and actively involved in community life. The deacons became more aggressive in using their Helping Hand Fund to assist people in crisis. A thrift shop was developed and housed in the Cuttingsville church, a sick-room library of convalescent supplies was established, and a Food Shelf was opened. A musical comedy about peace with an intergenerational cast of thirty was produced. Our very active youth group served the whole community and traveled in separate trips to Montreal, Maine, Boston, New York, and Washington. A very exciting, though poorly attended, Food Day raised consciousness and earned $1,500 for food programs.

The most significant outreach happened through the assistance of the sister of our church chairperson. She and her husband were missionaries in Rwanda, Africa. They helped us create a partnership with the Gahulire Baptist Church in Rwanda. Letters, tapes, pictures, and gifts were exchanged, and Bibles were sent. We learned that termites were destroying their school and that a new one could be built for $3,000. The church raised the money with a variety of efforts. In February 1988, twelve of us took $7,000 in money and supplies and traveled to Rwanda for a life-changing mission trip.

This all looks and sounds both effective and faithful, and it was! So, if the Shrewsbury ministry ended in disappointment, what happened and why?

First, I impatiently expected the church to grow from what it had been to what it could be faster than it was able to. Second, we had differing expectations. I wanted the church to become a close-knit, caring, Christian community that would reach out to others. Many lay people wanted the pastor to minister to their separate, interior, spiritual lives. Some wanted my ministry confined to church members and narrowly defined spiritual matters. Third, I wanted to spread the responsibility and power broadly throughout the church. Some wanted to vest the bulk of authority in a small group of leaders. Fourth, I hoped the members would become personally and actively involved in the worship, work, and ministry of the church, but many of our busy, over-committed, and personally stressed people could not move beyond partial commitment.

Finally, as a result of the legacy of conflict in the church, the combative style of some in the church and community, and the clash between pastor's and people's expectations, there was a continuing undercurrent of unrest and conflict. The historic pattern continued of people being dissatisfied or getting mad and leaving rather than working at tolerance, accommodation, and reconciliation.

I read, studied, prayed, and worked harder. I checked my perspective with a counselor and worked with our pastoral relations committee. I consulted with the pastor's support group I attended and consulted our denominational staff. No cure for the unrest and conflict could be found. When an invitation came from Iowa, I was ready.

Emmetsburg, Iowa

The people who survived the sword found grace in the wilderness. (Jer. 31:2)

July 1988, I received a letter from Don Gall, conference minister for the United Church of Christ in Iowa, asking if he could interest me in Iowa. The letter told of a conference restructuring that would place four half-time area ministers out in the four quarters of the state. Two of the positions would be combined with half-time pastorates in small churches.

Iowa? I'd been quoted as saying I'd go anywhere God called me except Nebraska—which was just across the Missouri River from Iowa. I'd been in New England for over twenty years and loved it. But my spirit was tired and my soul was hungry. I responded: "I don't think so, but send more information."

One of the two sites was Emmetsburg, the county seat of Palo Alto county in northwest Iowa. Cindy and I talked, comparing what was no longer productive for me with what might be very productive and satisfying and what the ramifications might be for our family. We'd just built our dream house in Shrewsbury—beautiful view, forty-four acres of meadow and woods. Noelle and Aaron were happy in school and Cindy had a secure job. We'd said "no" to the Midwest once before. On the other hand, the area minister job sounded challenging and tailormade for me, and the Emmetsburg church sounded all right. When offered the dual positions, we decided it was all right enough to say, "yes." I've never regretted that "yes."

Northwest Iowa, like much of the Midwest, has been hurt badly by the growth of agribusiness and the decline of the family farm, the farm crisis and drought of the 1980s, and the exodus of young people to places with more jobs and brighter lights. Our county population dropped from

12,721 in 1980 to 10,699 in 1990; and our small city declined from 4,621 to 3,940. Several factory buildings and Main Street businesses are empty. In the last two years, Emmetsburg's three clothing stores closed. There are twice as many people over age seventy-five as under five. It sounds like a dying situation, but it isn't.

There is much that is typically midwestern about Emmetsburg. The pride of the community is our state champion football and girl's basketball teams. Our neat, clean community is built around the southern tip of its most significant resource—Five Island Lake. In a remarkable display of community spirit and long-range vision, Emmetsburg voted recently, by a 90 percent plurality, to tax itself $400,000 to begin the long process of dredging the lake. An established economic development program is working hard to keep and attract business and industry. Emmetsburg is a pleasant and hospitable place to live.

Recent years were also difficult for our church. It was hit hard by the loss of several young, active families. Our church membership dropped from 398 in 1946 to 113 in 1980 to 88 when I arrived in March 1989. The previous ministry resulted in continuing loss and the inability to afford a full-time pastor. During the interim between pastors, the church discovered its east wall was bulging and the roof over the sanctuary was sagging. A church meeting was held to consider the church's options, including the option of closing the church. The church chose to continue. As an emergency measure, a post was erected in the middle of the sanctuary to hold up the roof. Exterior iron beams and four cables through the sanctuary were installed to hold the structure together. The building was stabilized. Now attention turned to the life and ministry of the church.

The state conference intervened and offered the prospect of calling someone to be half-time pastor of the church and area conference minister. I was recruited and called. The plucky spirit of the church asserted itself as the members organized to fix up the "manse." Over $4,000 was donated. The old bathroom was renovated, a new one was installed, carpet was replaced, much of the interior (including closets) was repainted, everything was cleaned. Sensing a new lease on life, many people worked very hard to get ready for the new pastor.

Having left my family behind to finish school, I arrived with my dog, a full pickup, and U-Haul trailer. A "Welcome to Emmetsburg" banner, food in the refrigerator and cupboard, temporary furniture, and an African violet on the table greeted me.

That evening the trustees were meeting. The sentiment voiced that night and often since, was, "We're on a roll!" They were . . . and still are.

As soon as the manse renovation was finished, attention turned to putting in a handicap-accessible bathroom on the main floor of the church. More money was donated. I advised putting in a counter big enough to use as a changing table. When they said there were no babies, I suggested there would be. The changing table was put in and six babies have come along.

Next to the sanctuary were two dismal Sunday school rooms. Attention turned to these. Money and ideas were donated. What was an embarrassing eyesore was turned into a very attractive, functional Friendship Room. The latest project has been the complete renovation of the storm-damaged entry way and balcony stairway. People are discovering that the tired old building they were taking for granted is an architectural gem and a fine space conducive to housing significant ministry and mission. The vision has grown from a little fix-up at the manse to a complete structural repair, renovation, and restoration by the building's centennial in 1996.

What has happened with the building is indicative of what is happening with the church. By God's grace, I'm pastoring a caring, classy, hardworking people. A humorous incident captures the serendipity here. The Women's Fellowship served a luncheon after our first worship service. Following lunch, I was part of kitchen chatter as dishes were done. I sat back on a counter top, not noticing that I was sitting on a piece of heavily-frosted cake. Conversation continued until I gradually became aware that the young voice repeatedly insisting, "Mister, hey mister, you've got cake on your butt!" was being directed at me. Sure enough, I did. Before I could invent some response or disappear to the restroom, one of the classiest ladies grabbed a sponge with one hand and turned me around with the other. I was sponged off as conversation politely continued. We've been taking care of each other ever since.

The principles for beginning a ministry enumerated in the Warwick section of this chapter were used here. And they worked. Innovation began with the first worship service and an outdoor Easter sunrise service a week later. With mutual trust and respect we've continued doing things differently. But even I was surprised when, after two months, I introduced to the church council a major reorganization plan for the church. I prefaced the presentation with the assurance, "This is not to be decided, but just talked about, and considered at some point in the future." Their unanimous response was, "Let's try it." We did and it's working.

Our first risky project came in the first year. I was saddened by the many abandoned farmhouses scattered around the countryside and envisioned out loud about what we might do with a farmhouse, if one could be inexpensively acquired. A realtor in the church approached a bank, which gave us a house and two acres eight miles from town. People donated money, fixed up the house inside and out, furnished it, and now we are trying to use the "Faith Farm" retreat center for ourselves and others. This project has not developed as we had hoped.

The church is slowly but steadily growing, many more people are involved in church leadership, and a new board of mission is moving the church into the community and world. With many older people and continuing erosion in our community, we are challenged by the loss of hard-to-replace people. We are working at building morale and self-esteem, strengthening our shared ministry, and planning for the church's future. Living in the shadow of larger, more prestigious churches, we are defining and fulfilling our special niche. We're the caring, outreaching, hard-working, fun-loving church where significant things continue to happen. Many were stunned on "Miracle Sunday" in June 1992 when forty-three individuals and families pledged $87,000 toward the building restoration. The total given or pledged is now over $107,000. The United Church of Christ in Emmetsburg is still on a roll.

After twenty years of experience in three very different small churches facing very difficult problems, I'm even more confident that *small churches are the right size, they're different, and new and faithful life is almost always possible.* In the next five chapters, I'll discuss how small churches can do things differently, faithfully, and effectively in the five fundamental areas of church life: worship, education, caring, mission, and organizational maintenance.

For Thought and Discussion

1. Look at the scripture references used at the beginning of each section of the chapter (1 Cor. 1:26–27, Isa. 54:2, Jer. 31:2). Is there any relevance for your situation in any of these passages?
2. How might the ten principles for beginning a ministry in the Warwick section apply in your situation or ministry? What virtues and cautions do you find in them?
3. In each of the situations, how did the surrounding context shape the church and the author's ministry there?
4. How were the three churches different? How were they similar?
5. What can you learn in these stories that can apply to your experience and ministry?

5. ♦ Worship: The Work of the People

Family reunions are fascinating rituals. Once a year a family clan will rent a hall, reserve a recreation area, or come back to the family homestead. The people of each generation who claim this as their family come from near and far to renew common ties. When they gather, family news is updated, changes are noted, babies are welcomed, new spouses are confirmed, departed members are remembered and mourned, family stories are told and embellished, feuds are resolved and exacerbated, indigenous rituals are observed. Though not much new happens, everyone goes home with roots, identity, and place in the family clarified and solidified.

Worship in small churches is a family reunion and more. People of various generations, who behave like an extended family and are connected by accident, choice, or blood come together to worship their heavenly Parent, identify who is present and absent, exchange greetings and regrets, receive and pass on good news and bad, baptize and confirm, marry and bury, pray and eat, and practice the rituals that tell them whose they are, who they are, where they belong, and what they need to be doing. This familial nature of their worship is one of the distinctive features of small churches. Unlike the family reunion, worship in a large church is more like a band concert in the park where mostly strangers randomly gather to picnic, observe, and listen to the music.

Carl Dudley suggests that small church worship is like a "'folk dance' in slow motion, a graceful gliding of people seeing the familiar and touching the friendly as they enter, take their places, renew their sense of the Lord's loving care, and 'depart in peace.'"[1] It is a folk dance because everyone is a participant, what each does is integral and related to what the others are doing, and the act of the dance recalls and recreates the culture that created the dance.

In contrast, large church worship is more like attending a ballet, in which some dance while most observe and critique. The critical question is, does one need to "dance" in order to worship, or can a Christian worship simply by observing the dancing of others?

A person can meditate alone. A person alone in a crowd can be entertained, informed, even inspired. But, I believe a person can only *fully* worship as a Christian by actively participating in worship with a Christian community, and a Christian community is a group of Christians who know and care about one another. "Christianity means community through Jesus Christ and in Jesus Christ," wrote Dietrich Bonhoeffer in *Life Together*.[2]

Søren Kierkegaard understood the inherent, active nature of worship when he compared it to a drama in which God is the audience, the congregation are the actors, and the minister is the prompter. Obviously, the larger the cast, the more likely that people will step on one another's lines and toes and some will simply stand by.

In worship, as in the rest of life, there is a bias toward bigness. Movie mogul Samuel Goldwyn once remarked that he wanted a "film which begins with an earthquake and works up to a climax." Television shows us only one type of worship—the Crystal Cathedral experience. Seminaries teach budding pastors how to lead large church worship but rarely how to call the small church folk dance. Our denominations at regional and national gatherings only provide one model of worship—the pomp-and-circumstance model carefully choreographed with a huge choir, professional-caliber liturgical dancers, a bevy of liturgists balanced to include the right combination of gender and ethnic groups, and famous preacher (sometimes projected several times larger than life on a video screen). Such worship is designed to thrill more than involve the audience of many hundreds. In light of these models, it's hard to be impressed with our little folk dances, even if we're pretty good at them.

The authenticity of worship is too often defined by whether "I enjoyed it" or "got anything out of it." The authenticity of worship is more correctly determined by whether God and a company of believers are enabled to touch one another. Annie Dillard, one of the most perceptive writers of our time, in her book *Holy the Firm* contrasts big and small church worship and what God might do in each:

> I know only enough of God to want to worship him, by any means ready to hand. . . . There is one church here, so I go to it. . . . On a big Sunday there might be twenty of us there; often I am the only person under sixty, and feel as though I'm on a archaeological tour of Soviet Russia. The members are of mixed denominations; the minister is a Congregationalist, and wears a white shirt. The man knows God. . . . "Good morning!" he says after the first hymn and invocation, startling me witless every time, and we all shout back, "Good morning!"
>
> The churchwomen all bring flowers for the altar; they haul in arrangements as big as hedges, of wayside herbs in season, and flowers from their gardens, huge bunches of foliage and blossoms as tall as I am, in vases the size of tubs, and the altar still looks empty, irredeemably linoleum, and beige. We had a wretched singer once, a guest from a Canadian congregation, a hulking blond girl with chopped hair and big shoulders, who wore tinted spectacles and a long lacy dress, and sang, grinning, to faltering accompaniment, an entirely secular song about mountains. Nothing could have been more apparent than that God loved this girl. . . .
>
> The higher Christian churches—where, if anywhere, I belong—come at God with an unwarranted air of professionalism, with authority and pomp, as though they knew what they were doing, as though people in themselves were an appropriate set of creatures to have dealings with God. I often think of the set pieces of liturgy as certain words which people have successfully addressed to God without their getting killed. In the high churches they saunter through the liturgy like Mohawks along a strand of scaffolding who have long since forgotten their danger. If God were to blast such a service to bits, the congregation would be, I believe, genuinely shocked. But in the low churches you expect it any minute. This is the beginning of wisdom.[3]

Annie Dillard perceives that the awesome and holy might be especially present and approached in the simple and the lowly. Small churches are the right size for authentic worship, and small church worship rightly done must be done differently, not just scaled down from the "higher churches."

Definition of Worship

If we're to worship rightly, we must know what worship is. Worship means to "grant worth to." The crux of my understanding of worship grows out of Jesus' greatest commandment: "You shall love the Lord your God with all your heart, and with all your soul, and with all your mind. . . . You shall love your neighbor as yourself" (Matt. 22:37, 39). Therefore, worship is the active response of those in the Christian community to God's love with the praises of their hearts, the yearnings of their souls, and the ponderings of their minds, so that they are able to love one another and all of creation as they love themselves. By this definition, worship should be right down the small church's alley.

A liturgical renewal movement is under way. In its attempt to recover the power and integrity of Christian worship, the leaders of the renewal movement have searched back to its roots. Those roots are found in Judaism, not in the Temple, but in the synagogue and the ritual meals of Judaism. The synagogue required at least ten men, the ritual meals were conducted by a family or small group.

Following those models the Christian church began, grew, and spread in the form of house churches. Acts 1:13, 2:46, 5:42, 12:12; Romans 16:3–5, Colossians 4:15; and Philemon 2 all cite the early church's use of homes for worship and holy meals. The earliest church worship was like a family reunion or a folk dance where Christian clans remembered, celebrated, and were equipped to serve.

When early Christians came together for worship in a house or borrowed room, they began their worship with the "kiss of peace," when *all* the people greeted one another. Their worship was marked by the active involvement of all—or at least the men. Everyone was encouraged to pray, not just the "president." Their preaching or proclamation was specific and maintained a discipline that was necessary for their survival. Their worship was centered around a common meal. Acts tells us that "the company of those who believed were of one heart and soul" (Acts 4:32). The worship of the early church was really a liturgy, which means the "work of the people," and they were the right size for all to participate in the work. A commonality and lack of hierarchical distinction brought together male and female, slave and free, rich and poor, gentile and Jew in the Body of Christ.

The rediscovery of the nature of early church worship has affected some contemporary understandings and practice of worship. It also points, however, to how far much of what is done in worship is from roots in the Bible and in the early church.

> Contemporary liturgical renewal is taking its cue from the period before the church became big, successful, and respectable; before the church's

worship had a chance to become pompous, dramatic, and extravagant; before the Sunday service degenerated into a preacher/choir performance for a gathering of isolated, passive individuals. Directives for contemporary worship renewal are coming from a church that was then still a family, gathered around a family table, eating a family meal.[4]

In a small church, I will probably never be driven to my knees by architectural splendor, as I was in St. Patrick's Cathedral in New York City. In a small church, I will never be stirred by the power and majesty of music from a great pipe organ, a semiprofessional choir, and the unison singing of hundreds of worshipers. I probably won't hear preaching that overwhelms me with the authority of fame and the power of amplified sound, nor will I have the assurance of being part of a mass movement. Although moving, these characteristics aren't the essence of true worship.

What is of the essence in worship happens all the time in all kinds of small churches. I can experience a sense of family, of solidarity, of community with those who join me in glorifying God. I can experience God in the vertical one-to-one, or more likely, in the horizontal, as God is made known through the intimate and dynamic relationships that exist among us. Rather than passively watching others do the work of worship, I can actively have the joy of playing my part as we *all* do the work of worship. Rather than only praying for the needs of me and mine, I can actively intercede in voiced concern and prayer for all the collective and personal pain and joy being carried or celebrated within my family of faith.

I love to go to Fenway Park in Boston to watch baseball the way the professionals play it. But I've had much more fun playing baseball and helping coach my son's Little League team. That's the difference I experience between big and small church worship.

Here's how everybody can play the game in a small church. Consider this hypothetical example of a church with fifty worshipers. Two people bring the flowers and decorate, two are greeters and help people feel welcome, two make and serve refreshments. Four children talk during ministry of children, two volunteer announcements, a woman and a child take the offering, two adolescents are lay readers, two children light and extinguish the candles. One preaches, twelve are in the youth-adult choir, ten are in the kids' choir, two accompany the music. Four share joys and concerns, one counts the "house" and turns up the thermostat, and two are too shy or new to do anything out loud or official. Forty-eight out of fifty help conduct worship and everyone participates through reading, singing, listening, praying, and giving. That's liturgy, the work of the people, and small churches can do it well.

The Place of Worship

The places where small churches worship are as varied as the Christian church itself, ranging from living rooms to cavernous sanctuaries that once housed large congregations. In small churches the room for worship is often the only room in the building, and, if not the only one, it's usually the principal room.

For many the worship room offers a real sense of a sanctuary or safe and holy place in the midst of a threatening secular world. Whether it is good theology or not, many people feel God is somehow more present or approachable there than in the world at large. Inside the holy place are holy things. Some are obvious like the cross, the Bible, the altar. Other holy things not so obvious might be a picture, vase, piano or organ. In Warwick, a picture of Jesus had special meaning, along with candlesticks and the pulpit chairs, which were memorial gifts. In Shrewsbury, it was the tiny, silver baptismal bowl. In Emmetsburg, it is the gold, dossal curtain behind the altar that has special value. The holy place is full of clues for the curious and landmines for the unsuspecting.

For many, it's the place where they've gone almost every Sunday of their lives, where they were married, where a son was baptized and a daughter confirmed, from where a parent or spouse was buried. It's a place of refuge, comfort, decision, security, and hope. It's where some of their best friends are. It's a place some have helped build, furnish, and maintain, while others have paid dearly to keep it open. For many, it is the most orderly, attractive, peaceful, and hospitable place in an otherwise chaotic, drab, stressful, and hostile world. Although it may appear modest to the visitor, the place is very important to those who worship there, and even to many who don't. To the latter, it may symbolize God, security, order.

The place is particularly important because it can make or break the worship experience. When the environment dulls our senses and there are no living symbols to beckon our souls, it is difficult to experience the transcendent. A sense of family is difficult to achieve if people are too scattered to even catch a cold from the nearest person. Flexibility and informality are out of reach if everything is screwed down or untouchable. Everyone won't know everyone if there's no room for moving and mingling.

In the six worship rooms where I've been the pastor, I've experienced much that is conducive to faithful and effective worship and some things that aren't. The first worship room in Warwick was difficult. Although not shabby, it was drab. It felt as if it had been furnished from yard sales. The open area between the front door and the Sunday school room was like a moat that separated the congregation at one end of the long, narrow room from the preacher, organist, and little choir at the other end. Within a year we moved the pulpit to the middle of the room with pews on both sides, which was some improvement. What the room lacked in aesthetics, it made up for in intimacy.

The new sanctuary we built in Warwick has both—aesthetics and intimacy. It can seat a hundred, but no one is more than twenty-five feet from anyone else. With five rows of pews, no one has more than four heads in front of him or her. Everyone can see and be seen, hear and be heard. The room has rich, red carpet and beautiful light fixtures. We bought fire-damaged pews for ten dollars each, painted and varnished them, and they are lovely. The altar was made by a carpenter in the church and the baptismal font by a potter who was a friend of the church. The pastor's stoles and the banners were made by church seamstresses. The Metcalf Chapel was the house of the Lord, but we were very much at home there.

The three Shrewsbury sanctuaries are each fascinating. All three are the right size and shape for immediacy and intimacy. The kerosene lights (never electrified), antique spindle benches, and old piano and pump organ in the Northam church contribute to its unique charm and historic aura. The Meeting House sanctuary has a nice square shape, a beautiful old tracker organ, and a breathtaking view to the west through large, clear windows. The Cuttingsville church has a beautiful stained-glass window that catches the worshipers attention.

For all but a few people, each place feels like it belongs to another time and another people. For most of the people now worshiping there, little has changed during their tenure. Antique wall lights from Donna and the large and beautiful banners made by Connie and Karleen were the only contributions from this generation of church members. It seems to me that many felt more like tenants than residents as they moved among the three sanctuaries.

The Emmetsburg sanctuary is a wonderful place for worship, with the potential for becoming much more so. The east wall is mostly large, old, beautiful stained-glass windows that bathe the people in a golden "light from heaven" during Sunday worship. The pews in a semicircle on a sloping floor face the chancel in one corner of a square room. All can see, hear, and feel connected to one another. The sanctuary is big enough for us to grow into and small enough so we don't rattle around. A ramp and a new bathroom a few steps from the sanctuary make worship easily accessible. Adequate space in the back and our new Friendship Room on the side facilitate hospitality.

The remodeling of the sanctuary in 1950 made our chancel and choir loft more modern and utilitarian. But it's not particularly in keeping with our 1896 romanesque architecture. The carpet is faded and the plaster is cracked. The sanctuary restoration we're planning will dramatically transform an already attractive space and allow us to make it our own as we move into the building's next century and our future.

J. A. T. Robinson writes: "The church building is a prime aid, or a prime hindrance, to the building up of the Body of Christ. . . . And the building will always win."[5] Any church can make its worship space more of an aid and less of a hindrance in the pursuit of its worship goals.

The place of worship should be a living museum that defines the people who worship there; it should be furnished with the indigenous things that help them feel at home. It should not feel like a lecture hall but like a stage or arena where all participate in the great drama of worship. It should be pleasingly attractive but not indulgently opulent. Some spit and polish, a coat of paint, a new carpet runner, brighter light bulbs, vibrant banners, live plants, and fresh flowers can do wondrous things to a dry and drab space.

The sanctuary should bring the worshipers and worship leaders closer together. Perhaps the back pews can be roped off or removed and the pulpit brought down to the main floor. The worship space should be as flexible as possible. In the new sanctuary in Warwick, the pews were moved into the round for communion, taken out and replaced with tables and chairs for a Sunday morning wedding feast and another time for a Good Friday seder-communion, turned one way for a wedding and another way for a drama. And each arrangement was simple and beautiful.

The appearance of the space can change with the change of seasons and themes if creative members are turned loose to use their flair to enhance the worship of God and the building of community. If God and God's church are alive their place of worship should not remain static.

Worshipers can worship in "spirit and truth" without having to be in the sanctuary on Sunday morning. We ran out of fuel one cold, snowy Sunday morning in Warwick and easily moved to a member's home for worship. We worshiped at the town hall and had outdoor services at a state park and in the woods. In Shrewsbury we worshiped at Meetinghouse Rock once each summer. We had a vesper service in late afternoon to take advantage of the stunning sunsets that could be seen from our sanctuary windows and had evening vesper services in Northam by the light of the kerosene lamps and candles. In Emmetsburg we've worshiped on an island at the lake and at our farmhouse retreat center. A church might worship at a factory or office building on Labor Day Sunday and on a farm on Rural Life Sunday. Small churches should take advantage of the flexibility made possible by their small numbers.

Size-Appropriate Worship

We make an enormous mistake if we don't tailor our worship to enhance the distinctive qualities of small churches. We should make sure our worship is characterized by what small churches do best and not weakened by its liabilities. The twenty-six qualities of small churches that I identified in chapter 3 ought to help shape the way we worship.

Worship is the primary activity of small churches and they generally do it well. If worship is our primary offering, then let's do it for all we're worth. As one pastor said to me: "The importance of worship which takes place in every small church is too easily overlooked. After all, every seventh day the congregation does this one thing if little else."

Not having to spend considerable time administering a program, the small church pastor can concentrate on knowing and caring for the flock and leading them in worship. The way we plan and lead worship can enable other expectations we have for the church. When we gather for worship many administrative decisions can be made before, during, or after the service; an enormous amount of caring can happen; worship can be a profound learning experience for all ages; mission can be initiated in response to concerns that are raised. Seeing our gathering for worship as more of a potluck than a banquet may not be neat and orderly, but it can be nutritious and satisfying. And I believe God can be glorified and magnified in the process.

Each church and worshiper has his or her preferred way of worshiping. Often that way has been shaped by a cultural tradition, a denominational tradition, or the church's own tradition. A church's theology impacts the way it worships. Frequently the way a church worships was introduced by Pastor So-and-So sometime past or by the present pastor. Often it has been handed down with no rhyme or reason. All too often it has not considered its size when seeking the appropriate way for it to worship.

I've used the same basic order of worship for twenty years, yet it continues to evolve. This order is, and I think all worship should be, in three acts: *Preparing* for coming into God's presence; *Hearing* through biblical and preached word what God is saying to us; and *Responding* to God's Word and goodness through prayer, offering, sacrament, and commission. This basic ordering of the worshiping experience fits any theological, denominational, or cultural tradition; allows for predictability, variety, and spontaneity; encourages active participation; and maximizes the possibilities of worshiping with a small number.

The skeleton of this way of worshiping looks like this:

We Prepare

> Prelude and Lighting of Candles
> Welcome and Announcements
> Call to Worship
> Hymn of Praise
> Call to Confession and/or Unison Prayer of Confession
> Silent Prayers of Confession
> Assurance of Grace
> Hymn of Faith or Thanksgiving or *Gloria Patri*

We Hear

> Ministry of Children
> Anthem
> Scripture(s)
> Sermon Hymn (optional)
> Sermon

We Respond

> Service of Intercessions and Prayers
>> Joys and Concerns of Our Community
>> Prayer Hymn (optional)
>> Preparation for Prayer
>> Silent Prayers
>> Pastoral Prayer
>> Lord's Prayer
> Offering of Gifts and Doxology
> Sacrament of Communion (first Sunday of month)
> Hymn of Service
> Commission
> Passing of the Peace and Time of Fellowship

Within each segment of the service a variety of things are possible. Most Sundays there is some variation but never is everything changed. A bulletin helpfully enables congregational involvement and greater variety but isn't necessary. Let's walk through this order step by step, and consider a few of the limitless possibilities for worship in small churches.

Prelude and Lighting of Candles. The prelude serves several purposes. It tells greeters and kibitzers in the rooms off the sanctuary that worship is beginning. It masks the sound of people moving about and greeting one another and of children struggling against quieting. For people who've been rushing since awakening, it's a time to catch their breath before beginning to worship. Good musicians will use it for their own warm-up and to set a mood for the theme of the day's worship or the liturgical season. For everyone, it's an opportunity to begin getting in touch with both neighbor and God.

People in many small churches argue about what should happen in the time before worship. Some (often people from larger or more liturgical churches and introverts) think it is for quiet, prayer, contemplative preparation. Others (often small church people, people from congregational traditions, and extroverts) feel they can't worship until they've made the rounds and reestablished contact with their friends. For many, this is necessary community building time and a prerequisite for good worship. Prelude music allows talkers and meditators to prepare for worship in their own way.

Welcome and Announcements. From the first word, I want every person to feel welcome and at home. So I welcome as warmly and genuinely as possible. What I choose to say distinguishes this from all other services, personalizing it for the people present. This is warm-up time for the worship ahead. We might rehearse a new or difficult hymn. Some small churches begin every worship service with hymn singing. I've worshiped in African churches that warmed up by singing hymns for half an hour before their worship "began."

Some consider announcements a harsh intrusion into the spirit of worship and, at best, a necessary evil. I believe they are important and an opportunity for others to participate. I encourage others to make their own announcements. Sometimes, for special events like the CROP Hunger Walk, we've had a short skit in this time. The announcements help relate the worship service to the rest of church life. They're particularly appropriate in small churches where most announcements relate to everyone rather than particular interest groups.

Call to Worship. If worship is a drama in three acts, the call to worship is the first scene in the first act. In this scene the actors are identified, the scene is painted, the theme of the drama is named. The call is *not* calling God into our presence but calling the community of faithful into God's presence. The call is crucial and should get the actors on their feet, acting together, centered on the present task, with extraneous thoughts left behind.

The call to worship takes many forms. Generally it's a short responsive reading. For variety's sake, this can be divided between left and right, men and women, choir and congregation, young and old, blue eyes and brown. In a tiny church each member or family could be called to worship by name. Individuals, families, or groups in the church can be enlisted to write the call or confession or a statement of faith. Some hymns are appropriate calls and can be read or sung. The call can be "lined out," a colonial practice in which the leader speaks or sings a line of scripture or song and the people repeat it back, using the same volume and inflection. Parts of many Psalms are good calls to worship.

We've had actors act a short drama that confronted the congregation with the theme of the morning. Once a hidden, preset alarm clock startled and called people out of their daze and into worship. A clown group, dance choir, or mime troupe can silently call a church into God's redeeming presence. In Warwick, a member who taught at a school for the deaf, taught our congregation to sign Psalm 46:10, "Be still and know that I am God." We used this regularly, and it brought everyone from youngest to oldest to a state of reverent readiness.

I wrote this call for small congregations:

LEADER: Come! Worship the Lord God who created all things, large and small.

PEOPLE: **Let us worship the Creator God.**

LEADER: Come! Worship the Lord God, who loves all churches, large and small.

PEOPLE: **Let us worship our Loving God.**

LEADER: Come! Let us celebrate the small church and its important place in God's good plan.

PEOPLE: **Let us celebrate and renew ourselves for our important calling as one of God's small and mighty churches.**

Hymn of Praise. Music, specifically hymn singing, can be either one of the weakest or one of the strongest aspects of our worship. Habit, environment, choice of music, and attitude are more important than quantity and quality of musicians. Music is at the core of our tradition.

It was the duty of the trumpeters and singers to make themselves heard in unison in praise and thanksgiving to the Lord, and when the song was raised . . . the house of the Lord was filled with a cloud, so that the priests could not stand to minister because of the cloud; for the glory of the Lord filled the house of God (2 Chron. 5:13–14).

Song was the voice of faith of our Christian ancestors. It was so important that Ignatius, bishop of Antioch, addressed the Ephesian church in musical metaphor:

Your accord and harmonious love is a hymn to Jesus Christ. Yes, one and all, you should form yourselves into a choir, so that, in perfect harmony and taking your pitch from God, you may sing in unison and with one voice to the Father through Jesus Christ.[6]

Everyone who sings in the shower, hums along with the car radio, or has an adolescent knows that music is the voice of the human spirit and a powerful influence on thought and behavior. Music in worship is not meant to be a performance, time filler, or change of pace. Some people have come primarily to sing their favorite hymns. Music tells the story of faith in poetry, builds personal faith, and binds together the faithful in the pews with those who came before. Dietrich Bonhoeffer describes the place of unison singing in the Christian community's worship:

Unison singing, difficult as it is, is less of a musical than a spiritual matter. . . . The more we sing, the more joy will we derive from it, but, above all, the more devotion and discipline and joy we put into our singing, the richer will be the blessing that will come to the whole life of the fellowship from singing together.

It is the voice of the Church that is heard in singing together. It is not you that sings, it is the Church that is singing, and you, as a member of the Church, may share in its song. Thus all singing together that is right must serve to widen our spiritual horizon, make us see *our little company* as a member of the great Christian Church on earth, and help us willingly and gladly to join our singing, be it feeble or good, to the song of the Church.[7]

The Hymn of Praise is an occasion when the congregation, with one voice, can praise the One who creates, sustains, and leads them forward. It should be a hymn of praise and gratitude. It's good that hymns harmonize with the theme of the service and have theological integrity. But what is most important with this hymn is that it be one that the people love to sing, that they sing well, and that energizes them for what is to come. Sometimes it should be a children's song, if your church loves and includes its young. Quick tempo is essential. How can it be a hymn of praise if it sounds like a 78 RPM record being played at 33 RPM?

Call to Confession and/or Unison Prayer of Confession. Confession is necessary for being ready to hear God's written and preached word. A time of confession is not a popular part of worship. Some have no sense of sinfulness and feel no need to confess anything. Some are so miserable that they don't want to be reminded of what they already know too well. For confession to have meaning and power, education and new language are needed.

Paul Tillich's sermon "You Are Accepted," helps me see that my sins are not a laundry list of infractions, but that I live in a state of sin, which is separation from God, others, and self. It's not what I've done, but who I am. Who in our fellowship is not experiencing being out of touch with himself or herself, out of relationship with important others, cut off from God? People who have nothing to confess have no motivation or reason for worshiping.

A time of confession in a small church may be especially difficult. The disruption of a major conflict, the pain of an interpersonal offense, the embarrassment of scandal involving a member, the estrangement within a family or between friends is powerful in a small fellowship. Members may have to deal with the risk of asking and granting forgiveness. When Jesus said we should not offer our gift at the altar until we are reconciled with our sister or brother (Matt. 5:22–24), he was speaking about relationships in small fellowships.

A personal invitation, scripture, news clipping, quotation, community event, or piece from a liturgy can call people to confession. People might be invited to share situations where they see sin and separation. We usually recite a short, contemporary prayer of confession. I wrote this confession for a small church gathering:

> Loving God, creator of the atom, ant, and hummingbird; we have learned that small means puny, weak, and insignificant. Forgive us when we use small size as an excuse for small vision and weak action. Teach us again the biblical lesson of Little David and Goliath, the leaven in the loaf, and the pearl of great price. Help us to be all that you have created us to be, without seeking to be more. Amen.

People can write anonymous confessions on slips of paper that they or the leader can read with the people praying: "Forgive us loving God." On Pentecost our people have written confessions or fears on slips of paper, which were brought to the altar and burned in a Chinese wok as the people sang, "Every Time I Feel the Spirit." In Emmetsburg our children led a clown worship service. Anonymous confessions were written on slips of paper and collected in a picnic basket. As we sang "Amazing Grace," the basket was opened and a helium balloon ascended to the ceiling trailing a sign announcing "Forgiven!" The congregation's collective gasp and hush communicated their understanding. Our corporate confession is followed by silence when our people are urged to get specific and to pray for the power to forgive and receive forgiveness.

Assurance of Grace. Forgiveness and grace are the radical promises of the Christian faith. For an assurance I use one of the biblical promises, a hymn like "Amazing Grace," a traditional or contemporary assurance, or a litany. A volunteer might describe a real experience of grace.

Gloria Patri or Hymn of Faith. The climax of our time of preparing should be when we rise and sing the *Gloria Patri* or a hymn of faith or thanksgiving to God, who has just freely wiped our slate clean. Often the liturgist faces the altar at this time. I look intently from face to face as we sing, affirming that God is not on the altar but in our midst. Forgiven, we're now ready to hear what God has for us.

Ministry of Children. One of the unique and beautiful possibilities of small churches is the way children can be an integral part of the whole. The ministry of children is a specific opportunity for the whole church to be family together, for children to learn from adults, and for adults to learn from children.

This time offers a world of possibilities. A story can be told to the children by the pastor or a lay person. (Often there are several better storytellers in the church than the pastor!) Sometimes we have a discussion with the children or with the whole congregation. I've had a series in which a different child each week brought in a bag something from home that reminded her or him of God, and the congregation had to try to figure out what that might be. Each one was funny and profound. Sometimes the children share a song, drama, or visual creation. I've had a child tell a story to the church. This is a good time to share some of the stories out of your church's history.

In this part of our worship I want our children to feel at home and to know they are important to us. I want our adults to get to know and love each child. It is a time to educate about matters of faith, Christian values, ways of the church, and discipleship. It's a time when a family of faith can laugh easily or share deeply. Most important, I want our children to experience how it felt when Jesus brushed off the disciples, called the young to him, held them, and made them his own. It is a time when we hear God's word for children *and from* children.

Anthem. In Emmetsburg, the choir likes to sing at this point so they can move into the congregation for the rest of worship. Ideally the anthem should be placed where that particular piece of music is most appropriate. If it praises God it should be in the beginning of worship. If its a biblical text it might be with the scriptures. If it's a song of faith it should be during the time we respond. What is most important about the anthem and the work of the choir is that they and the congregation *don't* see what they do as performance. Their first job is to help the congregation sing; their second job is to use their gifts to glorify God and inspire the people.

Small church musicians and choirs often fall into the trap of selecting music that is beyond their ability or that requires more singers or parts than are available. A wide assortment of music, however, is available for choirs of small numbers or limited ability. Many small church musicians feel a piano is better than an organ for accompanying a small congregation. Many churches without a good accompanist successfully use cassette tapes to accompany their choir or congregation. As I've worked with five lay choir directors in three churches, I've encouraged them to use a variety of music that will minister to the spectrum of musical tastes represented in our churches.

My dream in regard to music would be for the whole congregation to become the choir. During the last four years I was in Warwick, a tradition developed in which the whole congregation rehearsed Handel's "Hallelujah Chorus" after worship during Lent in order to sing it as part of our Easter celebration. When we couldn't get a skilled accompanist, we sang along with a recording and it was still magnificent.

A beauty of music in small churches is the informality and naturalness that is possible. In my first weeks at the Warwick church the choir took off their robes and became part of the congregation. Often a choir member would sing with baby in arms. In all three churches, even when the choir members weren't even semiprofessional, they sang well what they sang and expressed well what the rest of us felt.

Another beauty of small church music is that since professional quality is not expected, we can encourage people to use their God-given gifts, even if they're not of recital quality. A child with two months of piano lessons doing her or his best at playing an offertory can move a church to a more generous sharing of their own gifts. In Emmetsburg, one of our most faithful members is a woman of limited mental ability. But when she plays a piece on the piano by heart, we all are touched.

Scripture. I center worship in scripture, but it needs to be presented in various ways. In our fast-paced, visual world, people are no longer skilled or patient listeners. Much scripture is written as dialogue or drama and can be read as drama by two or more readers. Sometimes the congregation is asked to read from their pew Bibles in unison. Occasionally the scripture has been acted out. Sometimes I involve the whole congregation in a Bible study of the passage (a technique that is far more effective with a small church). The Emmetsburg church owns the excellent Zeffirelli *Jesus of Nazareth* videotape. In a small sanctuary a segment could be used as the scripture.

A congregation usually has several good readers and reading scripture is a way to involve them. But beware! One Sunday I asked a bright high school student to read the Old Testament lesson from the Jerusalem translation. I made the mistake of not rehearsing with him. The Jerusalem translation uses the Hebrew name *Yahweh* for God. Several times in his reading he referred to Yahweh as "Ya-hoo." Many snickers were stifled that morning.

Sermon Hymn. This is a bridge from the written to the spoken word. Some find here a message for their living that they won't find in the scriptures or sermon. For some this is a time to move, cough, and stretch. For some a well-chosen hymn is the preamble to the sermon.

Sermon. In 1857, Anthony Trollope wrote, "There is perhaps no greater hardship at present inflicted on mankind in civilized and free countries than the necessity of listening to sermons."[8] Perhaps there is also no greater hardship inflicted on preachers than preaching to a small church. There is the danger of not taking the preaching task seriously when there are "only" thirty people present. Beceause the preacher is so close to the congregation, he or she is particularly vulnerable: You can see who has fallen asleep, who's frowning, who's tuned out. Listeners can see when you're ill prepared, insincere, not serious. When you know your people well, you know where they're tender, pained, opinionated, and therefore—desiring to protect them or yourself—you are tempted to be vague or innocuous.

If you have more than one vocation, there may not be time to prepare the kind of sermon your people need. If you're preaching to multiple churches, it's hard to target one sermon for more than one congregation. Small church people who know you well and are close enough to read you clearly, can tell if they're getting heavenly manna or junk food. A church that receives manna may remain small, but it will be well nourished and offer nourishment to others.

Henri Nouwen says there are two essential aspects of preaching—dialogue and availability.[9] Both are particularly relevant for preachers in small churches. By dialogue he means the preacher's job is to preach truth that connects with the hearer's life experience. Vague abstractions don't work with the small congregation. Since they know that you know them, they expect you to "scratch where they itch." The sermon is the opening thrust in an ongoing dialogue.

Second, the preacher must be available. Being available means opening your own vulnerability and humanity to back up your good words. It means a willingness to walk with your people through their "valley of the shadow." The small church pastor preaches not just with words but with his or her whole life.

There is more to the distinctiveness of small church preaching. One preaches to two hundred or more. But one converses with seventy-five who are known pretty well and visits with thirty or forty who are good friends. In a small church there is the real possibility of verbal response during and immediately after the sermon. With only a handful of births, baptisms, weddings, tragedies, and deaths each year, the preacher can personally and specifically address both the events and the feelings that accompany them. Early in my Warwick ministry, our Sunday school superintendent's husband was killed late Saturday night in a motorcycle accident. My prepared sermon was scrapped and a new message that interpreted the tragedy and addressed our grief was crafted.

Despite the reputed conservatism of small churches, I've found in all three pastorates general tolerance and appreciation for my deviations from the normal fare. Occasionally I've used a piece of film, video, or audio tape as part of a sermon. People have appreciated the times I've costumed and created dramatizations of characters like Johnny Appleseed, Martin Luther, Noah, blind Bartimaeus, and Simon Peter. Sometimes the sermon has been a Bible study involving the congregation. Recently we had a "Ask-the-Pastor" Sunday when the sermon was my spontaneous response to questions submitted on notecards. The pastor isn't the only one able to preach. Often I've had lay people talk about the way faith and life intersect for them. The issue isn't how the Word is proclaimed but whether it's presented in a way people can relate to and use.

Service of Intercessions and Prayers. Following Preparing and Hearing, people need to Respond by affirming their faith, singing, praying, giving, and—as often as possible—communing. Small churches can do these things exceptionally well. Frequently the sermon is followed by a statement of faith, creed, or prayer of dedication.

Bonhoeffer describes the intent of prayer at this point of a small community's worship:

> We have heard God's Word . . . but now we are to pray to God as a fellowship, and this prayer must really be *our* word, *our* prayer for this day, for our work, for our fellowship, for the particular needs and sins that oppress us in common, for the persons who are committed to our care.[10]

A large church may list the sick and those in need. A sensitive small church will share the joys and sorrows of how it is with one another, what should be celebrated or grieved, who is in need, and what should be done. Joys and concerns will range from local to global. The smaller the church, the longer this can take, and the more important it is. What is shared sets the agenda for prayer and the church's work list for the days ahead.

Bonhoeffer continues: "Where Christians want to live together under the Word of God they may and they should pray together to God in their own words. They have common petitions, common thanks, common intercessions to bring to God, and they should do so joyfully and confidently."[11] The congregation may pray together via simple-sentence prayers; the leader may lead in a bidding prayer by stating subjects for the people to pray about; or the leader may be the spokesperson for the prayers that are on the hearts of the people. A small, faithful, fervently praying family, can be a mighty force for healing and wholeness. We conclude our time of prayer with the Lord's Prayer. Help people see that Jesus' model for prayer is corporate not private. His pronouns were and ours should be "our" and "us," not "my" and "me."

Offering of Gifts. To me the climax of worship is the response of the people with prayers and offerings. Churches usually have the same people (almost always men) usher. I like to see that honor passed around the congregation and include all ages and both genders. Rather than a time when individuals ante up to pay the bills, the offering needs to become the time when the people thankfully respond to God's goodness by committing their lives and resources to God's work in church and world. We have a child bring the Sunday school offering forward with the ushers during the Doxology. I like to have all money that comes to the church (donations in the mail, dividend checks, fund raiser proceeds) brought to the altar or table to be dedicated.

Sacrament of Communion (see under the heading Sacraments and Seasons, this chapter).

Hymn of Service. When worship ends, service begins. The ending hymn is also the beginning hymn. This is not the time for a new or difficult hymn. It should be an action hymn that gets people back on their feet and inspires them to discipleship.

Commission. In place of a passive benediction, I use an active commission to send people out to their daily ministries. This is similar to the commissioning of a ship when a champagne bottle is smashed against the boat's new hull before it begins a life of service beyond the harbor.

Passing of the Peace. This ritual goes back to earliest Christian worship. "Greet one another with the kiss of love. Peace to all of you who are in Christ" (1 Peter 5:14). Some churches pass the Peace (or refuse to pass it) as if they fear receiving leprosy. Most small churches, like families aren't afraid to touch. Our churches passed the Peace with a genuine greeting, handshake, or hug.

Sometimes I've changed the greeting. A touching worship experience in Shrewsbury happened on "Apple Sunday," when each worshiper was given an apple and greeted with, "You are the apple of God's eye" (Deut. 32:10). I came to Betty in her wheelchair. Betty is retarded and has cerebral palsy. I took her hand, looked her in the eye, and blessed her with, "Betty, *you* are the apple of God's eye!" Our new awareness of the inclusive magnitude of God's love brought tears to many eyes.

As the Peace is passed, the child acolytes carry the light from the altar candles out of the sanctuary and we all carry our light into world. This order of worship works because it allows and enables the liturgy to be the active and transforming work of all the people.

Sacraments and Seasons

Sacramental occasions and seasonal celebrations can be very special and holy times. Here are some thoughts about these times.

Baptism. I was raised as a Baptist and experienced "believers' baptism" by immersion. I'm now part of the United Church of Christ and our two children were baptized as infants by sprinkling. Either way, baptism is the initiation rite through which one enters the church. It is an act of grace by which one is identified and named as one of God's holy people. At baptism, the church accepts and takes responsibility for the spiritual (and more) nurture of the one being baptized. Only a small church can make this a personal and genuine promise as a whole church.

I try to make each baptism very special. Since it is the church not the pastor who baptizes, all baptisms are conducted during Sunday morning worship. Except for siblings, every person is baptized in a separate ceremony. A special service is printed with the person's baptismal certificate photocopied on the cover. Each service is different. If the child is known by our church, I invite our people to bring cards, notes, letters, and prayers for the child, which are read and given to the family to share with the child at a later time. The church's children can be invited to come have a ringside seat for the baptism. In a very small church the whole church can be invited to come stand in a tight circle. We sing this baptism song to the tune "Morning Has Broken":

> (Name), we name you: And with thanksgiving,
> Offer our prayers and sing you this song.
> We are the church: your spiritual family.
> Sing we our praises to Christ the Lord.

If I'm baptizing a baby, I ask permission to hold the baby. I hold it close, baptize the child, and carry him or her around the sanctuary so all can see and perhaps touch.

In traditions that sprinkle water, it's important that people have some experience with it. I run my hands through the water and use enough to really wet the child's head. Sometimes at the end of the baptism, I cup water in my hand and cast it over the congregation with the admonition to "Remember your own baptism." Willimon and Wilson capture the distinctive quality of baptism in small churches. "In baptism . . . the small church acts as a family, to name its own, claim its own, look after its own, and identify its own, until those whom the family claims respond as part of the family—the Family of God."[12]

Communion. Since most small churches love to eat together, it's a mystery why many don't treasure and look forward to the communion experience. People who care about each other enjoy eating together. The agape meal was part of the early church's weekly worship service. Perhaps its lack of appeal for so many has to do with the way we've made it so routine, sterile, and impersonal.

Bonhoeffer writes: "The fellowship of the Lord's Supper is the superlative fulfillment of Christian fellowship."[13] When we come around the Lord's Table, we do so remembering Christ's love and sacrifice for people and churches such as ours, we recall the saints (including our own saints and loved ones) who came before, we celebrate the presence of Christ binding us together, and we anticipate communing with Christ and his church in the time to come.

The Lord's Supper should be celebrated as frequently as the church is willing. Rather than using wafers or Wonder Bread cubes, our bakers bake bread for us. A Sunday school or confirmation class could make the bread or press the grapes. I break a whole loaf, the symbol of Christ's body and our common life, and worshipers tear off a chunk. We serve communion in various ways—in the pew, with people coming to the front, with the congregation gathered together around the table, by dipping the bread into a chalice. Once in Warwick, we went to the town hall and worshiped around breakfast tables, ending the service with communion. Another time our Sunday worship was a wedding feast in our sanctuary for a couple soon to be married. This celebration ended with table communion. Sometimes a family is asked serve communion. Wherever I've pastored, we've concluded communion by forming a family circle around the room, taking hands, and singing a song.

Marriage and Death Ceremonies. Often these are important, all-church occasions in a small church's life. When a new pastor handles one of these occasions well, the church believes it's in good hands. I treat weddings and funeral/memorial services as worship services, not as adjunct ceremonies. Usually a bulletin is provided, the congregation participates, and there is singing. Some of my best memories of weddings have been where there was a time for people to share blessings and visions for the couple. Memorial services have been enriched when people have been invited to share memories and stories. These are opportunities for evangelism when visitors can determine if this is a church where God is experienced and they would be at home.

Church Year. The church year offers a seasonal rhythm that helps a church experience the totality of the faith. Advent/Christmas, already a family time, is a natural for the small church family. Every week of advent can be a different church-family event. Advent workshops, caroling, cookie swaps, concerts, old-fashioned Christmas parties, and the children's pageant are wondrous. We've enjoyed a Kris Kringle project in which participants draw a name from a hat and perform anonymous caring deeds for that person throughout Advent. An Epiphany Party, twelve days after Christmas, allows the church to have Christmas to itself after the culture has finished its commercialization. Lent, Easter, Pentecost, and lesser seasons of the church year offer a multitude of opportunities for decorating, observing, and celebrating.

Other Seasons. There are other seasons the church can celebrate and invest with meaning. Emmetsburg is an agricultural area, so one spring we observed a "Blessing of Seed, Soil, and Sowers." Bags of corn and soybean seed and a tub of soil were brought to the front of the sanctuary. Two of our farmers helped lead a liturgy from an old Methodist worship book. The service included communion using corn bread, since Iowa is a corn growing state. Churches could do this together as an ecumenical community service.

In Shrewsbury, after a protracted and divisive community battle over a new school addition, our church conducted a service of reconciliation for the whole community. Those who came were very appreciative. At various times we've celebrated such occasions as a Passover Seder, Graduation Sunday, Children's Day, Family Life Sunday, Rural Life Sunday, First Fruits Sunday, Homecoming, Harvest Sunday, and Thanksgiving.

I believe we underestimate the importance of worship for our people and are blind to its greater possibilities. In small church worship we need to do what we do well, which is involve; we shouldn't do what we generally do poorly, which is perform. When people come to the familiar holy space, surrounded by holy objects, with people who are dear to them, as they experience the Spirit of God, they find peace, courage, direction, and hope. The power of all this presence is illustrated in a prayer offered by an old woman as she sat in her pew:

> Lord, I'm tired—so very tired. Please Lord, I don't want any advice. I've heard enough of that over the years. I don't want to be told what I must do. I've been told that often enough. Lord, I just want to sit here in quietness and feel your presence. I want to touch you and to know your touch of refreshment and reassurance. Thank you for this sacred little spot where I have heard your voice and felt your healing touch across the years. Thank you for these dear friends who share this pew with me. Together we have walked the tearlined lanes. We know what it is to be lonely. . . . We also know the comfort and strength of one another and the joy of your presence. O God, the child of my womb has become a drunk. . . . Daily I watch her die before my eyes. Where have

I failed, O Lord? How can I find the strength to continue? How can I help my dying daughter find herself?

O God, soon I will be going home to be with you and my husband. I am ready, even eager. But until that day help me to be a help to others. Give me strength to live this day and peace to enjoy it. Amen.[14]

As people do the work of worship together, they discover the grace by which they live.

For Thought and Discussion

1. How do you define and understand worship?
2. Is your church's worship the work of the people? How could it be more so?
3. How does the place in which you worship help or hinder your worship experience?
4. How does the author's development of the order of worship particularly fit and enable the worship of a small church?
5. How might a small church you know more effectively celebrate the sacraments and seasons of the church?
6. What new ideas and possibilities for worship are sparked by this chapter for your small church or one you know well?

6.

Education:
Learning the
Old-Fashioned Way

John Westerhoff, whose provocative ideas about Christian education are the basis of my own, tells the story of a person who, having looted a city, was trying to sell an exquisite rug. He cried out in the market place, "Who will give me a hundred pieces of silver for this rug?" A buyer bought the rug. A friend of the seller came over and asked: "Why didn't you ask more for that priceless rug?" "Is there a number larger than one hundred?" asked the seller.

Is there another, more effective way to do Christian education than the way we do it and have done it over the last half century? Yes, there is! Do we not know the value of the priceless faith we're seeking to pass on? We forget! Could we be giving our children, youth, and adults something of far greater value than we now are—especially in our smaller churches? Yes, we can!

In 1957, *Life* magazine called the Sunday school the most wasted hour of the week. Overstatement? Attendance has dwindled for decades. Of those who are left, not many can accurately be labeled disciples of Jesus Christ. For a majority it's been a rite of passage *out* of the church, rather than an avenue *into* vital church involvement. Those who graduate from our Sunday schools are likely to emerge with little spiritual discipline or sensitivity, with little ability or passion to share their faith, with values similar to their secular friends, and with little commitment or skill for righting the wrongs and meeting the needs of this world. We may have baptized them, but most haven't learned to be disciples or to obey all that Christ commanded (Matt. 28:19–20). Our priceless faith has been bartered far too cheaply.

Actually it hasn't been cheap. Many churches have sunk all they could afford into Christian education facilities, professional and semiprofessional Christian educators, the best possible equipment and materials. Those that could have sought to rival the public education establishment. Based on the evidence, both public and religious education have fallen well short of their goals. Larger churches, who've been able to invest far more, can't point to any more success at nurturing faithfulness than can smaller ones.

Maturity of Faith

My concern is not just about children, but about all people in the church. In 1989, the Search Institute in Minneapolis surveyed 563 congregations in six mainline denominations, ranging from the United Church of Christ to Southern Baptists, regarding the nature of mature Christian faith, how people become mature in their faith, and how people can be helped to arrive at that maturity. The survey's results are both fascinating and disturbing.[1]

Representatives of the six denominations agreed that a person of mature faith:

1. Trusts in God's saving grace and believes firmly in the humanity and divinity of Jesus
2. Experiences a sense of personal well-being, security, and peace
3. Integrates faith and life, seeing work, family, social relationships, and political choices as part of one's religious life
4. Seeks spiritual growth through study, reflection, prayer, and discussion with others
5. Seeks to be part of a community of believers in which people give witness to their faith and support and nourish one another
6. Holds life-affirming values, including a commitment to racial and gender equality, affirmation of cultural and religious diversity, and a personal sense of responsibility for the welfare of others
7. Advocates social and global change to bring about greater social justice
8. Serves humanity, consistently and passionately, through acts of love and justice

By this definition, only one-third of the adults in the six denominations can be considered mature in their faith. The study also discovered that small churches are at least as effective as large ones in nurturing mature faith.

The Search Institute research suggests that a church that is highly effective at promoting maturity of faith will have these characteristics: a climate of warmth, people experience receiving care from others, a climate of challenge, worship that touches the heart as well as the mind, lay and pastoral leaders of mature faith, and a strong and vibrant educational ministry. Of these characteristics of a church that effectively nurtures mature faithfulness, the one that clearly matters most, more than worship, is effective Christian education.

Churches have mistakenly concentrated on education for children and youth and generally ignored the continuing nurture of their adults. And they have operated under faulty assumptions and methodology. Through much of this century, the church has attempted to educate by instructing about the Bible, about Christianity, about the church, about faith, about right and wrong. It believed that if people knew *about* those things they would be good, faithful, Christian church members. With those assumptions, churches did their best to duplicate the public school model by trying to provide trained teachers, objective subject matter, attractive curriculum, up-to-date supplies and equipment, age-graded classes, separate classrooms, and para-professional educators. As a result, we've produced at worst, poorly educated atheists; at best, church members struggling to be Christian. What went wrong?

Two things. We forgot that faith cannot be *taught* by objective instruction. Faith is *caught* as one experiences it in the Christian community, has the opportunity to reflect on that experience, and then practices it in one's living. And we overlooked that the church had been doing a pretty good job of helping people be faithful.

The tragedy for smaller churches is that when the experts promoted the instructional, public school way, many small churches abandoned what they were the right size to do effectively and adopted the new methods. Unfortunately, they usually didn't have enough students, space, teachers, or money to implement the new approach, which, as it turned out, wasn't very effective after all.

The Old-fashioned Way

Anyone interested in helping people of all ages mature in the Christian faith should read and reread John Westerhoff's *Will Our Children Have Faith?* He writes:

Recently, I discovered the large, important world of the small church.
As a professional church educator, I had often ignored these thousands
of small churches and, like other church educators, I had gotten used to
talking about educational plants, supplies, equipment, curriculum
teacher training, age-graded classes. . . . Most small churches will never
be able to mount up or support the sort of schooling and instruction
upon which religious education has been founded since the turn of the
century.[2]

After admitting that he had ignored the small church, Westerhoff
confesses that he has come to see the old-fashioned Sunday school,
which was small and personal, as the prototype for Christian education as
it should be. He cites an address in 1905 by John Vincent, the great
Methodist leader of the Sunday school movement:

In the future the Sunday school will be less like a school and more like a
home. Its program will focus on conversation and the interaction of
people rather than the academic study of the Bible or theology. The
Sunday school will be a place where friends deeply concerned about
Christian faith will gather to share life together.[3]

After recalling the contributions of others to the Sunday school movement, Westerhoff summarizes:

The old Sunday school appears to have cared most about *creating an environment* where people could be *Christian together* and where persons
could *experience Christian faith* and *see it witnessed to* in the lives of significant people. The old Sunday school seemed to be aware of the importance of *affections, of storytelling, of experience, of community sharing,
and of role models.* While many of these remain in the rhetoric of the
modern church school movement, we seem to have created an institution more concerned with teaching strategies, instructional gimmicks,
and curricular resources than with *spiritual mentors;* more concerned
with age-graded classes for cognitive growth than with *communities concerned with affections;* more concerned with the goals of knowing about
the Bible, theology, and church history than with *communities sharing,
experiencing, and acting together in faith.*[4]

The quotations are important in helping us see we have been traveling
a dead-end road, helping us see where we went wrong, and helping us select another road that will lead our people and churches toward greater
maturity of faith.

What is being proposed here is a radical shift away from child-centered
learning about the Bible and about Christianity, to Christian education

for the whole church, implemented in experiential ways that fit the special character of small churches. We will be turning away from what most of the church has been doing recently and turning back to some of the old-fashioned methods used to nurture faith. And we will seek to make it appropriate for our changing context and culture.

The Growing Medium

Many of you reading this are gardeners and farmers who grow house plants, flower and vegetable gardens, and cash crops. If you were starting from scratch, what kind of growing medium would you choose for developing a faithful, loving Christian church of faithful, loving, Christian people? This is the fundamental question for Christian educators as they plan for children, youth, and adults. Here are eight characteristics of the medium I would want.

1. The growing medium must be *warm and hospitable*. One Sunday morning a mother went to awaken her son so he could get ready for church. He rolled over, grumbling and complaining. Finally his mother ordered: "Get up now and get ready for church!" He said, "Why?" She said, "Because you're forty-five years old and you're the minister!" In contrast, our daughter, Noelle, then four and thinking the day for church was soon, said: "Mamma, is tomorrow Sunday?" After being told yes, she exclaimed, "Oh neat!"

It's a safe guess that the fictional pastor's church wasn't a warm and hospitable place, in contrast to what Noelle experienced in our church. A climate of hospitality is required for a church to become faithful and loving. Henri Nouwen writes:

> In our world full of strangers, estranged from their own past, culture and country, from their neighbors, friends and family, from their deepest self and their God, we witness a painful search for a hospitable place. . . . It is possible for men and women and obligatory for Christians to offer an open and hospitable space where strangers can cast off their strangeness and become our fellow human beings.[5]

People of all ages are hungry for a place where they know they belong and are safe. The first planning question for those responsible for nurture in the church is how can we create a warmer atmosphere of hospitality? When people pose that question, they will ask further questions:

- Is the building exterior, entrances, and interior forbidding or inviting?
- Who are the nurturers / teachers and are they cold or warm?

- What are we offering/teaching, and is it the gospel of loving good news or a religion of condemnation?
- When people are present do they experience warm fuzzies or cold shoulders?

The planners and implementers will do *everything* in their power to see that *every* person is treated as if that person is an angel of God in disguise (Heb. 13:1).

Some small churches are described as tough to get into, a caring cell for insiders that doesn't care about those on the outside. Some are. But my experience is that most small churches, although it takes awhile to become part of the family, are open to inviting people to explore adoption into the family. In these churches, lack of hospitality is often more lack of intentionality than intentional snubbing. Directional signs; greeters; name tags; snacks; flowers; and invitations to come, stay, and come back can be signals of hospitality.

Judy, Bill, and Aunt Harriet visited our church soon after moving to Warwick. After worship, people shook hands and Judy, Bill, and Aunt Harriet drove home. Here is where the story takes an unusual twist. Carl and Rotha saw them leave, rather than staying for coffee. The Nordstedts left their coffee on the table, followed our visitors home and into their driveway, got out, and said, "Why didn't you stay for coffee?" That's hospitality! And Judy said that's why they came back and got deeply involved in our church.

2. The growing medium must be *holistic*. The whole church as it meets, eats, worships, works, learns, cares, and serves is where Christian education happens. It doesn't just happen in the designated hour when the learners are down in the basement, the parlor, or Sunday school room. The small church, where these functions flow together, where space is used for several purposes, where people assume a variety of roles, where people know and care about one another, is especially well suited to develop and practice a holistic understanding of Christian education. The key to this understanding is to recognize that every experience is a learning experience and every person is a potential learner.

In 1780, a layman in Gloucester, England, started the first Sunday school. Therefore, for almost eighteen hundred years the Christian church attracted people and nurtured faithfulness *without* a Sunday school. The whole life of the church was the growing medium. Even today, quality Christian education can happen, either with or without a Sunday school.

The core questions are what do we want to communicate about faith and discipleship and how can we use *everything* we do in the *whole* church to communicate that? In a small church that doesn't need to compartmentalize learning, the wise educator will work on improving and expanding the nurturing quality of all that is already happening, *before* beginning new programs. The pastor who takes this approach will be remembered as the one who helped us, rather than the one who came and changed everything.

When the men gather at the cafe every morning for coffee, the sensitive layman or pastor can use that opportunity for care and nurture. When the women's group meets—whether to gossip, study the Bible, wrap bandages, or plan the next money-raiser—the potential for real Christian education about important matters is present. When the deacons meet, they can rehearse how to more smoothly distribute communion, or they can think theologically about what happens when people come around the Lord's Table and who is welcome there. The mission committee might roll up their sleeves to raise money for the foreign orphan they support, or they might first reflect prayerfully, biblically, strategically about possible ways to feed tens or hundreds of children, rather than just one. The Christian education committee or Sunday school teachers might seriously study how one matures in faith rather than just doing Sunday school the same way it was done to them.

If the church teaches in everything it does and if worship is the primary time when a small church gathers, then the wise worship planner will carefully plan how that precious hour or so can be used to make and feed disciples of all ages—from the first musical note to the last. Every moment of that time is an opportunity to nurture spirituality, awareness of self and sensitivity to others, biblical literacy, theological awareness, critical judgment, moral character, passion for justice, commitment to whole-life stewardship, and evangelism. The foolish pastor who only thinks about the sermon's potential to teach and inspire is wasting two-thirds of the people's time.

3. The growing medium must be *individualized*. In small churches everyone has a name and knows almost everyone. Part of baptizing is christening or officially giving a child his or her "Christian" name. When one becomes a disciple, one is named. God called Abram, "Abraham" and made him father of a nation. Jesus invited Simon, named him "Peter," and called him to a life of discipleship. God renamed Saul, "Paul," and his life was transformed. Small churches are the best size to pay special attention to each and every person and to bring each one into full and

complete membership in the community. That's their special gift and responsibility.

Each and every person comes with special needs and gifts. Our daughter had meningitis as a toddler and has a serious hearing disability. In all three of her churches she's been loved, included, spoken to clearly. We all bring special needs, and part of nurturing us in the faith is seeing that those needs are allowed for and addressed. I know one small church that raised over $20,000 for an elevator so that a member who had become wheelchair bound could still worship with her church. The Emmetsburg church is updating its sound system for the benefit of those who don't hear well.

We bring more than needs. According to the Apostle Paul, each person brings special spiritual gifts. One can sing, another pray, another teach, another act. One can imagine, another communicate, another build. Small churches are the right size to identify those gifts in each of us, to provide an opportunity for using them, and to hold us accountable for developing them.

I remember in 1971 when little Andrea was so shy she refused to leave her mother's side at the organ. Thirteen years later, as an unusually mature high school student, Andrea was a valued deacon of our church. Shelly came to Warwick as a self-conscious young housewife. In our church she discovered she was a gifted actress and leader. I remember Karleen in Shrewsbury, who was helped to articulate, channel, and act on her passion for justice for disabled persons. I think of Jan in Emmetsburg, who came to us with a tattered ego and a broken family, trying to piece her life back together. Her new church welcomed her, gave her an opportunity to express her remarkable artistic talent, and gave her room to explore.

In Warwick we created our own church family album for every family with each person's unique characteristics. In Shrewsbury we often wore name tags. In Emmetsburg we put lots of photos on our bulletin boards and use our new copier to print pictures of new members and church activities in our newsletter. In each of the churches, we've quickly and significantly expanded the number of persons who have a specific responsibility in the church. Sensitive leaders of small churches will see that everyone of all ages is known, has a place, and is helped to grow. If God can know the number of hairs on each person's head, surely a small church can see that every person is known and needed.

4. The growing medium must be *familial.* We live in a world that separates people by gender, age, size, race, religion, and interest. Large

churches often talk about family. A small church *is* family—though not always a healthy one. Families are combinations of people in relationship with and responsible to one another. We knew this concept was working when six-year-old Sarah queried her mother, "All the people at church are part of *our* family, aren't they?"

The church's educational ventures can help all its people understand, value, and develop the relationships they have with one another. It can bring individuals, families, and generations together for family events like potluck meals, intergenerational learning, family retreats, field trips, picnics, work days, mission projects.

In Warwick we developed a church school rotation of traditional age group classes from September to Advent, an intergenerational experience during Advent, more age-group classes through Lent, and then interest projects for all ages from Easter to Pentecost. In Warwick and Shrewsbury, my wife directed a delightful intergenerational musical peace play entitled, "Alice in Blunderland." In Emmetsburg we replaced traditional vacation Bible school with a Special Super Summer Sunday Series, which included an ice cream social, going to the homes of shut-ins to do fix-it things, and going to a lake for a shooting-star watch with an astronomer. A Mission Fair was held with activities for all ages and various interests. In the space of a year, each committee in the church planned one all-church activity.

But what about traditional Sunday school and real, solid learning? Later in this chapter I'll share some ideas for Sunday schools, but there is no record of Jesus talking *just* to children or of him sending them away or out to play. Jesus' teaching style was to instruct so that all could understand. If he was serious that one can't enter the Realm of God except as a child, we adults need children around to model and remind us of those childlike qualities of joy and trust that Jesus prized. No child is so ignorant, no adult so wise that they can't learn together and teach one another.

Until fairly recently, young people learned their trade by being placed as an apprentice with a master of the craft who worked with the apprentice until he or she could practice the craft alone. The greatest gift a church can give a person young in the faith is a role model, mentor, or master to guide that person's maturation. The church could reclaim the essence of the godparent role and assign to each of its children at baptism or dedication a wise and caring adult to assist the parents in shepherding the child's development of faith. Teachers who have the gift for mentoring could be more intentionally recruited. Sponsors can be assigned to people who are being confirmed or are becoming church members.

For several years I was a part-time Christian education consultant. When I went to work with a group of teachers or a Christian education committee, I often asked them to identify the "most significant memory in their own Christian education." Ninety percent named a teacher, pastor, or parent. When we talked about recruiting teachers, I encouraged them to make a list of those in the church who had the special qualities of faithfulness they wanted their children to have and then to figure out how to get those people involved with their children so those contagious qualities could be caught. In a small church, everyone can learn from everyone.

Another story about Warwick's Rotha. A beautiful, unplanned ritual evolved that illustrates the familial quality that can permeate a small church. Rotha and her husband were gifted gardeners and were responsible for the flowers that graced our sanctuary from April to November. Each Sunday after worship a small flock of children gathered around Rotha as she took apart her flower arrangement to make a special bouquet for each child. The rest of us stood in awed appreciation of the way they ministered to each other. Rotha made the young feel special; the young made her feel appreciated.

In the small church family, the old give the young a history and tradition, the young give the old a hope and a future. Each generation is a link in a chain of faithfulness that must be preserved and strengthened.

5. The growing medium must be *ecological*. Whether urban or rural, we're all provincial, focusing primarily on ourselves and our own. Christian education should help us discover and strengthen the interdependence of God's *whole* creation. No one and no church is an island. What can we do in common with other churches? How can we make a difference in our community? What are the differences, and more importantly, what are the commonalities between denominations and the world's religions? How can we relate to other cultures and parts of the world? How can we learn to care for and replenish the resources of our precious environment?

In Warwick the church school organized an enormously successful community clean-up. In Shrewsbury our youth group raised hundreds of dollars by recycling beverage containers and families experienced an Africa Day when we ate, played, sang, and crafted in African ways. On World Communion Sunday in Emmetsburg, we sing hymns in other languages and break a variety of breads from around the world. We support artisans from the Third World by holding a Self-Help Handcrafts craft sale in cooperation with Church World Service. All three churches have become much more aware of and concerned about the rest of God's good world.

6. The growing medium must *affirm the Tradition as our own story*. Most laypeople I've asked say they want the Sunday school to "teach the Bible." Do they mean teach it the way an English teacher teaches Shakespeare? Do they mean teach it as if God dictated it word for word? Do they mean teach every book, chapter, verse, and word? I think most of them mean the Bible should be taught as the tradition out of which we have come, the story of God's relationship with our early ancestors in the faith, and the light and truth for our living.

I get excited when I understand that our historical tradition, which began somewhere back with Sarah and Abraham and "begat" down through the ages, includes the saints, pillars, and characters here in our own time and churches. We teach this as *our* tradition or story so that it becomes *our* family tree. In a sense, this means opening the canon of the Bible so that we also are people God speaks to and acts through. Suddenly the Bible becomes not an old, tedious tome but our own family biography.

Sarah, our young theologian who knew the church was her family, was also close to this understanding as she conversed with her mother after the birth of a sister:

SARAH: Is baby Beth God's daughter?
MOTHER: Yes, she is.
SARAH: Is Joshua [her brother] God's son?
MOTHER: [sensing the water is getting deeper] Yes, he is.
SARAH: And I'm God's daughter, aren't I.
MOTHER: Yes, Sarah you are.
SARAH: Then Daddy must be God's brother!

Sarah knew she was part of a serious and powerful tradition.

If we take the tradition seriously, we will emphasize and celebrate the special seasons and days of our family story: the advent and birthday of Jesus; the season of penitence we call Lent and Holy Week when we remember our Lord's collision with the principalities and powers of his time and our complicity with those of our time; our Lord's breaking the bonds of death at Easter; and the birthday of our church, which we call Pentecost.

Seeing scripture, the biblical characters, church history, and our own church's story as part of one intertwined tradition transforms the way we do Christian education. Rather than simply learning *about* those weird bathrobed characters, the learner becomes part of the story.

Questions like these will personalize the biblical story:

- What would you have done if you were Absalom and King David was your father?
- How can we act that out and maybe share it during worship?
- Would you rewrite that psalm in your own words describing how you feel today and then maybe we can chant or sing it.
- After hearing the story of the Prodigal Son, are you most like the father, the younger son, or the older one?
- If Jesus were retelling this story in our church, how do you feel he might change it?
- Hearing Jesus say, "Go into all the world," where do you believe he wants you to go and what does he want you to do? Is there any way our church is doing that? What else can we do?

When we affirm the tradition and make it our own story, we move from a spectator's role to that of a character in the plot.

7. The growing medium must be *Christian*. Ours is an incarnational faith—the Word became flesh and lived among us. The goal is not to entertain or interest people but to help them become authentic disciples of Jesus Christ. And that makes all the difference. We need to help people come to the point where they each can say: "Yes, I was given a Christian name, but now I'm ready to call myself 'Christian' and live as Christ's loyal disciple."

There must be a substantive, serious side to our educational ventures. We need to help people risk intensive Bible study, to develop a serious spiritual discipline, to begin seeing their whole life as ministry, to believe that God expects life-changing results from them and their little church. Your denominational leaders and publishing house have resources and ideas for you. Any educational venture becomes substantive and serious when people wrestle with the question: what is God calling us to *do* in response to what we just learned?

8. The growing medium that is all of the above must be *experiential, reflective, and lead to action*. It's experiential because that's how we best learn. We learn a little bit of what we hear, a little more of what we see or read, and much more of what we experience. But to learn what we've experienced, we need to reflect on it by asking ourselves how did we feel and what did we want to do? Experience reflected upon should lead us to action, because we can't *be* Christian, without *doing* Christlike things.

James 1:22–24 says: "But be doers of the word and not merely hearers. . . . For if any are hearers of the word and not doers, they are like those who look in a mirror . . . and, on going away, immediately forget what they were like." The church is not for fun and games but for making a difference. The key to transforming small and weak churches into small and mighty churches is to help them experience bearing fruit and making a difference.

Every Sunday school class session can end with a plan of action. Youth can be empowered to change their family, church, school, or community. Every women's circle can be challenged to adopt a significant mission project. The last question asked in every Bible study can be, "What would we do if we took this passage seriously, and how can we do it?" Every sermon can say, this is what God calls us to do.

I know a Sunday school in which each child "adopted" one of the church's shut-ins. We taught our Emmetsburg children clown ministry and took them to three nursing homes to lead worship. Our Warwick weekday church school bought fifty small trees and planted them at the homes of older people. Our confirmation students in Shrewsbury and Emmetsburg traveled to a soup kitchen and helped prepare and serve supper.

If a small church has a growing medium that is warm and hospitable; holistic; individualized; familial; ecological; affirms its biblical and historical tradition as its own story; seeks to be Christian; and learns through experiencing, reflecting on the experience, and then acting in significant ways, that church cannot help but grow a faithful, loving Christian community. All that is left is to respond to some common Christian education issues that face many small churches.

Space, Methods, Leaders, Materials

Small churches often struggle with inadequate space. This may be a larger problem than it needs to be if a church is trying to have more classes than they need. But it has been a problem in each of my three churches. In Emmetsburg we have one class in the sanctuary balcony and another in the cellar behind the basement furnace. Both of these spaces are also strengths. The balcony kids can look down on all the people who pass below and can bask in the wonderful light refracted through our windows. Creative Virginia likes teaching her small class behind the basement furnace because she and they can make artistic messes without anyone caring. This group could name its area, "Daniel's Den" and do things appropriate to that place, or they could name it "Catacomb Cave" and learn about the dangerous times of early Christianity. In Shrewsbury and Warwick we were short of space, so we used the living rooms in the houses of laypeople who lived next door.

Virtually any space can be made to work with some ingenuity, scavenging and recycling, a little paint, and some spit and polish. Working with a group of fifth and sixth graders, we started with an absolutely bare room and together made it our own. The goal is not to reproduce a public school room but a room that is alive and conducive to being, playing, studying, praying, and working together.

One of the first eye-opening experiences in Warwick happened when we decided to redecorate our single, drab Sunday school room. A gallon each of brick-red floor paint, bright yellow wall paint, ceiling paint, and a quart of white and a quart of lime green enamel were purchased with money squeezed from our tiny treasury. One Friday night a dozen workers painted ceiling, walls, woodwork, floor, tables, and chairs. Soon after midnight a team of spattered and tired painters shared refreshments and peeked through the door into a new room. Washed curtains and a moveable divider made of donated brightly colored fabric on a wire, gave us a cheap, cheerful room for our two classes.

There are good alternatives to closely graded classes and resources to help make them happen. A church using *learning centers* for one season or a whole year will have a variety of activities (usually focused on one theme) spread around a large room (a drama center, a crafts center, a quiet spot for reading, a music center) with written instructions or a teacher at each. Learners of various ages gravitate to the area that is of interest to them. This can be more fun, require less space, and be very experiential and familial.

There are *broadly graded* resources that make it easier to combine a wide range of grades and abilities. They offer a range of lesson materials and activities so individuals can participate at their own level and according to their interest. This approach enables learners to be teachers for one another. Fewer rooms and teachers are needed.

Intergenerational resources provide learning experiences so people from cradle to grave can learn together. They encourage people to see everyone else as someone to learn from and share with. These are usually centered around a theme or season and can be done during Sunday school time, family nights, church retreats, and vacation church school. Donald and Pat Griggs have a helpful book entitled *Generations Learning Together,* published by Abingdon. Episcopalians in Colorado publish excellent lectionary-based curriculum materials that are very useable by small churches. One of their best is a two-volume resource called *Growing Together: Celebrations for Your Entire Church Family,* which includes activities for listening, writing, reading, discussing, creating art, making music, improvising drama, playing games, and doing outreach. You can get their materials from Living the Good News, Inc., 777 Grant Street, Suite 302, Denver, Colorado, 80203.

Where to get *leaders and teachers?* I don't believe in asking for volunteers. I don't believe that just any warm body will do. When it comes to working with our children, I want only the "right" people. To me the right people are those who love and respect young people and are loved and respected in return, who care about the Christian faith and witness to it with their lives, who have a contagious *joi de vivre,* or passion for life. If you intentionally recruit people with these qualities and set aside the stereotype of a "teacher," you may find a surprising number of these special people.

I've found there are enough teachers when those responsible for the education enterprise and the whole church make sure that:

- A church places a priority on education
- Teachers/leaders feel appreciated and needed
- A sense of "team" is developed, rather than teachers feeling they are expected to be "Lone Rangers"
- Teachers are given good resources and training in how to use the resources and do the task
- Teachers are asked for a limited, specific commitment (one quarter or one year) rather than for an unlimited period
- Teachers are helped to see that their volunteering is a learning and fellowship opportunity for themselves
- Prospective teachers are helped to see that the invitation to teach matches their own particular gifts
- You're realistic about how many teachers you need—neither too few or too many
- Teachers are helped to believe that they can make a difference in their learner's lives

If there just aren't enough people willing to teach on a weekly basis, perhaps you can combine forces with another church or perhaps people will alternate weeks. If there isn't enough personnel for a conventional church school, your church can do education in other ways. Have periodic events like retreats and family days that provide a block of time for nurturing your people. Consciously turn the whole church experience into an educational environment for all ages and don't worry about not having a Sunday school. Teach parents, aunts and uncles, grandparents, and neighbors how to seed and nurture the faith at home and give them resources for doing it.

How about *resources and equipment?* All you *have* to have for Christian education is one person who lives the life and one Bible. Anything beyond that is gravy. Much of the Sunday school curriculum materials are difficult for small churches because they are too expensive, the lessons depend on too many students, the lessons have an urban orientation that is difficult for rural people, lessons are theologically or biblically objectionable, or they assume conditions foreign to many small churches.

You might adapt someone else's curriculum or write your own. I've done both. Or you might borrow curriculum samples from your denominational office, from publishers, or from nearby churches in order to find the one that fits your church. I've used a half dozen different kinds of curriculum materials and evaluated others. Based on my experience, I believe good curricula for small churches will:

- Be compatible with the prevailing philosophy and theology of your church
- Be attractive and appealing to your learners
- Be stimulating and rewarding for the teachers
- Present the Bible and church history as *our* tradition, ancestors, and story
- Have continuity and progress from subject to subject and level to level, so that after a few years, the learner will have a comprehensive grasp of your church's faith tradition
- Build self-esteem in the learners
- Use inclusive language and not stereotyped gender roles
- Use a discovery rather than rote-learning approach
- Help students think and act creatively
- Build relationships and Christian community
- Further integration with the rest of your church's life
- Be relevant for the experience of the learner
- Be ecological in connecting with the whole world around us
- Help students act on what they've learned
- Be appropriate for a wide range of grade and ability levels
- Provide teachers with clear, creative, practical resources and instructions
- Use a variety of methods, activities, and materials
- Be useable with a few (even two or three) students and require limited supplementary materials, resources, and equipment
- Be affordable

Small churches need to be crafty buyers and active borrowers and scavengers. Post or print a list of needed supplies and see what the congregation and community can provide. Don't buy pads of newsprint if your local newspaper will give you the ends of newsprint rolls or the nearest moving company will give you some of the paper they use for packing.

A cassette player can be used not only to play cassettes for singing, but for recording student's music, drama, or interviews. Record players and filmstrip projectors are useful. If you can come up with a TV and VCR, there are many good video resources available. The use of a camcorder will enable you to make your own videos. Can you share equipment with one or more neighboring churches? Does your denomination or ecumenical group have a resource center from which you can borrow or rent? Investigate what your public library, schools, civic groups, extension service office, civic groups, YMCA, and YWCA have that you can use.

Don't forget the most important resources—people. Musicians can be asked to teach a song, dramatists to direct a play, artists to lead an art project. Remember those wonderful older people in your church who may not be willing to be "teachers," but whom you want your young people to know? Ask them to bake, bring refreshments, come tell stories of what the church used to be like and what kids did back then. Ask them to share their hobbies, show your class around their neighborhood, farm, or woodlot. One church recruited an older person for each of their classes to be a "lover," one who was there to pay special attention to the child in need of special attention.

Youth and Adult Education

What if there aren't enough youth for a youth group? How many is not enough? There are many ways to engage in youth ministry. Any church in a community with at least one young person can have a youth ministry. Our Emmetsburg church doesn't yet have a "youth group," but we have two youth on the state youth council; a confirmation class of four, plus a postgraduate confirmand; youth are involved in worship leadership and on committees; several children and youth are sent to camp each summer. We have an active youth ministry, even without a "youth group."

During adolescent years many young people drop out of church and others are seduced into destructive activities. With all that our culture offers to tantalize young people, they're in need of a place and people who take them seriously and help then establish lasting values and commitments. Small churches are the right size to take youth very seriously and to give them that place where they belong and can make a difference.

Our Shrewsbury church had a very active and significant youth group, thanks to caring adults willing to work with them. That group was the only activity for young people in the community. The highlight of each year was a special trip to places like Montreal, New York, and Washington, D.C. That group remains a valued anchor for Shrewsbury youth.

The most important prerequisite for a church to be alive and vital and for its children and youth to be growing in faithfulness is for its adults to continue maturing in their faithfulness. Few adults are involved in any intentional continuing education in the church and few churches offer much that's very interesting. Here's a sampling of fairly easy and effective education possibilities for adults.

I led a "Sermon Wrighters" group that studied the next week's lectionary selections to see what sermon they contained for our church. This was very interesting for the participants and helpful for me, the preacher. One-day seminars led by available leaders have been offered. One was around the theme of spirituality and one around the theme of caring in the church. We've had pre- and postworship adult forums to which we invited people to speak on timely subjects, film series using commercial films available on video tape, Bible studies, and book and tape discussions.

John Westerhoff ends *Will Our Children Have Faith?* with this affirmation: "Our children will have faith if we have faith and are faithful. Both we and our children will have Christian faith if we join with others in a worshiping, learning, witnessing Christian community of faith."[6]

For Thought and Discussion

1. Where does education happen in your church and how would you assess its effectiveness?
2. Using the criteria for mature faith cited in this chapter, how does your church increase the maturity of its people?
3. Does your church do education in the old experiential and sharing method or the new instructional, public-school model?
4. What kind of growing medium does your church provide?
5. What are some different ideas and alternatives your church might explore?

7. ◆ Caring: "Look How They Love One Another"

Most of this book was written on the island of Vinalhaven, Maine, during a two-month sabbatical and vacation. This was to be the easiest and fastest chapter. After a day of reviewing collected material, reflecting, and planning, I sat down at the word processor to start writing. The words I expected to come easily and quickly did not. I didn't like the ones that did. What was wrong? After a long day of frustration, I gave up and went ocean rowing. There I found insight to my writer's block.

Twenty-four hours earlier I'd had a disagreement with my wife about whether or not I was being helpful with household responsibilities. Reconciliation did not come easily or quickly. It was difficult to write honestly and helpfully about caring in the church when I wasn't feeling caring toward her or felt cared for in return.

In addition, I was struggling for something significant to say beyond "small churches are caring cells"—knowing that some are and some aren't. I needed clarity of words concerning the desperate need of people in our culture to be cared for and to care, clarity about my own experience with caring in the three small churches I know best, and clarity about how to increase caring in other small churches. A significant level of caring is not easy to achieve, maintain, or develop within oneself, in relationships, or in a church. Yet there is nothing humans need more. After rowing and pondering, I was ready to work with my wife and to write this chapter.

Caring vs Individualism

Caring addresses a crying need in our culture. In 1985 Robert Bellah and some colleagues published *Habits of the Heart: Individualism and Commitment in American Life. Newsweek* called it a "brilliant analysis" and the "richest and most readable study of American society" since the 1950s. The authors see the presence of individualism as the central reality and problem of our culture and the most serious threat to our future. The book quotes from the sermon John Winthrop preached on board ship in Salem harbor in 1630, before the Puritans disembarked: "We must delight in each other, make others conditions our own, rejoyce together, mourn together, labor and suffer together, always having before our eyes our community as members of the same body."[1] We've consistently fallen short of this utopian dream.

After three hundred pages of careful analysis, the authors end with this diagnosis and prescription:

> We have never before faced a situation that called our deepest assumptions so radically into question. Our problems today are not just political. They are moral and have to do with the meaning of life. We have assumed that as long as economic growth continued, we could leave all else to the private sphere. Now that economic growth is faltering and the moral ecology on which we have tacitly depended is in disarray, we are beginning to understand that our common life requires more than an exclusive concern for material accumulation.
>
> . . . Perhaps enduring commitment to those we love and civic friendship toward our fellow citizens are preferable to restless competition and anxious self-defense. Perhaps common worship, in which we express our gratitude and wonder in the face of the mystery of being itself, is the most important thing of all. If so, we will have to change our lives and begin to remember what we have been happier to forget.
>
> We will need to remember that we did not create ourselves, that we owe what we are to the communities that formed us.[2]

The authors have clearly discerned that the individualism that characterizes our culture may be its undoing. They identify the community of faith that worships the transcendent and cares for one another as a better answer to our human need. Churches, particularly smaller ones, have a capacity for caring that can serve as a needed alternative, one based on interdependence rather than individualism. Our world desperately needs that which we in the church are uniquely equipped to be and do.

Tertullian observed of the second-century Christian church, "Look how they love one another." I wonder what it was about the church or churches he knew that caused him to notice the love they shared. Was it the way they met the spiritual and physical needs of one another? Was it the way they protected one another in the face of terrible oppression? Was it the way they somehow hung together, despite being Jew and gentile, slave and free, young and old, male and female? Was it the way they took care of one another? Did their loving, caring nature have something to do with their small size?

I've said small churches are the right size to be and do all that God expects of a church. Not everyone has concurred with that premise. But there is agreement that they're the right size to really care about one another. Carl Dudley writes:

> The single cell, a network of caring people, is the strength of the small church.
>
> For this reason, *per capita* membership attendance and financial support for the small church are significantly higher than for the larger congregations. By the same token, the absent member is missed, reminded, and sometimes reprimanded. Small church caring is not always gentle, but it is genuine. Often members have known each other for a lifetime, some families for generations. . . .
>
> To the outsider the small church is a prickly ball of Christian love. But if we try to imagine the intensity of the relationship within the group, the single-cell church would "feel" like a lump of bread—textured in the middle, and solid on the crust.
>
> The inner texture and the outer toughness are universal characteristics of primary groups. But the single-cell, small church has pushed the limits of caring far beyond the capacity of most small groups to know or care about their membership.[3]

Those who haven't experienced the caring that is the glue that often holds a small church together and gives it its shape and substance, may not understand what we mean by "caring." It doesn't mean that people are always nice to one another or don't get angry with each other. It doesn't mean that their life together is nothing more than doing favors for one another. It doesn't mean that everyone is a caring person or cares in the same way as everyone else. It doesn't mean the church will automatically win "Miss Congeniality."

It does mean that in a caring small church most members have a commitment to the welfare of the whole and to each of the parts. Often they will put the welfare of the whole ahead of their own. It means that church is more of an emotional experience than an intellectual one. It means that when one hurts, others are likely to hurt, and that people tend to look out for and defend one another from outside threats. It means that people speak of "we," not "they." It means that people know they belong, even when absent; and when one is absent, the others feel incomplete.

Nothing captures the quality of caring that tends to bind together small churches any better than Margery Williams's marvelous allegorical story *The Velveteen Rabbit*. A young boy finds a splendid velveteen rabbit with pink-sateen-lined ears in his Christmas stocking. For a long time the Rabbit was just one of many toys in the nursery. But one day the Rabbit asked the old, worn Skin Horse, "What is REAL?"

> "Real isn't how you are made," said the Skin Horse. It's a thing that happens to you. When a child loves you for a long, long time, not just to play with, but REALLY loves you, then you become Real."
>
> "Does it hurt," asked the Rabbit.
>
> "Sometimes," said the Skin Horse, for he was always truthful. "When you are Real you don't mind being hurt."
>
> "Does it happen all at once, like being wound up," he asked, "or bit by bit?"
>
> " It doesn't happen all at once," said the Skin Horse. "You become. It takes a long time. That's why it doesn't often happen to people who break easily, or have sharp edges, or who have to be carefully kept. Generally, by the time you are Real, most of your hair has been loved off, and your eyes drop out and you get loose in the joints, and very shabby. But these things don't matter at all, because once you are Real you can't be ugly, except to people who don't understand."[4]

The Rabbit knew it would take a long time to become Real. But he longed for that, though he didn't want to grow shabby. He became the Boy's favorite toy and time passed. Sure enough, his whiskers came off, the pink lining in his ears turned grey, he lost his shape. To the Boy he was always beautiful and that was all the Rabbit cared about.

The special quality of caring that is so often found in small churches doesn't happen overnight, it doesn't happen without pain, and it is not always pretty. It is never accomplished and can always grow deeper. It is real and makes one Real. And it's a prerequisite for a church to be a church. Elizabeth O'Connor, reflecting on the Church of the Savior community, writes: "Learning to be persons in community with other persons... is the most creative and difficult work to which any of us will ever be called.... We are to be liberating communities that free love in us and free love in others."[5]

O'Connor tells a story about Michelangelo pushing a huge piece of marble down the road. A neighbor called to the sculptor and asked why he was working so hard to move the huge rock. Michelangelo stopped to wipe his brow and answered: "Because there's an angel in this rock that wants to come out." There is in each of us, and each other, an angel waiting to emerge, wanting to be shaped and set free.

Caring at Each Level of Need

Abraham Maslow, an American psychologist, in 1943 proposed a psychological theory of how the angel in us emerges, known as Maslow's "hierarchy of needs." According to the theory all of our feelings, thoughts, and actions are directed at meeting our needs. The intriguing part of the theory is that the needs we're trying to meet are in an ascending sequence. Lower needs must be met before we're free to concentrate on higher ones. Here's a simplified version of the hierarchy:

Self-
Actualization
Ego, Status, Esteem
Love and Belonging Needs
Safety and Security Needs
Basic Physiological Needs
(food, shelter, clothing, physical comforts)[6]

According to the theory, we aren't able to attend to safety needs until our most basic physical needs are met, or focus on love and belonging until safety and security needs are met, and so on. The Velveteen Rabbit might say the higher we progress up the hierarchy, the more Real we become. When small churches are related to Maslow's hierarchy, it's clear why they have a potential for growing Real people by caring at each level.

Basic Physiological Needs. This is both the first level of need and the entry level for most churches. When there's a tragedy or crisis, church people are there with a casserole, a bag of clothing, an offer of housing, or a check. When I was sick and unable to get in our winter's firewood, twenty people from the Warwick church cut, hauled, split, and stacked several cords of wood—out of concern for the basic needs of their pastor and his family. Churches support Heifer Project, CROP, and One Great Hour of Sharing because they resonate to meeting basic human needs.

Safety and Security Needs. Many people experience the church as a lifeline. Some want their children baptized as a form of "life insurance." Membership and attendance go up during hard and insecure times. At crisis times people call on the pastor. Small churches that offer the "pew where I've always sat," the pastor who buried my mom and baptized my kids, and the people I've always known are common symbols and sources of safety and security.

Love and Belonging Needs. After a person's physical and security needs are met, attention turns outward. The second creation story in Genesis (Gen. 2:4–24) is a partial illustration of Maslow's hierarchy. A human was formed from earth and given life. God planted a garden to provide food—the physical necessities. Adam was put in the Garden of Eden—a secure environment. Then Adam was lonely. Beasts and birds were provided, but loneliness remained. Eve was created and human need for love and belonging were met.

To be human is to need to be in relationship with special others. In large churches, while I may be acquainted with many but really know few, I may not find the love and belonging I need. In a small church, when I belong and know many, this need is met. Barbara, who moved to Warwick after her husband retired, said: "I feel people here make me feel needed. There are useful things I can do that in a big church I didn't get a chance to do. I feel it's the place I should have been all my life." Her need to belong was met.

Ego, Status, Esteem Needs. There is often contradiction at this level of the hierarchy. A major problem of many small churches is low morale. From the culture and larger churches they've inherited feelings of insignificance. In relation to the world around, small church people don't get much ego, status, and esteem satisfaction.

On the other hand, everyone in a small church can be and usually is "someone." They are known. They are missed when absent. They're needed to keep the ship afloat and on course. Patty, a retarded member of the Emmetsburg church, proudly announces each fall during our Joys and Concerns that she got a medal at the Special Olympics. This woman, who would be a "nobody" almost everywhere, is a "somebody" in our church.

Dietrich Bonhoeffer describes the importance of the Christian community for each person:

> In a Christian community everything depends upon whether each individual is an indispensable link in a chain. Only when even the smallest link is securely interlocked is the chain unbreakable. A community which allows unemployed members to exist within it will perish because of them. It will be well, therefore, if every member receives a definite task to perform for the community, that *he may know in hours of doubt that he, too, is not useless and unusable.*[7]

Self-Actualization Needs. Another word for this is self-fulfillment. When people discover they're not useless, their ego, status, and esteem needs are being met, and the angel emerging from the chunk of marble is becoming a radiant beauty. The Bible is a book about "becoming." Abraham becomes the father of a nation. David, the youngest and smallest of Jesse's sons, becomes the King of Israel. Mary, a young peasant woman, becomes the "mother of God." Saul, the most feared persecutor of the church, becomes its strongest advocate. And we, at whatever age and stage of life, are still becoming.

Each of us is created as a gifted person upon whom our community depends. "A primary purpose of the Church is to help us discover our gifts and, in the face of our fears, to hold us accountable for them so that we can enter into the joy of creating."[8]

A small church is a laboratory for identifying, experimenting with, and combining the raw elements of our becoming. It's a stage where each person plays a crucial part in an unfolding drama. Plentiful needs beckon reluctant volunteers. A pratfall can be taken without grave consequences. Genuine efforts are accepted, because small church people are more concerned with persons than with the product. My greatest reward in ministry is playing some part in people's becoming—from young people who grow up to retired people who discover they're still productive. People need caring at every level of need, and small churches are the right size to do so, if they choose to.

Homogeneity and Diversity

Nothing is more basic to being a Christian church than caring for one another. Caring, however, does not come naturally or easily to all churches, including small ones. Some are indifferent, some deluded, some fair weather, and some downright hostile to any and all. Perhaps they've been hurt, angered, are led by emotionally ill persons, or are at the very bottom of the needs pyramid. But small churches like these are not normal. What is normal is for them to be serious about their care for one another. But why?

In foxholes, the most dissimilar soldiers watch out for and take care of one another because they depend on each other. Likewise, in small churches where everyone is needed, everyone is cared for. Someone observed that a pinched finger is more painful to the one who is hurt than the starvation of millions. In a small church where all know all about each other, each one's pain is felt and the person is cared for. People who want to "do" are likely to go to a big church, people who want to "be" choose smaller ones. People who want to "be" tend to be "people people," and folks like this are likely to put people before tasks.

Often the caring of small churches has much to do with their lack of diversity. Many small churches are fairly homogeneous. People in homogeneous groups tend to get along and care for each other more easily. Often people who are different have been weeded out or repelled. Often churches are comprised of those with similar ethnic, socioeconomic, and family backgrounds; similar needs and wants; similar life styles. Similarity may breed contempt, but it also makes caring easier and more natural.

In northwest Iowa, many of our communities are made up of families that go back several generations and share similar ancestry. Most of these communities are dependent in some way on farming. Their people have similar expectations in life. They golf together, drink coffee together, and go to church together. All but the smallest towns have multiple churches and people have sorted out by socioeconomic level and theological perspectives. Long before the current pastor arrived, these churches had determined their beliefs and rules. Their caring helps maintain the status quo they've carefully established.

Like the swimming duck—serene on the surface, but paddling madly underneath—there is more diversity than one might guess in these apparently stable churches and communities. The farmers and the bankers may see economic matters quite differently. Those who live on the farms and those who live in town may see county government and tax regulations quite differently. Parents who want their children to take over the farm and children who have absolutely no interest in farming will perceive family responsibility quite differently. Merchants who want people to shop in town and consumers who prefer to drive for better bargains don't see eye to eye.

Add to the pot other ingredients like different political loyalties, contrary views on controversial issues, personality differences, and labor and management tensions and small-town and small church life may not be so homogeneous after all. When we look alike, sound alike, think alike, and act alike, caring may come naturally. The greater the diversity, however, the more difficult and necessary it can be.

In 1971, Warwick was pretty homogeneous. (The exception to this homogeneity was the large commune. And the community's fears of the commune people helped solidify community homogeneity.) Most residents had been in town for some time, worked in the paper mills or manufacturing plants, and shared a similar economic level. In the 1970s, an influx of young adults seeking to be closer to nature, retired people finding inexpensive land in a beautiful setting, and well educated people willing to travel to work, brought diversity to this homogeneous community. The church was quite successful in building bridges between diverse people and helping them cross those bridges. In the process, they discovered they had much in common and cared about each other.

In Shrewsbury, where there is greater diversity, the church has been less effective in bridge building. Our relationships tended to be more careful than deeply caring. When political tensions ran hot, the best we managed was to not talk about the things that divided us—except to those who thought as we did. Often the divisions grew deeper. Frequently people who valued homogeneity more than diversity, solitude more than community, and being right more than being in relationship, left the church causing those who remained to feel more spurned, resentful, and tentative. The tensions took a tremendous toll on energy, vision, and ministry.

How to Live with Diversity in the Local Church, by Stephen Kliewer, is a book I wish I had used in Shrewsbury. It would have helped me understand much of what I didn't understand. And it could have given me handles for helping the church manage or bridge its wide diversity and build a spirit of sturdy tolerance and genuine care.

Kliewer identifies five styles (with five descriptive metaphors) that churches use to respond to diversity within them: Comfortable Indifference (The Rocking Chair), Frustrated Mobility (The Treadmill), Polarized Destructiveness (The Boxing Ring), Supportive Cooperation (Rowing the Boat Together), and Creative Interaction (Mulligan Stew). The latter two are prerequisites for a caring spirit to grow. The question is how to avoid easy indifference, frustrated immobility, and polarized destructiveness, and how to build cooperation and creative interaction. With strategic thinking, planning, and acting the first three styles can be minimized and the latter two maximized.[9]

Pastoring in the Midst of Pain

There is hurt and pain in every church. The responsibility for dealing with it begins with the leader, whose job it is to insist on fundamental ground rules for how people will be treated and to paint the vision of the church as a tolerant people, a caring community. The leader may need to risk enforcing those fundamental ground rules.

One of the most difficult and dangerous dilemmas for a pastor and church is deciding how to deal with someone who is a destructive force in the life of the church. When the church is unsure or unwilling to limit the influence of these persons, they are allowed to get away with murder.

Such a difficult and dangerous situation occurred in Shrewsbury. Recognizing the diversity of our congregation and the variety of available church music, I encouraged our part-time music director to use a wide range of music to minister to a variety of tastes. One Sunday she used "Prepare Ye the Way of the Lord" from the musical *Godspell,* as an introit. A former music director, who had left the church during the previous pastorate only to return when I arrived and whose sharp tongue was widely feared, accosted the music director after worship. Her long verbal attack left our director speechless and in tears. This was not the attacker's first serious run-in with people in the church.

I reassured the director of my support and then did what I had never done before. I called on the attacker and verified the account I had heard from eyewitnesses. I screwed up my courage and said: "You may not treat people like that in this church. . . . If you aren't able to work toward a spirit of harmony and tolerance in this church, you might be happier in another church." Looking for their support, I shared with the church leadership what had happened and what I had done. She withdrew from the church. There was greater tolerance, harmony, and courage to care in the church after that incident.

In each area of my ministry, I worked toward that greater tolerance, harmony, and courage to care. I preached that more than worshiping in a sanctuary, we should work toward a spirit of sanctuary where each would be treated with respect and care.

The church was encouraged to gather as often as possible for study, fellowship, and the work of the church, in order that we might break down walls of anonymity. Working with the nominating committee and all of our committees, we sought to include as many people as possible in the decision making and work of the church. The deacons become a caregiving group that took turns calling in the hospital and in homes. The Pastor Parish Relations Committee was established to break down walls, to prevent misunderstanding and resolve difficulties before they escalated, and to care for the pastor and his family.

As a teacher I helped the church understand the nature of conflict, that it has positive as well as destructive possibilities. I helped the church see the advantages of diversity as well as the difficulties. The church as a whole worked with me in changing the nature and style of our church. Although we did not solve all the problems or eliminate all the personality conflicts, significant progress was made. Moving a church from being a random collection of individuals to a caring community of faith is a long and rewarding road.

A caring church will care both for the church as a whole and for its individual members and families. The health of the individuals affects the health of the church and vice versa. A large church can carry on when some members, even leaders, aren't well. In a small church, when a member is disabled the church is often disabled.

In Iowa, the farm crisis of the 1980s took a terrible toll on individuals, families, and churches. In response to the farm crisis, Prairiefire Rural Action, Inc. was formed. Its director, David Ostendorf, suggested in an article that churches are "listening posts" on the front lines when people are in distress and they need to be looking for the symptoms that signal people's need for special care and response. Any church serious about caring for its people will find Ostendorf's list of symptoms helpful:

- Withdrawal from activities, apathy, loss of interest in others
- Not attending church, not contributing time and gifts
- Expressions of loss, hopelessness, signs of grieving or depression
- Tension and stress reflected in physical appearance or conversation
- Talking in veiled terms about the rural crisis [or any problem] or making light of it
- Saying that everything is going well; nothing is wrong
- Coming forward with a presenting problem (marital issues, questions; about how to locate an attorney, and so on) that masks a deeper concern about their situation
- Aggressiveness and acting-out behavior, including the behavior of children in affected families
- Noticeable loss of self-esteem, self-worth, giving up
- Family conflict and tension; coolness in family and community relationships
- Any signs of suicidal behavior[10]

A caring church will watch attentively for symptoms like these. It will have people willing and trained as sympathetic listeners, advocates, and referral agents. In one study carried out during the rural crisis, 55 percent of affected, church-related families said their church had offered *no* support to them and either condemned or ignored them. A caring response in crisis time does not happen automatically. If it's going to happen, the church must call people to care, identify people's caring gifts, train them, and support them.

Elizabeth O'Connor writes: "The primary purpose of the disciplines, structures of accountability, and mission of the Church is to build life together, to create liberating communities of caring. To each of us is given a gift for the building of a community of caring."[11] We need to be serious and intentional about that purpose and task. Jesus was.

Biblical Motifs

The Gospel writers included many teachings and encounters concerning caring in the narratives they compiled for the first-century churches. They are as relevant for our small churches as they were for theirs. Here are three examples, useful for Bible studies and sermons.

Luke 10:38–42. After a hard day of being with people, Jesus is invited to the home of Mary and Martha. It's Martha's nature to see that everything is just right. She scurries about picking up the house, getting out the good dishes, and putting out the guest towels. Water must be fetched from the well and fish from the fishmonger. To Martha, hospitality means preparedness, organization, and propriety. While Martha fusses, Mary is attentive to Jesus. To her, hospitality means being with, more than doing for. Enjoying the company of Jesus is more important than the way the house looks and the food tastes.

Small church caring and hospitality tend to be more like Mary's than Martha's. The priority is on being together rather than impressing each other. People would rather potluck than banquet. Meetings are as much for catching up and telling stories as they are for conducting business. What some consider gossip, small church folks consider necessary information. People who aren't comfortable with informality, bantering, or "wasting time" may not be at home in a small church.

Caring moments in small churches—and they are likely to be in moments more than marathons—are rarely in the counseling hour, by appointment, as part of the agenda. They are more likely to be on the street corner or front porch, in the parking lot, on the phone or over coffee, in the cafe, on the way out of church, or when the pastor happens to stop by. Community happens less in the "koinonia" groups than at the funeral luncheon, at the work bee, during sharing of concerns, or when the prodigal returns home. Mary would have liked a small church.

Luke 15:3–6. This is the story of the shepherd who discovers one sheep is missing, leaves ninety-nine others, and goes searching for the lost one. Would a good shepherd really leave the flock defenseless in the wilderness to look for one sheep? This is the wrong question. The story illustrates that the folly of God is more faithful than human practicality.

In a larger church, it's easier to get lost and stay lost. The shepherd is more likely to stay with the large and demanding flock. There are more than enough sheep to tend, needs to meet, and chores to be done.

This is a small church parable. The lost sheep is missed immediately. The flock feels incomplete without it (though sometimes a flock will purge an unwanted member). The shepherd knows the runaway's habits and favorite haunts and knows when the truant is ready to come back and how to approach it. When the prodigal is found, there is rejoicing that the flock is again complete.

The parallel breaks down if we assume the pastor is the shepherd and the laity are the flock. When the small church works as a community, all will look out for the others. According to James Fenhagen, "The sign of a congregation's capacity to care is not seen in the sensitivity of the clergy, but in the number of people who are being trained and supported in caring for one another."[12] Today's shepherd may be tomorrow's lost sheep; but in the family of faith, there are always caregivers on the lookout.

John 13:1–15. In addition to being an itinerant rabbi, evangelist, physician, and prophet, Jesus was also pastor of a small church of a dozen or so. Has there ever been a small church more frustrating than his? They slept when they should have been awake. Rather than bringing children to Jesus, they shooed them away. They fought over the power positions in their little church. The church treasurer sold out the pastor and hung himself. They misunderstood, were frequently faithless, and squabbled a lot. Jesus had the patience of a saint!

John tells of a meal Jesus shared with his little church. It was customary for guests to have their travel-soiled feet washed, usually by the house servant. Bypassing the servant, Jesus got up from the table, wrapped a towel around himself, and began washing feet. Peter was shocked and embarrassed that Jesus would wash his feet. Jesus said: "If I, your Lord and Teacher, have washed your feet, you also ought to wash one another's feet" (John 13:8).

In churches where ministers are sought first for their oratorical and administrative gifts, who washes the feet of the people? Jesus' model of ministry requires care of both soul and sole. Caring is concern not just for spiritual needs but also for social, emotional, and physical needs.

In washing the feet of his church, Jesus helps them feel at home. He is the consummate host. Nouwen writes: "The minister . . . is a host who offers hospitality to his guests. He gives them a friendly space, where they may feel free to come and go, to be close and distant, to rest and play, to talk and be silent, to eat and to fast."[13] The host prepares the space and creates the environment where the guests feel safe and can take risks, be ministered unto and minister to others. Does each member of my church feel as cared about as the members of Jesus' little church must have felt?

The foot-washing story suggests not only the style and content of caring but also the identity of the care-givers. Larger churches often prefer, and can afford, to hire their care-givers. In *Mutual Ministry*, James Fenhagen writes: "One of the great heresies of the contemporary church is the idea that the primary role of the ordained person in a congregation is to exercise a ministry of caring on behalf of the others who are responsible for his or her hire."[14] Smaller churches cannot as readily hire professionals to care for them and may prefer the do-it-yourself style. Washing one another's feet is the job of all, not the job of the servant or professional. Jesus demonstrates that it is the job of the leader to model caring and to train the cadre of foot washers. Perhaps the primary symbol for the pastor should be a towel and basin.

Caring Strategies

If a church is going to care effectively, it must *plan* to care. Identify caring strategies that fit the gifts and nature of your church and implement them. Here are examples of caring strategies:

1. Look for a pastor who has the gift of caring. In the interviews with candidates, the ones who do all or even most of the talking are not care-givers. A gift for listening is almost synonymous with a gift for caring.
2. Think up ways to help everyone know everyone's name and know about everyone. Use name tags at least occasionally.
3. Eat together a lot. Use any excuse for a potluck. Don't use an automatic dishwasher or paper plates. Dishpan hands and building community go hand in hand.
4. Be with parishioners the night before or morning of surgery and with spouse or family during surgery; don't wait until afterwards to visit in the hospital.

5. Begin every meeting with worship/meditation and community building (not just a prayer). Spend fifteen minutes around a question like: "What's the best thing that's happened to each of you since the last time we met?"

6. Have a daily ministry in the local coffee shops. A variation is to serve coffee one morning a week at the church—if it's on the way to wherever people go.

7. Recognize that life-passage times like baptisms, weddings, and funerals are primary times for offering and receiving caring. Plan these occasions accordingly.

8. Make communion a time for caring, not just for remembering and anticipating. Make it real and make it communal.

9. Sell get-well and greeting cards and encourage their use.

10. Send birthday and anniversary cards to all your people.

11. Structure the grapevine so that five telephone calls from you gets the word out to the whole church—not just announcements but also concerns and prayer requests.

12. Have the nurses in your church, perhaps a doctor and counselor, conduct a workshop on crisis intervention and hospital and nursing home visiting, to help people replace their fears with confidence and skills.

13. Start a Parish Nurse program in which a nurse in your church does health education and preventive health care with your and other people.

14. If you're the pastor, announce often how and when you want to be notified of people's needs. Because I'm both a pastor and an area minister, I say and write often: "I'm busy, but *you* come first. Call me and I'll make time."

15. Plan church retreats, or what I call, "A Time Away," when people can relax and be real with one another.

16. Don't just call on people or call people together when you want something from them (like money). Call them together simply to play, like regular Sunday afternoon volleyball and horseshoes.

17. Go down your list of people and make at least one "Hello, I was just thinking of you and wondering how you are" telephone call every day.

18. Involve your church in a mission project that includes an opportunity to know one another better and to care for each other.

19. If you're the pastor, do more pastoral calling than you have time to do or feel is necessary. Call both in people's homes and their place of work. Once I visited every member at their workplace or at home and took their picture working or doing something they enjoyed, and created a slide show for the church. It was a hit!

20. Persuade and train lay people to make pastoral calls. Use *Called to Care: A Notebook for Lay Caregivers* to train and equip your callers. It's excel-

lent and can be ordered from: United Church Resources, 1–800–325–7061.

21. Create ways to get your people into each other's homes—committee meetings, progressive suppers, cooperative window-washing parties, Bible studies.

22. Decorate and furnish your building (and turn the heat up) so people will linger rather than leave.

23. When making pastoral calls, take people—including children and young people—with you. In some ways my infant daughter was more effective in the nursing home than I was!

24. Find creative ways to help your children develop their caring aptitude. They're never too young to care.

25. Create a Prayer Partner plan. Identify a different person or family each week for the church to pray for or pair people to pray for one another.

26. Include the Passing of the Peace in every worship.

27. First and last, find at least a core of people who will do Bible study and pray faithfully, thankfully, and caringly for one another, the pastor, others in need, the whole church, and the community. Where there's honest prayer, there's care.

Elie Wiesel tells of a contemporary Hasidic rabbi who asked a disciple:

> "How is Moshe Yaakov doing?" The disciple didn't know. "What!" shouted the Rabbi, "You don't know? You pray under the same roof with him, you study the same texts, you serve the same God, you sing the same songs, and you dare to tell me that you don't know whether Moshe Yaakov is in good health, whether he needs help, advice or comforting.[15]

We in small churches have no excuse for not knowing how one another is doing and for not helping each other do better.

For Thought and Discussion

1. On a scale of 1 to 10, how well does your church care for its people? What ages, types, persons get forgotten?

2. Identify times when *you* were especially cared for by your church. And when did you feel forgotten?

3. Look at Maslow's hierarchy of needs and discuss how your church cares or could care at each level.

4. Does your church relish, avoid, or manage conflict?

5. Start with the list of twenty-seven strategies of caring in this chapter and brainstorm ways your church could be more caring.

8. Mission: Doing the Faith Outside the Doors

Listen, Christians

I was hungry
and you formed a humanities club
and discussed my hunger.
Thank you.

I was imprisoned
and you crept off quietly
to your chapel in the cellar
and prayed for my release.

I was naked
and in your mind
you debated the morality of
    my appearance.

I was sick
and you knelt and thanked God
    for your health.

*I was homeless
and you preached to me
of the spiritual shelter of
    the love of God.*

*I was lonely
and you left me alone
to pray for me.
You seem so holy;
so close to God.
But I'm still very hungry
and lonely
and cold.*

*So where have your prayers
    gone?
What have they done?
What does it profit a people
to page through their book of prayers
when the rest of the world
is crying for their help?*[1]

As I understand the church, it's a "3-M" company—Ministry, Mission, and Maintenance. *Ministry* happens when the church gathers to worship, to learn, and to care for one another. *Maintenance* includes all the household maintenance tasks a church does in order to carry on its Ministry and Mission. *Mission* encompasses all that the church does beyond its doors. The ultimate purpose of Ministry and Maintenance is to equip and strengthen the church for its Mission. Its Mission is to bring the caring and community building power of the Gospel to the world, which is asking the kind of questions posed in the poem "Listen Christians."

Churches of all sizes often get so involved in their worship, education, caring, and tasks of institutional maintenance that they don't get around to or lose sight of the needs waiting on the church's doorstep. Recalling Maslow's ascending hierarchy of needs, churches often perceive Ministry and Maintenance tasks as more basic needs and Mission as a need to be addressed *after* the more basic needs are fulfilled.

I've learned in the three places I've pastored, that many churches will move seriously into mission if someone, particularly the pastor, raises the issue and provides the leadership. Mission was not a conscious, church-wide priority in any of the three churches before my ministry.

One way of evaluating a church's commitment to mission is to look at what it does with its money. In 1971, the Warwick church designated $50 for mission out of a budget of $1,585. (Our independent treasurer refused to send the $50 because he disagreed with some ways the United Church of Christ used mission money.) In 1985, out of the $32,300 the Shrewsbury church spent, $950 went outside the church—about 3 percent. In 1988, the Emmetsburg church (with a stronger denominational connection and tradition) committed $2,300 out of the $29,000 it spent, for mission—about 9 percent. These churches were not organized to reach beyond their doors in other ways, either.

Mission has been a priority throughout my ministry. An active mission committee was established in each church. Those responsible for drawing up the church's budget were encouraged to make the same kind of commitment to mission support as they did to paying the utility bills. They did and led the churches in increasing that commitment annually. Mission projects were quickly and continually initiated. I tried to make the individual church's approach to mission a natural expression of the unique personality of the individual church and appropriate for their particular context. The people of each church were helped to see themselves as disciples in their daily living, not just members of a local religious organization. Each church was helped to not use its small size as an excuse for little action.

Small churches aren't usually known for being faithful and effective at mission. And there are good reasons why they aren't. Many are desperately seeking to survive and aren't thinking beyond their survival needs. Many have not had leadership that encouraged them to think about mission. Most have not had anyone encourage them and help them do mission in ways that are right for them. Many are so involved in caring for one another, and some are so involved in fighting with one another, that they don't have time and energy for reaching out beyond themselves. Small churches, which operate on a person-to-person level, often don't understand or know how to respond to the complex, systemic justice issues of our world.

Many have only perceived mission as money sent away to national offices to be used in some way by someone else somewhere else. (This often feels like one more imposed tax, and no one is enthusiastic about taxes.) Like Warwick and Shrewsbury did, many have ambivalence or hostility toward their denomination's way of doing mission and soliciting the money needed for it. When mission is defined as money sent, small churches without much money to send are intimidated because their little bit feels like a piddling drop in a huge sea of need. On the other hand, many small churches *are* significantly involved in mission in ways that they and outsiders *have never defined* as mission. Consider Warwick, Shrewsbury, and Emmestburg.

The Warwick church had not closed because they were committed to having a Sunday school in town. That was their mission, though no one ever called it that. Just by providing a Christian presence in the community through decades of struggle was a mission. When that handful of people lived the Word heard on Sunday morning during the week in their homes, the mills and factories where they worked, and in community life, they were doing mission.

The Shrewsbury church, although it did not have a denominationally connected mission, did have a mission. It worked to be one unifying church out of the three that had been, to unify a geographically large and diverse community, and to witness to what God was trying to do in that place. In times of personal tragedy or crisis in the community, the church was quick to respond. Many individual members were very involved in significant lay ministries—though they never labeled them that. Several worked in education and human services vocations. Daily these people spent themselves in responding to the kinds of needs raised in the "Listen Christians" poem. Some were leaders in working effectively to protect Vermont's threatened environment. Several served the community in town government and voluntary associations. A few were active members in Amnesty International. The church's buildings were used for community programs. Their budget showed a minimal concern for God's mission. Their lives showed an active commitment to God's whole creation—which is mission broadly defined.

The Emmetsburg church had a long tradition of active involvement in the United Church of Christ—at the association, state, and national levels. But their denominational support was more out of loyalty than conviction. It has been in their local service where they have been most active. In a strongly Catholic, Lutheran, and Methodist community, their participation and influence in community life and activities is way out of proportion to their size. Through several retired and active school teachers, the church has had a strong influence in building a very good education system. Their farmers have cared for their land. Virtually every person in the church was a solid, caring, contributing member of the community. Its building housed a free child-care program.

My task as pastor in each church was to:

- Be thankful for and affirm who the people were and what they were already doing
- Build on what the churches were already doing
- Make mission a priority of the whole church encompassing more than dollars sent away to somewhere else
- Help people see that mission is more an exciting opportunity than a matter of duty and loyalty
- Help each person to find their niche in the church's mission
- Not bog people down in organizational matters so that they lacked time and energy to do the church's mission
- Educate concerning all that God's mission needs to be
- Help people experience or at least hear about the needs
- Help shape an indigenous, customized mission effort for each church that grows out of its history, personality, and context
- Carry out mission in a creative and involving way

That's been my approach in each church. Each one moved from significant unintentional mission to more significant intentional mission, had a stronger reason for being, and made the world a bit better. My work with mission in these churches has been based on *nine fundamental assumptions*.

Fundamentals of Small Church Mission

1. *Mission is a life-and-death matter for small churches.* In a "bigger is better" world, little churches struggle to feel legitimate and valuable. Many have dwindled and languished because they've lost their reason for being. Churches have closed or been closed because they, or someone who had power over them, couldn't justify their existence. For small churches to survive, they must be helped to find their reason for being, their mission. To paraphrase Jesus: Churches who seek merely to survive will lose their lives, but those who lose their lives in mission will find life.

On a very pragmatic level, whether many small churches live or die will depend on whether the community around them supports, ignores, or abandons them. When the Warwick, Shrewsbury, and Emmetsburg churches reached out to serve their communities, they received both moral and concrete support. God's directive to Israel when it went into exile is relevant to the relationship between churches and their communities: "But seek the welfare of the city where I have sent you into exile, and pray to the Lord on its behalf, for in its welfare you will find your welfare" (Jer. 29:7).

2. *People want to make a difference.* A woman, walking on a beach no-

ticed an older woman picking up starfish and returning them to the sea. The younger one asked what she was doing. The older explained that the starfish would die if they remained stranded until the tide rose. "But there are millions of starfish on the beach, how can your efforts make any difference?" countered the younger. The older woman, throwing another starfish to safety, said simply: "But at least I can save this one." When people are helped to make a difference, they are empowered and their lives are changed. My ministry is to help people make a difference in the lives of others.

3. *Authentic mission grows out of a church's history, character or personality, and context.* Small churches, more than others, find meaning in their past. The symbols and stories of who they were help a church know who they are. Carl Dudley writes: "Memory is the strongest motive for ministry in the small cell of caring Christians."[2] A church's memory helps shape its character or personality.

My Aunt Elizabeth used a quote from my grandmother, who looked around the dinner table at a family gathering and pronounced: "Not a shabby one in the bunch," as the title of the little book she wrote about our family. That myth has helped shape the Ray character, who we are and what we do. We try to live up to our grandmother's myth of us.

The third ingredient is context, the surrounding situation. Appropriate mission must fit the current situation and present needs. For example, the three rural churches I've served found it easy to relate to Heifer Project International, an agricultural self-help program. A church whose mission is rooted in the memory of who it was, whose present character is shaped by that memory, and who lives out that history-shaped character in ways congruent with the past, with itself, and with surrounding needs and opportunities will have an authentic and faithful mission. Any other mission will be as cut flowers in the desert.

4. *People have to "feel" the need.* People in small churches are more likely to respond to what has touched them. Surveys, statistics, and sermons don't influence them as much as direct experience. Later I'll describe the ministry of Bill Briggs, whose strategy of providing direct experience of human need helped transform a quiet New Hampshire church into a beehive of amazing mission ventures. The mission trip I led to Rwanda transformed the twelve who went and impacted our church, because we could all feel the poverty of many Africans and the power of African Christianity.

5. *Small church mission needs to be hands on, person-to-person.* If I explain the systemic nature of injustice in the international economic alliances, people will yawn. If I invite them to work on a problem, they will shrug. If I give a name and a face to a systemic problem, they will act. Warwick would not have raised three thousand dollars for Heifer Project if it had not been for Steve; Shrewsbury would not have raised several thousand dollars for world mission if they had not experienced a partner church in Rwanda. The thrift shops begun by both churches are still operating.

6. *Small church mission is integral to the whole life of the church.* Working as it should, small church mission is inspired through worship, informed through education, and carried over from the members' care for one another. It is not a separate activity done by a separate group of people. No one is too young or too old, too conservative or too liberal to help. Theologian Emil Brunner's well-known quotation expresses the centrality of mission: "The church exists by mission, as fire exists by burning."

7. *Small churches are better at doing mission than planning it.* Feasibility studies and long-range planning may have a lot to recommend them. But they often feel like talking a problem to death. If it's broke fix it; if it ain't, don't. Small churches would rather follow the organizational principle of K.I.S.S. (Keep It Simple, Stupid). As a leader, it's my job to see a need and envision a solution, and to encourage others to help with that process. Then we seek to involve as many as possible in working that solution.

8. *More gets done when you're having fun.* The need may be serious and the work hard. But when your approach is creative and you enjoy being together and you're making a real difference, your work will be both productive and pleasurable. Plan on it. I remember the laughter when the Shrewsbury mission committee planned and carried out our Food Day "Cow Flop Drop," which raised $1,500 for hunger programs. (The way a Cow Flop Drop works is that a field is divided into many squares, which are raffled off. A cow is released to wander through the field. The person "owning" the square where the cow first "flops" wins the first prize. The sites of the second and third flops determine the second and third place winners.) Part of the value of the Emmetsburg Mission Fair was the fun we had selecting international recipes and tasting unfamiliar foods. Mission can be both fun and exciting.

9. *Love without limits.* More often than I want to remember, I've heard church people say we should take care of our own first. That's a natural reaction but *not* a faithful one. Jesus loudly and clearly said *all* people are our neighbors. To "think globally and act locally" is a good idea. But it's even more empowering for small churches to discover they can think globally *and* act globally. In all three churches we tried to strike a balance by doing significant mission at both the local and global levels.

History, Character, Style, and Context

The assumption stated earlier that authentic mission grows out of a church's history, character or personality, and context needs more amplification. When we talk about mission we're recognizing the need for change. Small churches are *not* opposed to change. They're opposed to what they perceive as wrong, needless, or threatening changes or right changes for the wrong reasons. Dudley and Walrath write about helping small churches with change in *Developing Your Small Church's Potential.* They see faithful and effective change in small churches as a dynamic process requiring three components—memory, vision, and organization.

Memory without vision and organization is simply sepia tinted nostalgia. Vision without memory and organization is simply pie in the sky. Organization without memory and vision is simply change for the sake of change. A church that is able to create change rooted in the memory of its storytellers, shaped by the beckoning vision of its visionaries, and built by those who know how to get things done will not be building castles in the sand.

We're in the early stages of a major project in Emmetsburg that illustrates what Dudley and Walrath are suggesting. We're working on our memory, vision, and organization. 1996 is the centenary of our building, which is in serious need of both exterior and interior rehabilitation. Surprisingly few people are left who have been in our church for a long time. Our historical records and our people's memory of our church history are quite sketchy. Our vision of our church's future is blurred by anxiety over continuing population and economic decline in the community and region and what this may mean for our church. Organizationally, most of the work of our church has been done by a few. So we're using our building issue to work on our memory, vision, and organization.

Memory. People are looking for pictures and records, asking questions of others about our history—particularly the history of our building. The next steps will include gathering people with recollection of the church before 1950 and interviewing them on videotape, to give us and people who come later a sense of who we were.

There will be a History Night, when records and pictures are displayed, acquired information shared, and a time line of remembered history created. We'll have a roll of paper taped to the wall with the founding date of the church on one end and the current date on the other, and a few major events in between. We'll go back to the earliest memory that anyone has, hear the story, note it on the time line, and proceed from there to the present. I believe our need to do something about our building will be the catalyst for helping us replace our amnesia with a potent memory.

Vision. From day one, I've preached the wisdom expressed in *Alice in Wonderland*: "If you don't know where you're going, you'll end up somewhere else." I've been helping our people envision along with me. In writing and in worship, I share my unfolding vision and encourage theirs. When officers and groups are asked for annual reports, they're asked to include what they planned to do this last year, what they did do, *and* what they believe should happen next year and in the years ahead. Our annual report is much more interesting now.

Over a year ago, as part of a UCC community-mission project, we asked our leadership and interested members four questions: what do you affirm about our church? what do you affirm about our community? what are your concerns about our church? and what are your concerns about our community? Just asking the questions and listening to the answers helped us believe we have power to build on what we affirm and do something about our concerns. People's affirmations were more powerful than their concerns, leading us to be more confident about our future.

As I've gotten to know these people, I've intentionally tried to create a "myth" for the future that they can live into. Our corner signboard now says, "We're a Caring People." In various ways I've repeated, "We're the community-minded church," and "We're an ecumenical church." All that is true and part of our character, but it has now been highlighted as a directional sign for us and others.

Organization. Organization is simply the way things get done. Every church has one, even if organization means benignly doing what the Chief Pillar says to do. The Emmetsburg church is good at getting things done, but often they did things without great forethought or without consulting many people. A principle of mine in all three churches has been to spread responsibility and power as broadly as possible, in order to encourage participation by the new, shy, and semi-interested. With surprising trust and willingness, the Emmetsburg church adopted a new form of organization, which has spread and increased responsibility; brought more people into decision making; improved communication; and is developing new leadership, improving communication, and enabling us to get more done. This new form is more consistent with our congregational tradition.

As we're remembering, envisioning, and shaping an organization that works, we're ready to make major building decisions. Experts were brought in to assess the condition of the building. We renovated and restored the main entry way, which gives us a taste of what more renovation and restoration would be like. My wife attended a conference in Chicago about dealing with church buildings as a sacred trust. Our state conference financial person has been in twice to help us work on the financial issues. The whole congregation's questions and ideas are continually being solicited. We have over $100,000 in hand or pledged and a plan for the additional $35,000 that will be needed.

I expect that by 1996, rather than surviving by practicing deferred maintenance, our church will be thriving in a building that faithfully kindles poignant memories and will effectively house another century of ministry and mission. My vision is that it will also be a beacon of hope for a community looking for reasons to believe in its future. As our church's memory is recovered, our vision focused, and our organization overhauled, we will be more faithful and effective and our mission beyond ourselves will be customized and strengthened.

A helpful book in looking at a church's character or personality and its context is *Handbook for Congregational Studies,* by Jackson Carroll, Carl Dudley, and William McKinney.[3] It is the result of a collaborative effort to understand churches called "congregational studies." Four approaches to discerning the nature of a church are to study its: Identity, Context, Process, and Program.

The section on Identity reports on a typology developed by Jack Carroll, Bill McKinney, and David Roozen that characterizes churches by their orientation to mission. Most congregations are a mixture of the four, with one dominating. The four are: *Activist, Civic, Evangelistic,* and *Sanctuary.*

The *Activist* orientation sees the world as the arena of God's redemptive activity, in which God is calling the church to speak out on issues and engage in actions to change and transform the world into a more just and loving society. An Activist church is likely to sponsor social action groups, promote social change through organized activity, expect the pastor to speak out on social and political issues, and so on.

The *Civic* orientation also believes this world is God's arena and that God calls Christians to act responsibly in public life. But the Civic orientation is more comfortable working within existing organizations and institutions. It emphasizes making them work better more than challenging or replacing them. The Civic church might sponsor forums on issues but would encourage individual involvement rather than joint action by the church. It would be inclined to work with other religious groups for community improvements, provide aid and services to individuals, and so on.

The *Evangelistic* orientation is more focused on the world to come. It calls people to salvation with the promise of eternal life. Members are urged to witness to their faith by sharing the message of salvation. These churches maintain an active evangelism program, reach out to members of other religious groups with the message of true salvation, protect its members from false teachings, and prepare its people for the coming world.

The *Sanctuary* orientation also has an otherworldly emphasis. It sees the church existing primarily to provide persons with opportunities to withdraw from the trials of daily living in the company of fellow believers. A sharp distinction is made between sacred and secular, spiritual and temporal. Christians are expected to live in this world, obey its laws, but not "be of this world." It will resist the many pleasures and life-styles of this world, prepare people for the world to come, and see patriotism as a religious obligation.

This typology helps interpret much church conflict and behavior. Each orientation has a different approach to and participation in mission. A church's orientation grows out of its remembered history and perhaps its denominational tradition. Each orientation has a different vision of what and where God is calling it to. For example, the Shrewsbury church had outspoken advocates of each of these orientations, which helps explain the tension I experienced.

Stephen Kliewer's little book *How to Live with Diversity in the Local Church* provides guidance in helping a diverse church with differing orientations find a way to be involved in mission(s), rather than being stymied by its diversity. He suggests that a church can and should choose a congregational style which will work for it, and offers four alternatives and strategies for getting there.

The *Uni-Faith/Uni-Mission* church is a homogeneous church united in faith and the way to express its faith. The *Uni-Faith/Multi-Mission* church has arrived at a common understanding of faith but chooses to live it out in diverse ways. The *Multi-Faith/Uni-Mission* church has a diverse understanding of faith but has a unified way of acting out its diversity. (The Shrewsbury church was multi-faith/uni-mission in its partnership with the Conservative Baptist Church in Rwanda. Each orientation in the church found value in its African partnership.) The *Multi-Faith/Multi-Mission* church accommodates diversity in both its understanding of faith and mission.[4]

Strategies for resolving the problems around multi-faith understandings revolve around finding one faith affirmation that all can salute (like "Christ is Lord") and then agreeing that each can define and develop their faith stance from that common fundamental. Strategies for encompassing multi-mission expressions revolve around encouraging and affirming a variety of mission involvements. The Church of the Savior in Washington, D.C., organized itself into several tiny and intensive "churches," each with its own major mission thrust. A practice there is that if anyone feels called to move into a new mission, that person stands in worship and articulates the call. If no one else is moved to join the call, it is assumed the call is premature. If one or more people "sign on," the church affirms the new mission and encourages them to proceed. This is a creative way of living with and benefiting from both multi-faith and multi-mission situations.

A church wanting to take its *context* seriously by understanding its relationship to it and determining its mission within it, might consult Carroll, Dudley, and McKinney's *Handbook for Congregational Studies:* "The more leaders and members are helped to see and understand the power of the context on their congregation's life and their participation in it, the greater the possibility they have of cultivating a more responsible and effective expression of their faith commitments."[5]

An inner-city small church's mission will be different from that of a suburban small church and different from that of a rural small church. Inner-city churches will more likely offer fellowship opportunities as an antidote to urban anonymity. Because of size and setting, an urban church will probably need to pinpoint specific needs such as school vandalism, housing, a dangerous street crossing, or language tutoring for a specific ethnic group. It will generally focus on a limited geographical area—a block, street, or neighborhood. An urban small church's building and physical resources are particularly valuable mission tools. Often program and meeting space is needed more than money in serving a community, and urban churches usually have under-utilized space. Also, urban churches can work with neighboring religious and community groups in tackling larger needs.

Suburban small churches may focus on family needs and issues. Many suburban churches have members who hold influential positions in business, industry, social services, and government. Such a church might help these persons explore ways of using their influence to meet needs. These small churches can help people who have chosen the suburb for its insulated qualities to become advocates for less privileged peoples in less protected places. There will be community issues like zoning, housing, schools, and drug abuse that the church can help its people and their neighbors address.

Rural churches have a unique mission. President Theodore Roosevelt's 1908 Commission on Country Life included the rural church in its report: "The time has arrived when the church must take a larger leadership, both as an institution and through its pastors, in the social organization of rural life."[6] As many rural communities face declining populations and economies and a changing way of life, the church is often one of the few remaining viable organizations. In contrast to urban and suburban areas, the rural church is often still at the center of community life—physically and socially. Its building is a community meeting place, the church is a center of communications, and many church members are community leaders. The church has the potential to be a strong influence at several levels of community life. Protection of the environment, farm issues, rural poverty, zoning, rural medical and legal care, and quality education are a few of the issues that rural churches can address.

Moorland, Iowa is a tiny farming community of 220 people. The barely surviving UCC church averaged fifteen (no children) in worship when Jerres Jane Mills became their part-time pastor in 1989, while primarily pastoring in Manson, twenty miles away. She started having one-day-a-week office hours at the church. One afternoon two children wandered in to check out what happened there. An after-school story hour was started. That led to a winter boot exchange. The church co-sponsored a picnic for the seasonal Hispanic farm workers working in the area. The Moorland church is finding life as it reaches out to the needs around them.

It is important to get a concrete understanding of your context. Is it a city block, a neighborhood, a town, a city, or a larger region? I keep reminding myself that our context is not just Emmetsburg, since we're interdependent with the agricultural region around us and at least a fifth of our members come from a small town and area called Cylinder. A map of your community or county with pins for each member will tell you something about the community you serve. Also consider where your people are employed. Your context may be larger than you think.

Documents that will help you understand your context are at your library, local government offices, extension service, and chamber of commerce. Look for local histories, census reports, maps, land-use plans, back files of local newspapers, chamber of commerce and economic development publications, real estate and welcome wagon brochures. In Emmetsburg, we had a task force visit the mayor, the sheriff and police chief, the superintendent of schools, extension agent, and a poverty worker. They gave us valuable insight on our area. It's helpful to talk with people who normally don't get interviewed—students, merchants, drop outs, regulars at the neighborhood tavern, street people.

Now the fun begins. Take a video camera or tape recorder and take a walking tour of your neighborhood. Take your time. Get off the sidewalk and go in places—alleys, back yards, side roads, buildings. What do you see or not see? Whom do you see and not see? What have you never noticed before? Ask questions. What things—physical or social—need to be fixed. Let your curiosity get the best of you. Then do a windshield survey from your car. Drive slowly. Use that video camera, tape recorder, or at least a notepad to record what you see. Follow your hunches. Begin drawing some conclusions. What are the themes and trends you've discovered? What encourages, discourages, frightens you? If Jesus had been walking or driving with you, what would he have noticed, who would he have been interested in, what would have disturbed him? As you begin to bring together your church's history, personality, style, and context, what mission ideas are beginning to feel congruent for your church? What's the next step?

Two Mission Planning Processes

Following are two methods for helping a church determine its mission. The first is a twelve-step process that takes seriously who the church uniquely is and how it understands "mission." It uses the gifts already present in a church and addresses surrounding specific needs and opportunities. It can be used along with other ideas in this chapter. This process can be worked through by the whole church (sometimes working in small groups), a mission committee, the official board, a task force, or an ad hoc group over a couple of long evenings, a day, or a weekend. Someone skilled in enabling a group should lead the process. Use lots of newsprint to keep track of your work. Have refreshments to keep you going. Here's the process:

1. Begin with some community building around the question What are your hopes and fears for our church and community?
2. Do Bible study around one or more of these passages: Amos 5:21–24, Matthew 5:44–45, Luke 4:16–22, Luke 10:25–37, and Ephesians 2:13–14. Ask yourselves these three questions:

   • What is God saying through this passage?
   • Through this passage, what might God intend for us in this time and place?
   • If our church were to take this passage very seriously what would we do and how would we do it?

   (Then, without lingering or hurrying, work your way through the following steps/questions, being honest and creative.)

3. What is your church's present definition(s) of mission?
4. What does your church see as the key reasons for its existence or what is its mission (calling) as a church? Consider both your history as well as your present convictions.
5. List the ways your people are already engaged in mission? Is there rhyme or reason to it? Is it balanced or all local or global?
6. What is unique about your church—its history, personality, style, and context?
7. Answer the following three questions:

   • What does your church do really well?
   • What special gifts are present in your midst?
   • What issues and needs do you already care deeply about?

8. Identify up to fifteen specific needs and opportunities that surround your church. (Decide how large an area you want to include.) Arrange them by their importance—1 to 15. Narrow them to your top three or four. (It's O.K. to combine some that are naturally related.)
9. As you begin to consider how you might reach out in mission, what are the limiting factors or handicaps you'll have to keep in mind?
10. What resources—both physical and human, both in and outside the church—are probably available to you that might be used as you reach out in mission?
11. As a result of your time and work together:

    • What specific action(s) do you feel called to do?
    • How will you enlist the rest of your church?

- How will you do it?
- Who will do what?
- What help do you need?
- What are the next three steps?
- Who's in charge of calling you together as you proceed to implement your mission project?

12. With all the gusto you have left, hold hands, sing the doxology (or Hallelujah Chorus if you're musical), pray, have one more cookie, and go home with God's blessing.

This process can be done quickly or extended over a period of time, depending on your people's style and endurance. It should help your church members make a real difference in ways congruent with their history, nature, and context. It's compatible with my assumptions about mission. It requires a leader who knows the people and can gently but persistently keep them working at the task.

There is another exciting and effective method of moving a small church into mission. Rev. Bill Briggs, battered and bruised after difficult ministries in difficult times in Chicago and Buffalo, retreated in 1972 to the tiny (twelve active members) Franconia Community Church of Christ in Franconia, New Hampshire (population eight hundred). It was a church of older members who were despairing about their future. Their building was in good shape and they had some invested money.

Bill wrote about the wonderful things that happened in Franconia in a little, exciting book, *Faith Through Works*:

> God works in mysterious ways. . . . To our growing wonder, the Franconia church gave birth to a succession of challenging and exciting missions. The dozen or so meek and aging church people sought the most difficult work in their community and performed it with joy and humility. Their example attracted the "young" members they had expected me to attract. Their numbers increased ten-fold in ten years. People wanted to join in the Good Work. . . . We had evolved a model for church development.[7]

Their simple and effective model can be used or adapted anywhere. It is a five-step process:

Church ⟡Core Group ⟡Experiencing ⟡Reflecting ⟡Responding

First, out of the *Church* a *Core Group* "whose members are literally in love with each other must be developed." The Core Group gets to know and love one another as they engage in disciplined prayer and mission-oriented Bible study. When they are a cohesive and caring group, it's time for *Experiencing*.

The second stage is for the Core Group to Experience the need in this world. One Core Group of four people helped deliver a bus to a Catholic mission in Guatemala. Another visited the Church of the Savior's Sojourner Community in Washington, D.C. A third visited a self-help poor people's project on the coast of Maine, developed by a Catholic nun. It's important that the Core Group personally experience real need so that their subsequent action is a compassionate response and not merely a vague and half-hearted action.

The third stage is to come back and come together for "real thinking" and "real praying," for *Reflecting* on what they've experience and what a faithful and effective response could be. Real thinking looks back to the source of the need or problem and ahead to the nature and consequences of possible actions. Real praying opens the group to God's revealing and seeks the courage to respond to God's leading.

The fourth stage is *Responding* with appropriate and faithful action. The Core Group uses three criteria for right action: is it appropriate to the scriptures? is it appropriate for the receiver of the action? and is it appropriate for the Core Group? When they're sure the criteria is right, they're ready to come to the church seeking not their permission or money but their blessing. With the congregation's blessing and the participation of many, the mission was carried out. The pattern was that from completed missions new Core Groups were born. This all sounds pretty basic, but the results were dramatic.

Using that simple process, a number of creative projects emerged. The Noah's Ark craft cooperative provided a needed outlet for area crafts people and raised money for other mission efforts. The four retired women who had gone to Guatemala returned and told their story. A 6.2-mile road race (which became an annual event) was organized to raise money to support a land reform program in Guatemala, which led to purchasing and delivering a van to the mission in Guatemala. A wood co-op was established to help poor people procure their winter firewood. A nursing home ministry was established at the Willows Nursing Home. One person was so passionately concerned about the horrible plight of Southeast Asian boat people that a refugee task force was established, ultimately resulting in bringing many refugees to a new life in New Hampshire.

Like an unstoppable chain reaction, one mission project after another happened and met a variety of needs. And a dying, despairing rural church found in mission their avenue to new life. The unique aspect of the Franconia story is the way experiences were used to inspire wonderfully creative ideas that made tremendous differences.

The appendix to Bill's book describes the brainstorming process that was used once the group had done its Bible study and identified its area of need. The Core Group met and shared every idea that came to mind, no matter how silly, ambitious, or expensive. Affirmation of ideas was expected and interruptions encouraged. Ideas were recorded and later sorted and evaluated. Here's a very brief segment from a brainstorming session around a kitchen table:

> Shellfish cooperative.
> What's a shellfish cooperative?
> Coupon exchange.
> Skate exchange.
> Garden seed exchange! . . .
> Start a day camp.
> Take an inner city kid into your home for two weeks in the summer.
> Or a workcamp for spoiled suburban kids!
> They could harvest vegetables!
> Fix up an old school bus.
> Build a barn.
> Start an annual event to fund a scholarship.[8]

In a small church there may be things that cannot be done, tasks that are too large or complex. Because of smallness, however, there are ventures we can do, a mission we can effect. The potential for intimacy and immediacy makes possible a kind of mission that is difficult in larger settings. Philip Hallie, in *Lest Innocent Blood Be Shed,* tells the remarkable story of how hundreds of Jews and refugees were saved from Nazi arrest by the Reverand Andre Trocme and his little church in Le Chambon in France during World War II. Trocme enabled the kind of intimate caring and commitment in the Le Chambon church that is the spirit of mission in small churches at their best:

> For the rest of his life he sought another union, another intimate community of people praying together and finding in their love for each other and for God the passion and the will to extinguish indifference and solitude. From the union he learned that only in such an intimate community, in a home or in a village, could the Protestant idea of a "priesthood of all believers" work. Only in intimacy could people save each other. And because he learned this well, the struggle of Le Chambon against evil would be a kitchen struggle, a battle between a com-

munity of intimates and a vast, surrounding world of violence, betrayal, and indifference.[9]

In mission is the hope of the world and the salvation of the church.

For Thought and Discussion

1. What is your church's definition of mission? Is it narrow or broad?
2. List all the ways your church is engaged in mission.
3. What in your church's history, personality, style, and context is relevant for discovering your mission?
4. Which of the theories, methods, and examples found in this chapter seem most useful for your situation?
5. If your church tailored its mission to its unique history, personality, style, and context, what would it look like?

9.

Maintenance:
Keeping the Ship Afloat
♦ and on Course

What is it that makes the world work? A doctor, an architect, and a government bureaucrat were arguing among themselves about whose profession was the oldest. The doctor got in the first punch: "Why, mine's the oldest. Didn't God operate on Adam and remove a rib to make Eve?" The architect countered: "That's true, but mine's still older. Right at the beginning, God constructed the universe out of chaos." With a smug smile, the bureaucrat sat back, allowed just enough silence, and offered the last word: "And who do you think made the chaos?"

The *primary work of the church is ministry*—through worship, education, and caring for one another—*and mission*, or serving those outside the church. But this primary work doesn't happen automatically or by happenstance. Although a small church needs far less bureaucracy or organization than a larger church, it is no less important. The work of ministry and mission is the *what* and the *why* of the church. The work of church *maintenance* is the *how, who, when, where*, and *how much does it cost* of church life. (And by "maintenance" I mean far more than building upkeep.)

The Oxford American Dictionary definition of *maintain* is: 1. to cause to continue, to keep in existence; 2. to keep in repair; 3. to support, to provide for, to bear the expenses of; 4. to assert as true. If the church's maintenance tasks aren't attended to, it will wander off course or founder on the rocks.

Scripture provides handy labels for the tasks of the church. The priests and preachers lead worship, the rabbis educate, the pastors (lay and ordained) care for the flock, the deacons (servants) lead the church's mission, and the bishops maintain the church. One year in Warwick, we commissioned our church leaders and gave them each one of the above titles. The pastoral leader often carries all these titles, but the wise one will share each title and task with lay leaders.

Titus 1:7–9 describes the qualities the bishops or the maintainers of the church need to faithfully and effectively carry out their functions: "For a bishop, as God's steward, must be blameless, he must not be arrogant or quick-tempered or addicted to wine or violent or greedy for gain; but he must be hospitable, a lover of goodness, prudent, upright, devout, and self-controlled. He must have a firm grasp of the word that is trustworthy."

A church that pays no attention to its maintenance will soon have no church to pay attention to. Its worship will lose focus and power, its education will be mediocre and fragmented, its caring will be haphazard and unreliable, and its mission will be directionless at best, nonexistent at worst. On the other hand, a church that only pays attention to maintenance will be a beautiful, well-oiled machine going nowhere. It will be all form and no function.

Ten necessary maintenance tasks of the church are: self-esteem and morale, money, buildings and equipment, new members, leadership, organization, communications, conflict, planning, and tending to outside relationships. Each of these must be approached in ways appropriate to the size and unique nature of small churches.

As with everything else about small churches, size is a crucial factor in each of the maintenance areas. Small size can be either problematic or advantageous, depending on one's orientation and approach. A Baptist official takes the problematic stance:

> Church leaders have concluded that any church of 200 is marginal. Such a church will have difficulty in adequately supporting its minister, providing essential maintenance of physical property, and carrying on an educational program. Very little will be left for mission in the community or in the world. The church will be forced to turn inward simply

because the fight to survive will absorb the energies, the financial resources, and the time of the members. . . . A small membership means a
church that is hard pressed to maintain an organization and committee
structure that permits it to participate fully, completely, and in a satisfying way in the life of the denomination and the community. Such a
church will have an inadequate budget in most instances, which in turn
may lead to a high rate of turnover in pastors. Even if a pastor were content to accept the salary that would be offered, he or she would not be
content to accept the limited program of service and ministry that
would be possible on a starvation budget.[1]

Small churches, when seen through these conventional lenses of traditional assumptions, have problems upon problems.

Sadly, the corporate world knows more about the virtues of smallness
than does the church. Tom Peters and Nancy Austin, in their excellent
book *A Passion for Excellence,* gives the advantageous view of small size:

We observed small groups producing higher quality, more personalized
service and faster innovation than larger entities. It turns out that
scale—small scale, via team organizations and decentralized units—is a
vital component of top performance. The bottom line: ownership is inevitably lost in big groups. . . . ownership and commitment, pride and
enthusiasm . . . are virtually impossible in a giant, overly specialized organizational unit.[2]

Peters and Austin cite many examples from the business and corporate
world where operations are kept small or downsized in order to produce
greater quantity and quality of product or service.

What is true in the business world can be true in the church. When
small churches learn to carry out their maintenance tasks as well as their
ministry and mission tasks in customized and size-appropriate ways, they
will, as Peters and Austin write, "outperform the bigger ones time and
again."

Self-Esteem and Morale

The dominating and most debilitating problem in a high percentage of
small churches is low self-esteem, resulting in low morale. Comments
like "We're just a little church," "I'm just a small church pastor," "We
only have thirty in worship and twenty in Sunday school," and "We
don't do as much as the big church on the corner," are as common and
difficult to eradicate as dandelions. Low self-esteem is a cancer that kills

small churches. It reduces the amount of available money, results in poor building upkeep, repels new members, discourages leaders, erodes organizational effectiveness, changes communication from positive to negative, causes church fights, undermines planning, and limits relationships with those outside. In short, it undermines the ministry and mission of the church. Efforts to enhance personal and church self-esteem and build morale need to top a small church's priority list.

Lyle Schaller identifies some of the reasons for weak morale in smaller churches:

1. Congregational leaders underestimate the size, strength, resources, assets, and potential of their church
2. Members tend to forget the victories, ministries, accomplishments, and activities that could be sources of satisfaction
3. Churches tend to follow a problem-based approach to church life, resulting in their feeling weighted down by their long list of problems, rather than focusing on possibilities
4. Most pastors, seminary faculty, and denominational helpers come from large church backgrounds and bring large church perspectives resulting in a lack of understanding of smaller churches
5. Churches receiving some kind of subsidy find this kind aid erodes their morale
6. The frequent change of pastors causes small churches to feel rejected, if not used
7. People who don't remember the good things that have recently happened often remember the "good old days" when the pews, Sunday school, and offering plates were full.[3]

In addition, a powerful sense of loss permeates the experience and memory of many small churches, particularly rural ones. People grieve over the loss of children who've moved away, loss of church families, loss of a favorite pastor, loss of people who've died, loss of schools and businesses, and other losses. Morale dies when the prevailing mood is one of loss, despair, and death.

Poor self-esteem and low morale can be turned around and elevated. To begin working at this, church leaders need to identify the areas where morale is low. The following morale continuum can be used to assess church members' morale. A 1 is very low and an 8 is very high. People should mark where they believe the church's morale is for that area. Have people fill out the Morale Inventory on pages 145 and 146 and then discuss their perceptions.

The categories are interrelated. They represent attitudes that feed on

Low Morale					*High Morale*		

1. Feel under siege in the surrounding community

Trust the community to be friendly toward church

| 1 | 2 | 3 | 4 | 5 | 6 | 7 | 8 |

2. Fear financial failure

Not worried about money

| 1 | 2 | 3 | 4 | 5 | 6 | 7 | 8 |

3. People generally negative and pessimistic

People generally positive and optimistic

| 1 | 2 | 3 | 4 | 5 | 6 | 7 | 8 |

4. Mainly recall loss, defeats

Recall wins, successes

| 1 | 2 | 3 | 4 | 5 | 6 | 7 | 8 |

5. Folks feel abused, forgotten

People feel cared about

| 1 | 2 | 3 | 4 | 5 | 6 | 7 | 8 |

6. Think only of taking care of themselves

Commitment to a mission beyond themselves

| 1 | 2 | 3 | 4 | 5 | 6 | 7 | 8 |

7. Leadership is incompetent, uncaring

Leadership is able and/or caring

| 1 | 2 | 3 | 4 | 5 | 6 | 7 | 8 |

8. People resist new ideas

Open to new ideas, ways

| 1 | 2 | 3 | 4 | 5 | 6 | 7 | 8 |

9. Attend out of habit or duty

People enjoy attending

| 1 | 2 | 3 | 4 | 5 | 6 | 7 | 8 |

10. Visitors are not welcome

Visitors happily received

| 1 | 2 | 3 | 4 | 5 | 6 | 7 | 8 |

11. Church preaches/practices a theology of judgment

Church preaches/practices a theology of grace

| 1 | 2 | 3 | 4 | 5 | 6 | 7 | 8 |

12. Faith is a duty performed   Faith is joyous living

   1   2   3   4   5   6   7   8

13. People suspicious of others   People trust each other

   1   2   3   4   5   6   7   8

14. Building looks/feels cold,   Building looks/feels
    drab, uncared for   warm and attractive

   1   2   3   4   5   6   7   8

15. Pastors don't stay long   Pastors stay/feel at home

   1   2   3   4   5   6   7   8

16. People give no more than   People give generously
    they have to   and gladly

   1   2   3   4   5   6   7   8

17. People have many excuses   People volunteer readily

   1   2   3   4   5   6   7   8

18. New people must wait to   New members welcomed into
    become church leaders   leadership and power

   1   2   3   4   5   6   7   8

19. Attendance is poor   Most people come to
    at worship, meetings, events   everything

   1   2   3   4   5   6   7   8

20. Conflict is constant and   Conflict happens but is
    cancerous   handled and resolved

   1   2   3   4   5   6   7   8

21. Anticipate bleak future   Positive about future

   1   2   3   4   5   6   7   8

one another, moving the tide one way or the other. A church with high morale should identify why it is in that enviable state and work to strengthen it. A church with low or fragile morale can, with wise leadership and a core of conscientious people, conceive and carry out strategies for raising self-esteem and morale.

Addiction recovery programs use a twelve-step program to radically transform people's lives. Here is a different twelve-step program for your church and its leadership, which, if followed for twelve weeks, could radically transform your church's self-esteem and morale:

1. Use the twenty-one-category Morale Inventory with your church members; discuss and analyze it, get commitment from those present to try raising morale; and agree to pray for one another and for your church for twelve weeks.
2. Ask a leader/consultant from your denomination (or neighboring church or counseling agency) to spend one or more sessions with your church working on morale issues and doing some leadership training.
3. List all the successes of the last two years and twenty strengths of your church.
4. Take steps to make being together more pleasurable—turn the heat up, paint the walls, brew coffee and tea, and bring on the high-calorie sweet rolls.
5. Capitalize on your church's strengths (and every church has several). For example, if you have charming children, celebrate them, involve them more in the life of the church.
6. Plan a sure-fire success, make it succeed, celebrate it; and then plan a second, and a third.
7. Identify one significant, solvable problem; brainstorm every conceivable way of working with it; plan a strategy and accept responsibility for attacking the problem; work the strategy; evaluate what happened and start over.
8. Pick a significant mission project your church will enjoy doing together and do it.
9. Make your worship more enjoyable and effective. Sing favorite hymns; make new, beautiful banners; have shorter sermons that accentuate the positive; introduce some innovation in your worship for a trial period; pray that the Spirit of God will move in your church.
10. Do one interior and one exterior spruce up, fix up project in the next twelve weeks.
11. Ask everyone who can, to give 10 percent more money to the church for twelve weeks. Keep track of and use the extra money for something the church will feel good about. Some people may make the additional 10 percent a habit.

12. As a last resort, if disruptive, destructive persons threaten to leave, accept their offer.

High morale is a prerequisite for real effectiveness. High morale can be nourished; low morale can be turned around. Warwick's high morale resulted in people saying, "We can do anything we want to do." In Emmetsburg, some successful special projects resulted in people saying, "We're on a roll," and they're still rolling. This twelve-step program works. Try it—or at least some pieces of it.

Money

A carnival strong man once squeezed a lemon dry and then offered one hundred dollars to anyone who could squeeze another drop? A little old lady accepted the challenge, and squeezed half a cup from the already flat lemon. Flabbergasted, the strong man asked the little lady how she did it. "It's simple," she said, "I'm the treasurer of my little church."

Money is frequently perceived as a life-and-death squeeze in small churches—and frequently it is. It is around money matters that some people dispute my belief that small churches are the right size. If it weren't for the problem of money, more small churches would be happy with their size, more pastors would choose to pastor small churches, and many small churches would not close. Here are some background, principles, and strategies for dealing with small church money matters.

Background. Because of inflationary costs, even small churches which are *not* getting smaller are getting poorer. With the rising costs of insurance, salaries, buildings, utilities, maintenance, and other perceived needs, the costs of institutional survival are spiraling. In *The Small Church Is Different!* Schaller points out that in the 1930s a church that averaged thirty to forty in worship could financially support a full-time pastor. He says that by the 1980s, it took between 120 to 140.[4] By the mid 1990s, it might take 150 to 175 worshipers in the average church to support a full-time pastor along with the rest of the costs of operating a church.

Churches never have enough money. Rare is the person or the church who's been heard to say, "We have enough money." In a consumptive culture we always think we need more than we have.

I believe churches have *more than enough* money. No church ever closed simply for lack of enough money. Churches close for lack of faith, courage, and adaptability. Can't afford a pastor? A faithful church can function beautifully under gifted and committed lay leadership—*if* it is willing to share the work. Can't afford a building? In New Testament times and still today, some of the most vital churches were and are house churches. Most people *could* give far more money than they *choose* to give.

Money raising and stewardship are not synonymous. Stewardship is living my whole life as a response to the love of God and the Lordship of Jesus Christ. Financially supporting God's ministry and mission through my church is a small piece of whole-life stewardship.

Most churches aren't good at talking about stewardship or money. In fact, pastors and churches often conspire to avoid talking about them. One Iowa church called a pastor with the agreement he would never talk about money. For over a decade he kept that promise as the church withered. Pastors in small churches are nervous about money talk because they know the people so well and their salary and benefits are such a large part of church costs. People in small churches are nervous when money is mentioned because it is their money that's being talked about. The matter is all the more difficult because few pastors have been taught to deal effectively with money matters.

Principles. Financial support of the church has increased significantly in the three small churches I've served. I believe much of that increase is because of the principles I preach and practice. Strategies are important, but these principles are more important.

1. Money is a spiritual matter. Church people prefer to separate matters of the spirit from matters of the wallet. Jesus would have none of that. He said: "Where your treasure is, there your heart will be also" (Luke 12:34). I preach stewardship because the more we concentrate on stewardship the less we have to concentrate on raising money. I preach generosity because generous people are happier people. I preach thankful giving because when people give they complete and continue the cycle of generosity initiated by God.

2. People will pay for what they value and value what they pay for. Many churches, of all sizes, aren't worth more than a dollar in the plate. Daniel Biles's book *Pursuing Excellence in Ministry* is on my short list of essential books for ministry. He quotes two pastors on the subject of quality ministry and money. John Siefken became pastor of the divided, debt-ridden Prince of Glory Lutheran Church in Madison Heights, Michigan, in 1969. "People would ask me, 'What are you going to do about that huge $100,000 debt?' I told them that I wasn't going to do anything

about it. . . . Instead, we focused on good worship, good teaching, good outreach, and hoped the debt would go away." They did and it did. Peter Rudowski, a Lutheran pastor in Cincinnati, said: "Congregations don't need to do fund-raising. Do the ministry consistently well and the money will be there."[5] A primary factor in generating finances for a church is to have a church worth supporting.

3. A church (at least most churches) is a "Best Buy." It provides twenty-four-hour-a-day support. It cares for the body, mind, and spirit, from birth and baptism to death and burial. It cares for my needs and the needs of people around the world. In contrast to the TV evangelist empires, our local churches are far, far more responsible and cost-effective. This bargain is a taken-for-granted treasure.

4. Raising or making money should not be a church's all-consuming fixation. A tragedy in many smaller churches is that most of their energy goes into raising money, leaving little energy for being and enjoying being the church. The following strategies may help avoid this trap.

Strategies. Churches have two choices when it comes to meeting their financial needs—live on less or generate more. There are many strategies for living on less money. The two largest church costs are pastoral compensation and building costs. In the next chapter I'll deal more with the complex and difficult issue of compensation. Like anyone else in the congregation, the pastor deserves a fair compensation, which takes into consideration education, experience, ability, need, community standards, as well as the church's ability to pay. If the church can't pay a fair wage, it should contract to pay fairly for less time. It can do this by sharing a pastor with another church or freeing the pastor to earn income elsewhere or spend time on other things (like education, parenting, or retirement).

Buildings are the other heavy expense. Utility costs can be cut by implementing energy-saving measures and regulating use of the building. Costs can be cut by having volunteers do janitorial and maintenance work. Costs can be cut by sharing a building. The church building on Vinalhaven Island in Maine is used by three churches—St. Timothy's Episcopal at 8:00 A.M., the Union Church at 10:30 A.M., and Our Lady of Peace Catholic at 1:30 P.M. Many churches rent their building to outside groups. Wise and courageous churches don't tie their future to a costly building that weighs them down like a millstone. The church and the building are *not* synonymous.

Churches tend to cut every ounce of fat from their budget. This is penny wise and pound foolish. I encourage putting a little fat *into* the budget. Mission giving has increased every year of my ministry. I encourage extra money for stamps for more communication, extra money for adult education to enrich the people who pay the bills, extra money for community outreach, extra money for public relations, and so on. A skeleton budget only keeps the church on life supports. A budget with some fat allows the church to live, to attract others, to do the things that people value and support.

There are seven sources of financial support for the church: rents and donations for building use, in-kind contributions, memorial gifts, estate bequests, fund raisers, special appeals, and pledged regular giving. A prudent small church will use each source, give each its due, but rely mainly on the regular support of its own people.

Rents and Donations for Building Use. Contributions toward building costs can help make the building a bearable burden. On the other hand, a church may decide to encourage free use of its building by community groups as a local mission. The Warwick church did this and received more in donations from grateful groups and individuals than we could have generated in rent.

In-kind Contributions. Large churches are run like a business. Small churches work more like families in which people share chores as well as contribute to the family kitty. Often janitorial, secretarial, building maintenance and improvements, and music responsibilities are volunteered. The Warwick building addition and renovation happened mostly with volunteer labor. Volunteers painted the parsonage in Shrewsbury. Work parties are regular events in Emmetsburg. Money is saved, the "home" is cared for, people's talents are used, and the family grows stronger.

Memorial Gifts. Gifts in memory of a loved and respected person can provide both necessities and frosting items. They allow the church to remember special people twice—through the act of giving and as they use the gift. A wise church will have a list of desired items and a memorial policy to regulate how gifts are received, how they'll be used, and who is responsible for them.

Estate Bequests. These can be a blessing, a curse, or a combination of the two. Shrewsbury's large endowment has allowed the church to rely on it rather than on itself. Since they haven't had to put as much of their treasure in the church, they haven't had to put as much of their heart there, either. On the other hand, the bequest from the Alice Anderson estate was a helpful transfusion in restoring life to the Warwick church. And, if it hadn't been for her generous estate, she might soon have been quickly forgotten by most. I'm also thinking of two small Iowa churches whose endowments insured their survival through the hard times that preceded their current vitality.

A carefully crafted and encouraged endowment policy and program insures the future of the church, encourages the generosity and faithfulness of the living generation, enables creative outreach from the church, and assures the benefactor an honored place in the family memory. Small churches, whose future is precarious, should be encouraging people to remember their church in their wills with the same faithfulness with which they remember their checkbooks on Sunday. Create an endowment policy that will help not harm the church. Help people imagine the lasting contribution they could make. Do a good job of remembering the saints and angels your church already has, so future saints and angels will be encouraged.

Fund-raisers.   There are many critics of small church rummage sales, food sales, church fairs, strawberry festivals, and Lord's acre auctions. I think they can be fun and effective sources of money, fellowship builders, and evangelism strategies. The Warwick church's Christmas fair, apple pie sale, semiannual auction, and May dinner theater raised about a quarter of their budget and provided much church and community enjoyment. Fund-raisers keep the Emmetsburg Women's Fellowship strong and helpful to the church. The big annual event in tiny Rossi, Iowa (population sixty-eight), is the church's God's Portion sale, which generates up to $15,000 (a dozen eggs may sell for $50 at their auction).

Fund-raisers aren't businesslike. They may not look like serious stewardship. But they are a way church and community can preserve a vital organ in their ongoing life and have fun doing it. Early in the Warwick church revival, a ways and means committee was formed to raise needed funds. An unplanned consequence was that this committee became an effective avenue for assimilating new people in the church. The purpose of the church is *not* to raise funds, but fund-raisers can be *one* means of fulfilling some of its purposes.

Special Appeals.   If a family desperately wants or needs to do something, it usually finds a way to do it. With its family way of doing things, a small church can work the same way. Money to replace the furnace, renovate the sanctuary, or complete a special mission project comes more easily from a special appeal than from squeezing it out of the budget. In the process, people are energized and discover the joy of generosity, limited ways of thinking are expanded, and great things are accomplished. Rather than fight the special appeal or project mentality, I've learned to appreciate it and work with it.

The Emmetsburg building is an architectural gem in a community that has too few. It needs rehabilitation and restoration. A new building would be twice as expensive and half as attractive. Moving in with another church isn't a good option for this church. Over a five-year period, through a combination of budgeted money, fund-raisers, special gifts, and willed money, a major amount of money will be raised to do the job in a church that can't afford a full-time pastor. And the church will be stronger for it.

Pledged Regular Giving. Most important, regular giving is the lifeblood of both individual Christians and the church. Small churches go about this differently. People know each other too well to be comfortable with an every-member canvas. The smaller the church the less formal it needs to be about these processes. But from tiny Warwick to hundred member Emmetsburg, the following principles have proven effective:

- The pastor should set an example in his or her giving, provide clear leadership, know the church's giving pattern, and talk neither too little nor too much about money.
- It's helpful and appreciated when the whole church helps develop an easily understood and challenging budget, which underwrites what the church believes, values, and wants to make happen.
- Everyone is asked and expected to make a pledge, with the understanding that the pledge can be raised or lowered.
- Regular, proportional giving is the expected norm.
- Increased giving as a fruit of spiritual growth and greater faithfulness is encouraged and expected.
- Suggesting people reach the average level of giving lowers the total; encouraging increased giving by your top givers raises the general level. (We don't make public how much people pledge, but we do make public the number and amounts of pledges.)
- People are more generous when they're helped to reflect on the real value of their church for them and the potential of their gift to make a real difference for others.
- People are more generous when the church goes out of its way to express gratitude and affirmation for their efforts.
- People are more generous when morale is high.

- People are more generous when they are helping their church be faithful rather than just surviving.
- Like it or not, the amount people give is often a vote of confidence or no confidence in the church's leadership.
- People only give when they are asked, and the amount they pledge and give is directly proportional to the effort expended in the process of asking.
- Variety in stewardship, fund-raising approaches is far more effective than using the same stale approach every year.

Small churches must find ways to afford being small. Pray your church never erodes to the plight of the fifty-people church that put all of twenty-two cents in the offering. The exasperated pastor prayed: "May the good Lord guide, preserve, and bless these parsimonious people. I can't. Amen."

Buildings

Small churches meet in all kinds of places—homes, offices, tiny chapels, another church's building, one-room country churches, new buildings that just fit, old buildings that still fit and work, and others fit for another size and time. Some churches are at home in their building, others are in exile in theirs. A church's building enables or disables its ministry and mission. When the latter is the case, alternatives need to be considered—*with the greatest of sensitivity.*

A church building is not a rational matter to most people. For some, it's simply a building where people meet. But for more, it's an album of memories, a priceless treasure chest of holy moments and great happenings, a haven of security, a beacon of hope, or a symbol of despair. The sensitive new pastor will spend considerable time decoding what the building symbolizes for the church and community.

In addition to their value to the congregation, church buildings are valuable to their surrounding community. An intriguing study of church buildings was done in 1990 by Chicago's Community Workshop on Economic Development, entitled "Good Space and Good Works." It found that 77 percent of Chicago's religious buildings house at least one *community* program or organization. One fifth house six or more. But this is not without cost. Almost half of these religious groups spend 20 to 40 percent of their budget on building maintenance and energy costs. The study concluded that church buildings are a "sacred trust," worthy of being preserved whenever possible.[6]

In the beginning, the Metcalf Chapel in Warwick was merely a colonial house where a few people gathered weekly in the shadow of the Unitarian "church on the hill." It became a home full of activity. In Shrewsbury, it didn't make economic sense for a worshiping church of fifty to keep and have to keep up three separate church buildings. But each of the remnant congregations brought building loyalties and/or legal restrictions to the merger. We lacked enough people, will, imagination, and energy to find significant ways to use all three. The Emmetsburg building was a mirror image of its people and community—grand, gray, weary, and in failing health. Except for necessary repairs and the building of a concrete ramp, not much had happened with the building for forty years. Each building offered problems and possibilities that we had to address.

Sometimes churches with disabling buildings are forced to reconsider building options because of economic crisis, broken mergers or federations, offers to buy their building, structural deterioration, fire or storm damage. Then something has to be done quickly.

Other fearless churches evaluate their building requirements and alternatives before they're confronted with a crisis. These churches have the opportunity to rethink the nature of their church—a building or a people—and their purpose—maintenance of a building or ministry and mission. Churches are best able to make tough building decisions when the subject is initiated and pursued by trusted church leaders, supported by outsider helpers.

If a church chooses to retain its present building, it needs to make some building decisions. Are there ways to expand the use of the building by renting or sharing it—particularly with another church? Can it be made more energy efficient? Should there be some restoration to recapture lost charm and integrity? Should there be upgrading to make it more accessible, flexible, efficient, and consistent with its current size and ministry? And where will the money come from for these modifications?

Invested money may be used—either the interest or perhaps the principal. Sometimes low-interest loans and grants are available for historic restoration. People formerly involved in the church may be willing to provide financial assistance. Some members may be willing to use part of their estate now to help their church rather than willing it later. Many people are surprisingly generous when it comes to contributing to a building project, particularly when they've had a hand in the decision making. The existing community often has a vested interest in a church building and can be tapped in creative ways.

If the decision is to abandon the building like an ill-fitting snail shell, there are different decisions to make. What to do with the old building? Should the church tear down and rebuild on the present site? The UCC church in Manson, Iowa, made this choice. They tore down the Christian education wing and a week later a tornado swooped down and demolished the rest of their building. They now have a lovely building that just fits them. When the decision is to move to another building, can some of the holy objects be taken along to ease the pain of leaving a beloved place? Can people be helped to deal with the painful feelings that are part of such a wrenching step? Doug Walrath's book, *Leading Churches Through Change,* can be very helpful here.[7]

Finally, as a church deals with its present building, it needs to consider all the invisible signs that are posted around it:

- The lack of signs indicating where to park, where to enter, where to find the pastor's office and bathrooms that say, "Visitors are not welcome here."
- Steep stairs that say, "People with disabilities should go elsewhere." (Our association recently ordained a woman who was wheelchair bound, who had left a church of another denomination because she couldn't enter their building.)
- An ill-equipped or nonexistent nursery that says, "We have no place for children here."
- A shabby exterior or interior that says, "We don't care about our church."

Ask a stranger to go through your building to identify the "signs" you no longer see. A building speaks volumes about the people who inhabit it.

New Members

C. Peter Wagner says in *Your Church Can Grow,* "But whether a church is large or small, it should be a growing church. . . . If smaller churches are growing they eventually will become large churches."[8] Carl Dudley says in *Making the Small Church Effective:* "Most small churches have already grown much bigger than they ought to be."[9] And Lyle Schaller says in *The Small Church Is Different!:* "The natural size of the worshiping congregation is that of the small church. . . . The large congregation runs against the laws of nature."[10] Who's right? To grow or not to grow? If not, why not? If so, why and how?

Small churches feel pressures to grow from denominational officials trying to reverse declining membership totals, from the pressure of rising costs, from a culture that equates quality with quantity, from pastors reaching for success, and from church members seeking to measure up. At the same time, Christ gave us Good News to share and the order to make disciples. And part of being faithful and effective churches is maintaining a healthy membership.

Some small churches are growing, some aren't, and some choose not to. There are many reasons small churches may not grow: their present size works for them, low self-esteem causes them to hide their light under the proverbial bushel, people fear growth means loss of intimacy or loss of control, few if any immigrants are looking for a church home, the church has little to offer, its prophetic- or suffering-servant style doesn't attract many newcomers, they don't know how to grow and still stay small, or they simply haven't thought about growing. Some of these reasons are valid, some need to be challenged.

Wagner is right: every church should grow. But he overlooks varieties of growth—in spiritual depth, in an ability to face and solve problems, in prophetic witness, in the quality of care for those in and around the church, in the maturity of its interactions, in the quality of its educational ministry, in its ability to use each other's gifts, in its compassionate service to a world in pain. A church growing in these ways will probably grow in size.

There are four ways for a small church to grow—by addition, multiplication, division, and adoption. A church growing by *addition* snatches prospects as they happen by. This is the simplest and often the least effective. Often as many are lost as are gained, if the church doesn't work hard at assimilating its new people.

It can grow by the *multiplication* of small groups, a strategy promoted by Lyle Schaller.[11] In his scenario for small church growth, a *new* pastor *unilaterally* starts a series of *homogeneous* interest groups that are adjunct to the core life of the church. They are primarily for those on the fringe and outside the church. What was once a single-cell church is now a multicell church. The cells have little in common and little interdependence. If the strategy works, the once-small church becomes a middle-sized church. This strategy, in which an outsider (the new pastor) unilaterally transforms the church by changing its nature, replacing its leadership, and making it into what it never was, is artificial and lacks integrity.

The third form of church evangelism is the most historical—growth by *division*. Like cell division, the church grows to the point where its qualities of intimacy, caring, and personal involvement are strained. The church intentionally divides and a new church is started. Many churches have been started in this fashion. With today's escalating costs, however, few churches are willing to split off good members.

Fourth, growth by *adoption* into the church family is the most appropriate strategy for small churches. Adoption is preferable to topsy-turvy growth that transmutes a church from rabbit to elephant. Growth by adoption is slow but sure. People (often already known and vouched for by some in the church) are attracted and invited. They are welcomed and officially or unofficially sponsored by people with the gift of hospitality. They are involved in church activity, responsibility, and power sharing as quickly as they're ready. Opportunities are provided to learn the family story, style, and expectations of the church. There may be a new-member ritual, but adoption really happens over time. Growth by adoption is a matchmaking process, which understands that one church is not right for every person. When the match doesn't take, people will sooner or later wonder "What happened to what's-her-name?" Growth by adoption concentrates as much on assimilation as attraction.

The three churches I've served have been serious and intentional about growth by adoption. The Warwick and Shrewsbury churches tried to say clearly who they were, what they believed, and welcomed anyone who wanted that kind of church. We tried to demonstrate warmth, hospitality, and caring in everything. Careful assimilation and keeping a small church feel were part of the plan. In Emmetsburg, with several churches and a shrinking population, an even more intentional strategy has been needed. Word of mouth, newspaper ads, and frequent newspaper articles have been used to make the church known. Moving vans and new neighbors are watched for. When someone new is identified, a deacon takes a loaf of homemade bread, welcomes them to the community, and invites them to church. Visitors are greeted warmly, given a vital worship experience (we hope), and their visit is followed up by a personal letter and a visit. The effort was made in all three churches to build morale and create a lively church, in part so our people would be evangelical about their church. In each place, the church has grown slowly but surely.

Perhaps your church would like to grow by adoption. The following evangelism planning process, worked at carefully and creatively by key people in your church, will help you develop effective strategies for attracting, adopting, and assimilating new people. Record all information on newsprint as you go through the process.

1. Why do you want to grow? How many of your people want to grow? What price will you pay? Are you willing to pay it?
2. What's keeping you from growing? Attitudes? Demographics? Other reasons?
3. Specifically, what does your church have to offer? What's attractive about you? What are your specific gifts?
4. What specific problem areas in your church do you need to address in order to be more attractive and ready?
5. What particular kinds of individuals and groups might be naturally attracted to your church? What kinds of individuals and groups are unchurched or have unmet needs in your community or area?
6. Who are your warmest "gatekeepers" (those who let people in) and "magnets" (those who attract)? How can these people be more effectively brought in contact with visitors and prospects?
7. Based on the above conclusions, list five specific, appropriate outreach strategies for your church.
8. Pick the two most appealing and promising and give a skeleton to each, including:

   - Its theological rationale
   - How it would work
   - Who would do it
   - Who you would target
   - How the strategy particularly fits your situation
   - Steps in developing and implementing it
   - How you would assimilate new people who respond

9. Select the strategy that is appropriate for your church.
10. How will you move from here to implementation?

God doesn't call the church to grow but to be faithful and effective. A faithful and effective church will pursue fitting and intentional ways of sharing the Good News of the Gospel and inviting others to join their band of disciples.

Leadership

Jesus said: "The sabbath was made for humankind, and not humankind for the sabbath" (Mark 2:27). Substitute "church" for "sabbath," and the key to church leadership is clear. It is the people who are important. Around the world, millions of people are working for their churches. Often they experience little satisfaction and appreciation, while millions of others choose not to work. For too long and for too many, church has been a thankless activity. How can we better call forth, care for, equip, and appreciate all the people who make the church work?

By leadership I mean the people who do the work. In Emmetsburg, between 1988 and 1990, we had a net increase in membership of two, from eighty-eight to ninety. But our active membership increased from forty-five to fifty-six. The number serving in an office or on a board or committee almost doubled from twenty-two to forty-two. A board of mission, an altar guild, a retreat center committee, two historians, and two librarians were added. Each board and committee is more active. Several people serve in two or more capacities, but no one complains of overwork. Plus we have an active women's fellowship, choir and Sunday school, nominating committee, and part-time custodian, music director, organist, secretary, and half-time pastor. Another half-dozen people are moving toward assimilation and church involvement. This church has become more active, more ministry and mission are happening, and people are finding more satisfaction in their work. Warwick and Shrewsbury records show the same increased involvement.

Churches need to rethink how they call, equip, care for, and appreciate their leaders.

The Calling Forth of Leaders. Each person has unique gifts to employ in the church's ministry and mission. As a pastor, one of my goals is to help all church participants find their special niche, to equip them, assist them, and see that they find satisfaction in their ministry. The nominating-committee meetings are the most important meetings in the church year. The goal in those meetings is not to fill slots but to increase the ministry and mission of the church, to match the peoples' gifts with opportunities to develop them, to help new people find their place in the church, to rotate people so they don't get stuck in one place and power doesn't become entrenched. The by-laws of all three churches require rotation, which has proved healthy for each church.

The Equipping of Leaders. The ability to exercise leadership should not be assumed, but leadership skills can be taught. Orientation and training should be provided annually. If money or equipment are needed to do a job, do whatever has to be done to provide it. Volunteers, in particular, should be provided with what they need. In the last year, we've gone into savings to provide our secretary with a new copier and typewriter.

The Care of Leaders. Provide refreshments at your meetings. Make the meeting space pleasant. Humor is a necessary ingredient of good work. Workers should help set their own direction and define their tasks, rather than inheriting them from on high. Maintaining relationships is as important as doing tasks. Meetings should be long enough to get something done and short enough to get people home early. A carefully planned agenda helps insure that something worth coming for happens at each meeting. Distribute the work so no one is overworked. I do my best to shield our workers from criticism. I want all leaders to be able to say of their jobs what Rose Webb, our financial secretary, said of hers: "I know how to do it, I do it well, and I love to do it."

The Appreciation of Leaders. Volunteers can't be thanked enough. After all, appreciation and job satisfaction are their only compensation. In Shrewsbury and Emmetsburg, we've presented "Feather-in-the-Hat" awards to unsung heroes and second-mile leaders at each annual meeting. The award is a weird hat decorated with a peacock or pheasant feather. The church nominates people to receive the awards. A musician plays a fanfare. I make a flowery but genuine speech, announce the name, and place the hat on the recipient's head. He or she wears the hat for the rest of the meeting, pictures are taken, and they wear their hats at the next worship service. Garnet, who had taken care of our altar cloths for over twenty years, was so proud of her hat that it was placed on her casket. There aren't enough ways to say "thank you," but use as many as you can.

Organization

The goal of organization is not bureaucracy but significant accomplishment. Large churches must be well organized in order to get anything done; small churches don't. The genius of small church leadership is knowing how to have *just enough* organization. At the end of the Carter administration, Vice President Mondale addressed the difference between efficiency and effectiveness:

> First of all, I would relax a little bit in terms of this emphasis on "working better." In other words, my old friend Hubert [Humphrey] used to say you can read the Bible from the first word to the last and read the Constitution all the way through, and you can read the Magna Carta and you will never see the word "efficiency" mentioned once. Our system is not supposed to run on time. When issues are serious, when they are controversial, they are supposed to simmer for a while. They are supposed to slow down so that the public is engaged.[12]

Government may or may not work well that way, but I believe small churches do. That's part of the magic of diminutive size. They don't have to be well organized, punctual, businesslike, or efficient to be effective and faithful. Rather than trying to be well organized, they need to organize to work well. In some small churches this may mean simplifying or organizing in a different fashion. In others it means don't touch anything because you'll screw up what already works pretty well.

Organizational principles that I believe work well in small churches are these:

- Involve as many people as possible (it's not neat or fast, but it's fun and effective—in the long run)
- As much as possible, spend your energy on what you *can* do, rather than what you *can't* do
- Remember there are few life and death matters
- Allow as much time for "family" interaction as for business (if not more)
- Give everyone a say, rather than have some speak for others (the best ideas come from the funniest places)
- As much as possible make decisions by consensus, rather than by majority rule or decree (the Pennsylvania Dutch had a saying, "All of us are smarter than any of us")
- Communicate decisions, actions, and plans to everyone, rather than only to those who need to know
- When possible work as a whole, rather than in subgroups
- Remember that small churches would usually rather do it than plan it (so don't get bogged down in detail)

These principles aren't out of the Harvard Business School manual for institutional organization, but they generally work quite well in small churches.

The story is told about a group from a small church that died in a tragic accident and went to heaven. Saint Peter met them, welcomed them, but said: "I'm sorry we're full right now. You'll have to go down below until we have room." Early the next morning, Saint Peter's phone rang. It was the devil: "Will you please get these small church people out of here! They've met, organized, and put on a church dinner. And now they're just a few dollars short of air-conditioning the whole place!" Small churches can get things done, in their own way.

Communication

Communication is crucial in small churches. People expect to know what's going on and often make a fuss when they don't. In small churches people assume other people have heard, when frequently they haven't. Churches that are the right size to involve everyone can't involve them if *all participants* don't know when, where, what to bring, and what's going to happen.

Attempting to save money, many small churches don't have the tools of communication that larger churches take for granted—a secretary, typewriter, mimeograph or copier, bulletins, postage, newsletters. Communication tools cost money, but they can save and even make money, too.

Actually there are many tools of communication—some are free and some are overlooked. Listening is one of those. I can't communicate what I haven't heard. Lay and pastoral leaders who take the time, listen without distorting, and communicate clearly what was heard are the first line of communication. The pastor who values communication will learn who talks to whom, who can't be trusted with information, and how people find out things in her or his church and community. It is as important for a pastor to listen well as to preach clearly.

A pastor who can't write clearly and convincingly is at a terrible disadvantage. Our bulletin is full of news. Our secretary and I work hard at making our newsletter interesting and informative. When the church needs to consider a particular matter, I write a special letter to the membership. I write many notes to people. To save money and symbolize belonging, the Emmetsburg church has mailboxes at our front door for every member or family. I write letters to the editor of the local paper to express views on community matters and frequent articles about church news. Small-town newspapers are generally grateful for any well-written news release. Because of our frequent articles, a regular reader of the local paper would guess our church has more going on than other churches in the community. And because written communication is so important, we don't cut corners on postage.

There are other ways to communicate. Radio, TV, and cable stations must carry public service announcements. Use them. Rather than having your poster-maker make five posters by hand, have him or her make one beauty, run it off on a copier, and print fifty. Organize the grapevine. Set up a telephone tree so that five calls from you to five others who call five others gets the word to everyone. Can the message on your exterior signboard be changed? If so, do you change it? Can it be read by someone driving by at thirty-five miles per hour?

It's a mistaken assumption that what is said or read is heard and understood. That is seldom true. News worth communicating should be repeated several times in several ways. The Gospel is Good News. The church has good news. Too often churches keep this good news a well kept secret.

The new pastor of the church thought the sanctuary was too dark. She began promoting the idea of a new chandelier. In sermons, in meetings, in the newsletter, around town, she talked about the chandelier. At the church meeting called to decide, discussion went back and forth. Finally, the Church Pillar stood and spoke the last word: "I don't think we need any chandelier! We can't afford one! We've gotten along just fine without one! We don't have any place to put one! And, besides, nobody here knows how to *play* one!" He and the rest voted "No." Good communication gives light; poor communication generates heat.

Conflict

Little is more painful or predictable in churches—large and small—than conflict. Even when the waters are calm, the currents move and the winds of change threaten. Small churches are particularly susceptible to conflict, for a number of reasons:

- Since small numbers bring people into closer contact; toes are more likely to get stepped on
- People knowing people better makes them less polite and more real
- Low morale and fear of the future lower tolerance and raise anxiety
- Sporadic and often ineffectual pastoral leadership, intrenched families and leadership, and laissez-faire organizational patterns set the stage for conflict
- In rural and small town settings, the flowing together of church and community issues increases the likelihood of conflict in one realm infecting the other
- Just as families fight, so do churches—some habitually
- The greater care people have for one another and their church, the more they are free to fight, knowing the storm can be weathered

Speed Leas of the Alban Institute, in *Moving Your Church Through Conflict,* writes about the kinds of conflict found in the Family Church with up to 50 people on Sunday and in the Pastoral Church with 50 to 150. He says that in the Family Church, conflict between the pastor and church usually doesn't last long; conflict is often not out in the open but repressed; when there's deep conflict, it has often been long standing; and conflict in these very small churches is often between particular families. Conflict in the larger Pastoral Churches usually grows out of a history of tensions; there's not the same feeling of unity that can hold things together; the role of the pastor is to be a bridge between groups, but often the focus of the conflict is the pastor, and often he or she is used as a scapegoat for intergroup rivalries or conflicts.[13]

Leas has also been helpful in identifying five levels of conflict, detailing what to expect in each. He describes Level I as Problems to Solve. These problems can be dealt with rationally and are problem oriented, not person oriented. Conflicts at Level II are called Disagreements and are more difficult. People's objectives become less problem solving and more self-protective. Level III conflicts are Contests, in which sides form. People focus on trying to win and avoid losing, and people become invested in the fight. Issues tend to coalesce into clusters of problems, and sorting them out becomes complex. Level IV, Fight/Flight conflicts, move from wanting to win to wanting to hurt the other side. People's concern is no longer the good of the whole group but the good of their subgroup. People are unforgiving, cold, and self-righteous. Level V conflicts are Intractable Situations in which the goal is to destroy the enemy. Each side knows God is on their side as they fight to the death for universal principles. Leas offers strategies for working at each level. At least by Level III, someone from the outside, such as a denominational person or consultant, should be brought in to work at resolving, managing, or deciding the conflict.[14]

In *Resolving Church Conflicts*, G. Douglass Lewis offers seven principles for managing conflict, which can be helpful to small churches and their outside helpers.[15]

1. *Help others feel better about themselves.* Self-esteem and morale are so important that effort here is the best preventive measure for minimizing conflict. In the midst of conflict, it's helpful to ask, "How can I help other persons feel better about themselves?" People are helped and affirmed when they are listened to, and when their goals are taken seriously, and when their strengths are appreciated.

2. *Strive for effective communication.* Make sure people know and understand what is going on in the church and between people. Practice and teach listening skills. Bring people together to seek understanding and for rumor control.

3. *Examine and filter assumptions.* People assume much more than they actually know. Generally assumptions about reality are more serious than the reality.

4. *Identify goals, what is wanted.* Help each party find understanding about what each is trying to accomplish. Ask "what" questions, not "why" questions. "Why" questions feel judgmental ("Why did you say that?"). "What" questions don't put the other person on the defensive as easily ("What did you mean when you said. . . ?").

5. *Identify the primary issue.* Conflicts are usually clouded by secondary issues. Keep asking what the real issue is here until all parties see it and agree on it.

6. *Develop alternatives for goal achievement.* The ultimate goal is not compromise but finding ways for everyone to achieve what they most want. As much as possible make the issue the problem and not the other party, and brainstorm every possible solution.

7. *Institutionalize conflict management processes.* Many small churches resist institutionalizing anything, but establishing a Pastoral Relations Committee or commissioning some other group to prevent, monitor, and work on relational problems can be helpful.

A church fuss is frustrating and a full-fledged church fight frightening to the participants and an enigma to the leader attempting to untangle the feelings, issues, and fighters. The analysis and theory of Speed Leas and Douglass Lewis provide helpful handles in determining what is going on and what can be done. In the realm of church conflict, "an ounce of prevention is worth a pound of cure." Small churches may be particularly reluctant to air their dirty linen with an outside helper and wait until it's too late to seek help in resolving or managing their conflict.

The most difficult conflicts occur when a church is plagued by one or more church killers. Usually they are alienated or disturbed people who've gained power through long presence and intimidation. They can split churches, drive away healthy people, and destroy pastors. Hopefully strong, healthy, and resolute lay leaders will identify such a killer and demand that his or her disruptive behavior cease. In the absence of such leaders, a strong pastor may be able to force such a change or removal from the situation. Sometimes such people can be converted by sweetness or co-opted as an ally. These situations are always sticky and traumatic.

There are many ways to minister to persons or a church in conflict. One strategy is to be an enabler of communication. In Warwick, I was the mutually agreed upon interpreter between town officials and an aggrieved person. A church can be a forum where issues and feelings can be aired, considered, resolved, or understood. It can reestablish the old tradition of *sanctuary,* in which guns are checked at the door and the church building is a place in which people trust they are safe from attack. Sometimes the conflicting parties can be encouraged to coexist in the same space, even when they are still feeling hostile. Leaders can implement the search for alternatives, so that all parties can win all or part of what they want rather than settling for winners and losers. Sometimes it is necessary to allow people to retreat from church without being made to feel disloyal. Developing problem-solving and peacemaking skills can become part of the church's educational endeavor. At its best, the church is a channel of God's grace, where through all of church life, the Spirit of God can work confession, forgiveness, and reconciliation.

Carl Dudley is right. Small churches:

> . . . can afford to fight, because they are not held together by rational commitments, nor the outcome of any particular decision. The ties that hold most small churches are in the past: family and people, space and territory, history and tradition, culture carrying in the Christian faith. These are commitments of the heart. The pastor (or church members) who shares an appreciation of these elements can heal the most divided church and mobilize the most withdrawn congregation.[16]

Planning

Planning turns some people on—and many off. Most churches, particularly smaller ones, don't have articulated goals for the church and even fewer are working toward any identified goals. Yet all churches have goals—to stay open, to have a Sunday school, to keep or get rid of the minister, to make the budget, and so on. But, too often, these goals don't aim beyond institutional maintenance.

Goals aren't written down for various reasons. The pastor may prefer to do things his or her way. People may fear that specific goals would divide the congregation or mean more work. Some think setting goals smacks of corporate America and doesn't belong in the church. Others might feel goals would constrain the Spirit moving in their midst. Most likely, small churches haven't articulated goals because they haven't thought about it or don't think they're needed.

Clear and mutual goals are important for smaller churches. With limited resources, churches can't afford to waste energy or squander assets. Goals can rally people and enthusiasm around common desires or concerns. They can help people feel they are being heard and their wants addressed. They can bring hidden agendas out in the open. They can move a church beyond institutional maintenance toward being and doing what God calls a church to be and do. Goals can be particularly helpful when a church is in a transition—when a minister has left or a new one has come or when the membership or community is changing.

Lyle Schaller suggests that goals should meet three criteria (which form the acronym SAM). A goal should be Specific, Attainable, and Measurable.[17] Without these three criteria, goals are meaningless and fraught with frustration.

Planning doesn't need to be boring or tedious. In fact, it can be fun and energizing. It should involve as many people as possible and result in real change and concrete action. I developed the following quick and simple process for a small Maine church. I used it with a church in Iowa whose morale and bank account were sinking. In both cases, this process was the catalyst for a dramatic turn-around. With the Maine church it was part of a Saturday retreat. In Iowa it was part of a Sunday afternoon and evening all-church event.

Having a person lead the process who can ask the right questions and keep the process moving is essential. Begin with serious worship and community-building time. Supply plenty of refreshments and meet in a comfortable setting. Have a pad of newsprint and a reliable recorder write down the group's responses. People should be in a circle or semi-circle. You may want to work in smaller groups for part of the process.

1. List on newsprint ALL of your church's Strengths; Resources; Opportunities; and Goals.
2. On separate sheets for each of the three ministry categories (Worship, Christian Education, and Caring), brainstorm first Church Needs and then Church Possible Responses for each category. These should be ideas, activities, innovations, strategies, and projects. Nothing should be labeled a dumb idea or too grand.
3. On a sheet labeled "Local Mission," list Local Needs and Local Possible Responses; and then on one labeled "Global Mission," list Global Needs and Local Possible Responses.
4. Go through all your sheets of Possible Responses and beside each entry put a symbol from each of the following columns (for example, A-2–N):

A. Easy	1. Imperative	N. Now
B. Realistic	2. Important	Y. Within a year
C. Conceivable	3. Symbolic	F. Future
D. Unrealistic	4. Fun, maybe frivolous	X. Forget it

5. Decide collectively:
   - Which will be done first (tomorrow?), second, third, simultaneously?
   - Who will do what?
   - When will it be done?
   - Broad strokes of how it will be done?
   - How will you know if it was faithful and effective?

6. Celebrate, praise God, congratulate one another, and go home.

The process ought to yield directions and projects ranging from imperative to fun, easy to difficult, accomplishable now and into the future. A church that follows this or a similar process every year or two, and follows through on their intentions, will discover their shared life is much more faithful, lively, and productive.

Outside Relationships

Small churches don't and can't live in a vacuum. Each is part of a surrounding neighborhood or community. Most are in some kind of relationship with neighboring churches. Most are related to a denomination or association of churches. A wise church will pay attention to each of these relationships and recognize their interdependence with each.

Healthy relationships with the community, neighboring churches, and the denomination aren't always easy. The community may be perceived as uncaring or hostile. Declining population or differing theology and style often result in more competition than cooperation between churches in a community. Denominations have often neglected or maligned their smaller churches, and the churches may have dropped out of the relationship rather than work for their rightful place.

Within its community, the church needs to take the initiative. For example, the Warwick church offered free use of its building to community groups, published a newsletter for the whole community, and operated a Helping Hands project for anyone in need. The Shrewsbury church Christmas Eve and Meetinghouse Rock worship services were community events. The deacons and pastor called on all people from the community who were hospitalized and organized caring responses to people in crisis. In both Warwick and Shrewsbury, thrift shops were developed for the welfare of the community. The Emmetsburg church donates from its budget to community projects, hosted a child-care program, and hosts arts council events and ecumenical programs.

Creative thought can generate a wide variety of opportunities for churches to cooperate. Pastors can meet weekly to study the lectionary and support one another. Churches could buy supplies cooperatively and share office equipment and even office staff. Sunday schools, confirmation classes, youth groups, vacation church schools, camping, and adult education experiences can be carried out ecumenically. Pastors might swap pulpits occasionally. Rural churches might do a joint "blessing of the seed" service in the spring and a harvest service in the fall. Buildings and pastoral leadership can be shared. Where there's a will, there are a thousand ways.

To strengthen relationships between small churches and their denomination, the initiative needs to come from both directions. Our Iowa UCC conference provided the primary leadership in developing a regional summer Rural Institute for pastors. The Iowa strategy of placing half-time area ministers around the state was chosen particularly with small churches in mind. Small churches need to speak up and make their wants and needs known. They need to speak out about what they see and don't see happening in the church. And they need to honor their covenant with their denominational partners, recognizing we're all in ministry and mission together and integral organs in the Body of Christ.

Even the humblest home and family requires careful maintenance. Without that careful maintenance they both disintegrate. The same is true with a church, no matter how small.

For Thought and Discussion

1. What is the level of your church's morale and how could it be elevated?
2. How does your church deal with money? Which of the author's principles and approaches have most promise for you?
3. What building questions are facing your church? What building possibilities do you envision?
4. In what ways could your church be more effective in inviting and including new people?
5. How could your church improve the ways it calls forth, equips, cares for, and thanks its leaders?
6. Is your church more efficient or more effective in the way it is organized? How does it go about getting things done?

7. How does communication happen or not happen in your church? Can you think of ways to get the word better heard?
8. What happens when conflict rears its head in your church? How effective is it at preventing, defining, resolving, and managing its conflicts?
9. What are your church's stated and assumed goals? How could it move toward more intentional directions?
10. With whom is your church in relationship outside of its membership? How could those relationships be more satisfying and productive?

10. The Shepherd of the Flock

Like everything else about small churches, ministry with them is different, very different. The assumptions, expectations, needs, and tasks are different. To be faithful and effective, a compatible personality is required. Not everyone can be or should be a small church pastor. Pastors who are starting in a small church in order to get to a large one should start somewhere else.

In his book on leadership, *Getting Things Done*, Lyle Schaller contrasts two different pastors. Sally Carson is the pastor of a small village church and Terry Carter is the pastor of a rapidly growing new church. Each was asked to list in order of importance twenty pastoral roles they fulfill. These are the first ten on each of their lists:

Sally (small church)
1. Shepherd
2. Pastor
3. Friend
4. Equipper
5. Counselor

Terry (large church)
1. Leader
2. Preacher
3. Administrator
4. Visionary
5. Motivator

6. Visitor
7. Teacher
8. Nurse
9. Preacher
10. Cheerleader

6. Evangelist
7. Fund-raiser
8. Planning consultant
9. Shaper of traditions
10. Organizer[1]

Notice how the roles fit the needs of two very different churches and probably the style of two very different pastors. Neither the lists nor the pastors are interchangeable. Sally and Terry would not be happy or effective in each other's church. "Shepherd," the role Sally ranked first, is the fundamental role that fits pastors of small churches—rural and urban. The shepherd is the one who protects, loves, guides, serves, and cares for the flock.

André Soltner, chef at Lutece in New York, one of the world's premier restaurants, describes his approach to his vocation—the same approach needed for small church ministry:

> I am more than thirty years a chef. I know what I am doing and each day I do my absolute best. I cook for you from my heart, with love. It must be the same with service. The waiter must serve with love. Otherwise, the food is nothing. . . . People ask me all the time what secrets I have. I tell them there is nothing mysterious about Lutece. I put love in my cooking and love in the serving. That is all.[2]

The faithful and effective pastor of a small church puts love in his "cooking" and love in her serving.

Scripture provides us with the model for this style of ministry—the servant model. Isaiah 53:4 describes the servant leadership Israel will need to lead it out of exile: "Surely he has borne our griefs and carried our sorrows." In the Gospel of John, Jesus voluntarily models servant leadership as he washes the feet of his disciples and tells his followers to do the same. When the disciples bicker over who has the most status, Jesus contrasts the way of the world with his way: "In the world the recognized rulers lord it over their subjects. . . [but] among you, whoever wants to be great must be your servant" (Mark 10:42–43). Paul reminds the little church in Galatia, "Through love become slaves [or servants] to one another" (Gal. 5:13). The closest word for ministry in the Greek is *diaconos*, which means "one who serves."

Today, shepherd and servant images aren't fashionable models for ministry. One sounds archaic; the other sounds demeaning. Neither offers what is considered most attractive in our society—power and prestige, money and security. Nevertheless, they are the images that scripture teaches and that best serve small churches.

Steve Burt, in his illustration-packed book *Activating Leadership in the Small Church,* describes six qualities of an effective small church pastor. They're all ingredients of a shepherd and servant ministry.

- The good small church pastor has a people-first theology and practice of ministry.
- He tends to be "in culture," meaning he lives and relates to the culture in which he's pastoring.
- She's willing to be a character and has character.
- He's usually patient and understanding.
- She earns authority by sharing power and giving it away.
- He believes people are basically good, not depraved.[3]

We've inherited a neat, clean, but invalid distinction between minister and laity. The stereotype of a minister is the full-time professional Christian with four years of college and three years of seminary who's standing up front. The laity are the amateur Christians sitting in the pews who work at secular vocations and avocations and pay the professional. This distinction doesn't work theologically or in practice.

The word *laity* comes from *laos,* which means "the whole people of God." The ministry in the New Testament church belonged to the *diakonos,* which was everyone. The early church didn't distinguish between professional and amateur or minister and laity. It is more valid to blend ministers and lay people into "all the people of God who serve." The minister is part of the laity, and the laity are all ministers.

Also, small churches are facing some practical problems concerning ministry. Most persons who feel called to "ministry" want and expect to be ordained and to serve one church full-time. Seminaries primarily prepare students for full-time, single church ministry. A majority of churches want and expect to have at least one full-time ordained person. These expectations are no longer feasible for a large percentage of churches and pastors. If at least one hundred in worship is required for a church to afford a full-time pastor and 60 percent of the 375,000 Protestant congregations in the United States and Canada average less than one hundred in worship, most pastors will be serving more than one church or serving on less than a full-time basis, and most churches are not going to have their own full-time, ordained pastor.[4]

Additionally, in some denominations and in some parts of the country, there is a serious shortage of ordained or ready to be ordained pastors. There are plenty of candidates for medium-to-large, well-paying suburban churches. But poor churches in rural areas and some not so poor churches in remote rural areas are having great difficulty attracting able candidates. And the situation is getting more problematic, as churches get smaller and the average age of pastors and students in seminary rises. Many pastors will be retiring soon and new pastors will not be staying in ministry as long.

The variety of people serving small churches poses a semantic quandary—what to call people serving in the pastoral role. In this book, I've intentionally used the term *pastor* rather than *clergy* or *minister*. I've not used *minister* to refer to the pastor, because everyone in the church is a minister. I've not used the word *clergy* because clergy are ordained, and we have many, and will need to have many more, nonordained people serving as pastors of churches.

A Pastoral Crisis

The shortage of trained pastoral leaders points to a pastoral crisis facing the Protestant church. By way of illustration, in the Iowa Conference of the United Church of Christ, by the year 2000, we project that out of two hundred churches, only eighty-three will have full-time ordained pastors. This is not unique to Iowa or the UCC.

The Chinese language has two characters for our word *crisis*. One character means "danger," the other means "opportunity." The danger is that there won't be nearly enough faithful and effective pastors for many churches. The opportunity comes in being forced to rethink, retheologize, and redo how pastoral leadership is provided.

A new understanding of ordination is needed. If ordination is how one's qualification to be a pastor is determined, lay pastors and the churches they serve are deemed less than fully legitimate. Theological education must be rethought. Rather than only preparing people to be full-time ordained pastors, seminaries need to equip many people for bivocational ministry and others to serve multiple churches. Theological schools need a variety of training methods, in addition to the three-year, on-campus, full-time model.

Every level of the church must rethink ministry itself, redefine credentials, and learn to live without neat categories like *lay* and *ordained*. Denominations need to do some radical reworking of practical issues like pastoral compensation, insurance, and retirement programs. The small church leadership crisis is raising real dangers for the church and opening up wonderful opportunities.

The crisis of too few faithful and effective pastors for small churches is of enormous importance. As important as lay people are in small churches, these churches will not realize their considerable potential without effective pastoral leadership. Since they can't compete with their larger, better-paying cousins in the pastoral leadership marketplace, the wider church needs to begin seeing and responding to *smaller churches and their communities as a new mission field.* The church will then start recruiting and equipping missionaries or small church specialists to serve as shepherds in this new mission field.

Small churches have had three kinds of relationships with pastors, resembling three kinds of male/female relationships. Many churches have been tantalized and plagued by a succession of *one-night stands* with a variety of pastors and imposters. A succession of college and seminary students, lay preachers, supply pastors, Bible school products, incompetents, and charlatans have come along, raised expectations, preached the same often-heard pitches, added a little life, and moved on. Each time, the congregation becomes more convinced that they don't deserve a lasting relationship and more certain no one wants such a relationship with them. Each time the church's self-image and reputation as "one of those churches" becomes more firmly established. The members become resigned in the belief that this is all that life has for them.

Some luckier or wiser churches and pastors find one another, become lovers, and *live together.* Each finds a little security in the other. If they are not mismatched, they share times of euphoria and times of contentment. But since each suspects the intentions of the other, there are times of suspicion, resentment, and withdrawal. Eventually boredom sets in. Sooner or later, one feels used or sees a more intriguing partner and the arrangement is broken. Each tends to move on to a similar arrangement with a new partner. Most pastor-church relationships are of the living-together variety.

Some trusting and courageous churches and pastors buck the prevailing trends and commit to a *marriage.* In these relationships each party makes a commitment "to have and to hold from this day forward, for better or for worse, for richer or for poorer, in sickness and in health, to love and to honor." Each partner trusts and cares deeply about the other. Although living separate lives, they grow together. They are proud of each other's strengths and tolerant of each other's idiosyncrasies. They run and accept the risk of being jilted. They grow and mature so that the relationship remains fresh and fertile. Sometimes, despite great effort, they grow in different directions. When the marriage has been good and satisfying, the parting is both thankful and painful. Each wishes good for the other.

The challenge is how to prevent one night stands or how to make short pastorates into more intentional ones, how to encourage more than simply living together, and how to help pastors and churches create and sustain strong and enduring marriages.

Making a Good Thing Last

Many small churches have served as proving grounds for novice pastors learning the tricks of the trade, as dumping grounds for pastors who haven't worked out elsewhere, or as fields where tired and retired pastors have been put out to pasture. They have not always been the landing place for pastors riding the rapid shuttle from church to church. Such has not always been the case. Historians Robert Lynn and James Fraser tell how it once was:

> Americans have not always valued the large church more than the small one. In fact, in the eighteenth century. . . no absolute distinction was made between the large and small church. . . . A study of the graduates of Yale College from 1702 to 1775 shows that 79 percent of those who were ministers served one parish all their lives. . . . A mere 7 percent had more than two parishes. In those days, it seems, an individual was called by God to a lifelong commitment to the people of God. . . . The eighteenth-century New England Congregationalists did not view the successful pastor as one who changed churches. . . . There were no essential spiritual distinctions between the minister who labored in a small Connecticut hamlet and the pastor of the prominent church in New Haven or Boston.[5]

Things have changed. Small churches and their pastors expect short-term relationships and therefore don't commit to one another. Schaller points out the drawbacks of short-term relationships: "From a congregational perspective the most productive years for the typical pastorate are years five, six, seven, and eight. The minister who moves on after three or four years deprives his congregation of what often potentially could be the most productive and effective years of ministry in that place."[6] While serving in Warwick fourteen years, I experienced the satisfaction and joy of seeing tremendous development in the church and in people. Serving only four years in Shrewsbury, I experienced the frustration of unfinished starts and unfulfilled relationships.

There are several reasons pastors change churches frequently. Economics is the obvious first reason. Pastors can't, or feel they can't, live on the salary that's provided. Beyond that, many pastors are on a career track leading to big success. Some have more of a sprinter's mentality than a marathoner's. Some pastors and churches fear intimacy and keep one another at arms reach. Often pastors and churches are mismatched and just can't dance to the same rhythm. Many churches have been through so many pastors and many pastors have marched through so many churches that neither party has any hope or expectation of a solid, enduring relationship. Finally, there are a few churches that chew up and spit out pastors and a few pastors who abuse churches.

Here are ten guidelines that can encourage more marriages and fewer one-night stands.

1. If you're a pastor, believe that ministry is a calling and life-style, not a profession or career. Discern to what kind of calling God is beckoning you and what kind of life-style is right for you. Believe that God is more likely to call you to a marriage than a one-night stand.

2. If you're a pastor, try to wait for the right place. If you're the church, wait until you feel you're calling the right pastor. I know this is easier said than done. But if pastor and church are as choosy as one should be in picking a spouse, the chances are greater of a good and long relationship.

3. Make a lasting relationship a mutual and articulated goal. Mutually commit to the marriage-vow goals. See each pastorate as a book with several chapters. Believe God intends you to stay together for the long haul.

4. Start right. Greet your new pastor with bountiful hospitality. Greet your new church as if you couldn't wait to arrive. Listen to one another and learn each other's story. Have some quick successes and build a solid foundation.

5. Love each other. Dudley says small churches want their pastor to be a lover. Your pastor will find it harder to leave if he or she feels deeply loved. Tell each other you love one another. Do things that build love and trust.

6. Don't expect just smooth sailing. Any long voyage has troubled water and turbulent weather. Particularly in those times, the captain and crew need one another and need to care for each other.

7. To both pastor and church: maintain your health, self-esteem, and morale. If you're the pastor, take some pride in being a maverick who chooses to stay, religiously follow your spiritual discipline, seek out and commit to a serious clergy support group, cultivate hobbies and a life outside the church. If you're the church, have fun working and playing together. Tend to the things that raise morale.

8. Live simply. Moonlight if you need to supplement your income. Pay

your pastor as well as you can and help him or her be able to afford to stay. Recognize there are more important things than money.

9. Both pastor and church need to keep growing if they don't want the relationship to stagnate and deteriorate. Read and study together. Start and use a church library. Smart churches expect pastors to pursue regular continuing education and know it is in their own interest to grant time for it and help pay for it.

10. Don't confuse faithfulness with success. The goal of discipleship is not applause. Thomas Merton, while teaching in an obscure college, supposedly was asked: "Why do you waste yourself in a place like this?" He answered: "Because it is my vocation."

As a pastor for over twenty years and a staff person in two state conferences, I've seen very, very few bad pastors or bad churches. I have seen many bad matches. When the relationship between a man and a woman or between a church and a pastor fails, the natural tendency is to blame the other. It's the husband's, the wife's, the church's, the pastor's fault. If only she, he, they had just done or not done this or that. Rather than playing the Blame Game, it would be wiser to use the concept of "No Fault Divorce."

It used to be that before a marriage relationship could be terminated, one participant had to be judged at fault. Realistically, we know that rarely if ever does blame rest solely with one partner. A stressed or broken relationship is a mutual problem. When reconciling between a pastor and church is not possible or desired, both parties will be less injured and more capable of building a new relationship, if they agree to a no fault divorce.

The marriage encounter movement has identified five stages in a marriage relationship. Many pastor-church divorces can be prevented and better relationships enabled, if both parties understand each stage and give attention to what's happening in each.

First is the *attraction* stage. This is when pastor and church first meet and begin courting. This shouldn't be rushed. Both of you should be very clear about what you're looking for, what kind of church or pastor is wanted. Pray a lot. Check out each other's references. Don't allow yourself to make a match out of desperation. Pay attention to your gut feelings and then engage all your rational tools.

Take time for multiple, in-depth interviews. You might go on a retreat together. Perhaps the denominational person responsible for the church could be invited to sit in on one of the interviews. Compare preferred styles, theologies, methodologies. Are your down-the-road goals similar or compatible? Use all your denomination's matchmaking resources. (Frequently bad mistakes are made when these resources are ignored or circumvented.) Put food in the fridge and flowers on the table for the new pastor and help unload the moving van.

Next comes the *illusion,* or honeymoon, stage. A church will get the new pastor's best stories and sermons the first few weeks. The church will be on its best behavior and put its skeletons in the closet. Both parties will be trying extra hard to do it right—this time. Make the most of and enjoy this stage as long as it lasts.

If you're the pastor, use this early time of ignorance to learn as much as possible. Call, visit, go out for coffee, pot luck, party. Listen carefully to all that's said and read everything that's between the lines. Learn how things work, who has to be consulted about what, what's holy and un-changeable and what isn't. Make sure the first worship services, the first funeral, baptism, and wedding are very special. Make sure your first changes are wise and important ones. Begin to formulate and communi-cate your vision and goals and encourage the church to help define and refine them.

If you're part of the church, give your new pastor time to get used to the water. Help her or him locate the rocks and undertow. Even though you know your name, tell the new pastor your name until he or she's got it down pat. Don't forget, no new pastor comes with all the attributes and none of the faults of the previous pastors. Go way out of your way to care for each other.

Yet, inevitably, in a matter of hours, days, weeks, or months, the bloom will be off the rose and you are now in the stage of *disillusionment.* Old problems and habits will emerge. The honeymoon may well vanish in the first spat. The new pastor will discover this church is not God's finest church. The church will discover this is not God's finest pastor. This stage can be very painful.

Tragically, this is when premature "divorces" happen. The period of disillusionment needs to be recognized, planned for, and lived through. An outside "counselor," like your denominational staff person, should be brought in to help clarify expectations, define misunderstandings, and find new understandings. For the pastor, this is a time for going away for a few days, working harder, doubling efforts to build morale, achieving goals, calling on people you'd rather avoid, starting a new program, at-tending a relevant continuing education event, resolving problems. Most important, this is a time for listening more and talking less, a time for confessing that neither party has all the answers. If the church doesn't already have a Pastoral Relations Committee, use your denominational resources to start one.

The fourth stage is *realistic love*. If it has been a good match, this is the fruitful period in the marriage. This is the time when good memories are made, a time of faithfulness and effectiveness in your mutual ministry. Usually, but not always, it takes three or four years to get to this point. In Emmetsburg, we seem to have jumped right from the honeymoon to this stage. This is the time when each partner has earned the other's trust, and when you've learned to compensate for each other's shortcomings and capitalize on each other's strengths. It is the time when love grows deep and long.

Because of death, retirement, or the need to make a change, the last, inevitable stage is *termination*. All good things come to an end. The pastor and church that have successfully passed through each stage will be very different than each was in the beginning. Parting will be painful but not as painful as a premature divorce filled with regrets and recriminations. Each will be better equipped for whatever comes next.

Marks of a Good Ministry

There is a myth that not much happens in small churches except surviving, loving and fighting, and saying hello and good-bye to pastors. This may be true of some churches, but it's not my experience. When it is true, both pastor and church should be held accountable. In contrast to the myth, here's what is supposed to happen in a church.

In *Pursuing Excellence in Ministry*, Daniel Biles expresses the essential task of the church: "The critical, strategic difference between the churches that stand out for what they do and those that wallow in mediocrity is nothing more or less than a commitment, a passion, an obsession with doing things well in ministry."[7] He sets out the three most important areas of concentration in a church's ministry:

> Mission, pastoral leadership, lay commitment: these are the basic foundations of excellence in parish ministry. They are concretely expressed in activities which are the basic work of the community of faith: worship, education, and care and outreach. In strong churches these activities are marked by a commitment to quality and united by one purpose: to get the Gospel communicated, so that believers might be strengthened in their faith and unbelievers brought to faith in Jesus as their Lord and Saviour.[8]

Biles goes on to identify seven qualities of a faithful and effective ministry:

- The pastor must "plan to stick around!"
- He or she must focus on the basics of ministry and cut down on lesser and outside distractions, and commit to quality in everything.
- Practice a pastoral "Ministry by Wandering Around," which means leaving the security of home and office and being out and with your people.
- Promote mission, not just "bodies and bucks"; or pursue a vision of what God is calling the congregation to do in the local and global world.
- Constantly seek new ways to improve what you and the church are doing in your mutual ministry. (If this rubs against the grain of a conserving church, remember there are fresh ways to build on old values.)
- Do the things that cause people (in and outside the church) to sit up, take notice, and climb on board.
- Last, enlist and involve the members in a shared ministry, always thanking and affirming your co-workers. [9]

These qualities of effective pastoral ministry fit all sizes of churches, but they can be particularly effective in helping a small church move from survival issues to real ministry and mission.

Paying the Pastor

Except for the rare small church whose members are all tithers or that owns an oil well or that has inherited a large sum from Aunt Sally, there is no problem more vexing than finding enough money to pay for quality pastoral leadership. Even with the best of intentions, fairness feels very expensive.

The minimum salary recommendation in our UCC conference for 1991 was $17,000, which was lower than in other denominations and parts of the country. In addition to this minimum base salary, when a church offers a housing allowance or provides and maintains a parsonage and pays for utilities, offers a Social Security offset payment, health and dental insurance (it's over $5,000 for family coverage in our health plan), retirement, an auto allowance, continuing education, money for conferences and professional expenses, vacation supply, and perhaps other benefits, they're looking at a compensation package approaching at least $35,000. Yet when our small, rural churches offer this kind of minimum compensation package, we often still have difficulty finding good candidates for them. Many, many churches—even if they want to be fair and responsible—simply cannot afford this much for pastoral leadership.

As a seminarian, I made a commitment to spend my ministry serving small and probably rural churches. In 1971, Warwick employed me at thirty dollars a day for two days a week. Throughout my ministry, I've been considered a very faithful and effective pastor. But it was not until 1991 that my compensation climbed all the way to the minimum recommended levels. Fortunately, my wife—except for a few months off to have our two babies—has worked as a teacher throughout my ministry. This may work for a pastor who has a spouse, but a church cannot count on a double income.

The struggle to make ends meet doesn't end with the end of ministry. Because of built-in inequities in most retirement systems, pastors who choose to serve small, poor churches may also be choosing to spend their retirement years in relative poverty.

So what are a church and a pastor to do? Times have changed for both. Being a church costs more today. In addition to pastors costing more, so do buildings and their utilities and upkeep, support staff, program materials, and so on. Although churches want to maintain and expand their mission and denominational support, it's getting harder and harder.

Times have changed for pastors, too. Few businesses give discounts to pastors, as they once did. Many pastors, new to ministry, arrive in their first or second church with an enormous debt from college and seminary and often a family to support. Medical costs, even after insurance, are much greater today. What were once luxuries are now considered necessities by many if not most people, including pastors—appliances, a second car, a full closet, adult toys (boat, camper, VCR). When I went to college and seminary, it cost my parents and me a few thousand dollars. It will cost my family many, many thousands of dollars to send our kids to college. Times have changed for all of us.

Small, poor churches and pastors wanting to serve them are caught between a rough rock and a very hard place. But there are ways of coping with the gap between what churches have and what pastors need. And having to struggle for solutions between the rock and the hard place may push many of us—pastors and churches—into new forms and greater faithfulness. Since we're in it together, here are some options and responses for churches and pastors.

1. Place greater emphasis on serious stewardship, tithing, and including the church in wills—with pastors setting an example (but *not* setting the *only* example). One of our Iowa churches was going to offer a minimum salary in their search for a new pastor. When confronted with their needs and the reality that a minimum salary might only attract a minimum pastor, they dug deeper and voted overwhelmingly to raise their

cash salary to $3,000 over the recommended minimum. By offering more, they found a fine pastor, who should help generate more than enough income to cover the difference. It has been estimated that twelve to twenty tithing families can underwrite a full-time pastor's salary and the rest of the church budget.

2. Help churches and pastors see the virtues of tentmaking or bivocational ministry and tool up for that kind of ministry. This takes the burden of total compensation off the church and allows the pastor to earn more than most small churches can pay. (See the last chapter for a discussion of bivocational ministry.)

3. Find creative and effective ways to form and enable shared ministries between two or more churches. There are many possibilities: merging or federating two or more churches, blending or yoking two or more churches, a larger church or a denominational body sharing a staff person with a smaller church, or several churches sharing a team of pastors. (See chapter 12 for more details.)

4. Identify, train, and equip gifted lay persons for lay ministry in their or another church. This is a radical shift from the contemporary emphasis on pastors being credentialed by intensive theological education and ordination to the biblical emphasis on identifying and using spiritual gifts for ministry.

5. Offer compensatory compensation. A church that can't afford a full-time pastor and a pastor with wide interests and commitments might swap time for money. For example, the church, rather than granting a one-month paid vacation, might grant three months for study, travel, writing, and so on. Or a church might provide a retired pastor on a pension with a parsonage and partial salary and benefits.

6. Customize the pastor's compensation to be as advantageous to the pastor as possible. Take advantage of all that the tax laws allow—such as declaring as much salary as housing allowance as is honest and allowable. Take part of the salary and set it aside to cover medical deductible expenses if needed and give it as a bonus if not needed. Offer services like free baby-sitting, providing wood for the wood stove, meat for the freezer—if the pastor is agreeable.

9. Pastors need to remember it costs less to live in some parts of the country. The pastor who came to the church in Iowa that raised the cash salary $3,000 saved a considerable amount by moving from urban New Jersey to rural Iowa.

The Wisdom of Others

I've received helpful correspondence from gifted and committed pastors of small churches. Here is some of their wisdom. Rob Carr, a pastor in Kansas, writes:

Pastoral care is the key to everything. I learned that if I was experienced by the congregation as caring, available at the drop of a hat, compassionate, able to grieve and celebrate with them, everything else would fall into place.

Arlyce Kretschman, pastor of the Second Baptist Church in Walworth, New York, writes:

> Above all else, small churches want the pastor (and his or her family, if there is one) to be an integral part of the church family. They want him or her to "settle in," to understand them as a people, to become comfortable with their family ways, to love them and open themselves to be loved by the people.

George Spencer, a Baptist pastor in Central Square, New York, writes:

> Generally speaking, small church pastorates are far too short to get anything done with long term results. . . . Small churches need a better vision of the things they *can do!* . . . Would I do this kind of ministry all over again [after thirty-eight years]? Yes! But I would have more laypeople directly share ongoing parish life with me on a week to week basis.

Roberta Smith Patterson, United Methodist pastor in Springview, Nebraska, writes:

> I found the congregation to have low self-esteem. They didn't like themselves. They had no direction, they had no goals or objectives. . . . People were discouraged and dejected. What I have brought to these people is faith, and spirit, and enthusiasm, and optimism. For you see, as pastor, I live my faith, and I believe strongly in the power of the Holy Spirit at work.

Small churches have great needs and the greatest need is for strong and loving pastoral leadership. The financial rewards are minimal; the spiritual rewards and emotional satisfactions can be tremendous. Many of us would rather be big fish in a small pond than small fish in a big pond. Only a special person can be a good pastor in a small church, someone

- who would rather be her or himself than project an image;
- whose own sense of worth can withstand anonymity and who can give worth to others and see worth in all;
- who appreciates the potential of a tiny mustard seed or a bit of yeast;
- who is creative enough to make a silk purse out of a sow's ear and practical enough to make good use of a silk purse;
- who has the sensitivity to ignore the pressing crowd in order to feel

the touch of the hemorrhaging woman or see little Zacchaeus up in the sycamore tree;

- who has the very special knowledge and skills of the general practitioner;
- who knows God calls the church to be faithful and effective, not big and successful.

For Thought and Discussion

1. How does your church define *ministry*?
2. What qualities do you think are required for faithful and effective ministry in your church, a small church?
3. What kind of relationships has your church had with recent pastors?
4. If your church has a pastor, in what stage is the pastor-church relationship?
5. How does and how could your church cope with the issue of adequate compensation for their pastor?
6. What does your church need from their pastor? What does their pastor need from the church?

11.   *The Rural Setting*

Not all small churches are in rural and small-town settings, but a large majority are. Most rural churches are small, but not all. Medium-sized and large rural churches will likely feel and act much smaller than they are because they tend to be full of family connections and their people are likely to interact throughout the week. Rural America, like many of its churches, is in serious trouble, and the restoration of both is intimately related.

The relationship between rural and urban America is symbolized by a front page article in the *Des Moines Register,* 5 June 1990, titled "New York Garbage Rolls Through Iowa." The article described how the New York boroughs of Brooklyn and the Bronx, faced with limited and expensive landfill possibilities, had contracted to ship their garbage through southern Iowa to a landfill near Trenton, Missouri.

The article suggested that this may be a harbinger of the future. A spokesperson for the shipping company explained: "This is just a real neat way to do it. . . . This is a grand industry for any town that can accept it. We'll keep going to Missouri, until someone gets crazy and says, 'We don't want those rail cars here.' Then we'll go someplace else."[1]

The shipping of urban garbage to rural resting places is the completion of a logical cycle, since most urban garbage was originally extracted from rural places as food, fiber, and chemicals. The chickens are coming home to roost.

The Rural Problem

Rural land, once holy ground for native Americans, is now the playground, often depleted ground, and dumping ground for the nation. What was on it and in it, what passed over it and ran through it has been cultivated, harvested, harnessed, hunted, mined, pumped, and processed, in order to feed, clothe, house, heat, transport, electrify, entertain, and enrich America. The most fertile land was set aside and used to feed America and much of the world. Now much of this agricultural land is being paved, built on, or blown and washed away in the name of productivity, profitability, and progress. The native people who loved the land were displaced by immigrant people who cared for the land who were replaced by machines that could not care.

This is the same land that Chief Seattle spoke of in 1854, as native American land was transferred to immigrant Americans:

> Every part of the earth is sacred to my people. . . . We are part of the earth, and it is part of us. . . . We know the white man does not understand our ways. One portion of the land is the same to him as the next, for he is a stranger who comes in the night and takes from the land whatever he needs. The earth is not his brother, but his enemy, and when he has conquered it he moves on. . . . This earth is precious to [God] and to harm the earth is to heap contempt on its creator. . . . So if we sell you our land, love it as we have loved it. Care for it as we have cared for it. Hold in your mind the memory of the land as it is when you take it. And with all your strength, with all your mind, with all your heart, preserve it for your children and love it—as God loves us all.[2]

Long before Chief Seattle, Moses described a similar land into which he was taking the Israelite people:

> For the Lord your God is bringing you into a good land, a land flowing with streams, with springs and underground waters welling up in valleys and hills, a land of wheat and barley, of vines and fig trees and pomegranates, a land of olive trees and honey, a land where you may eat bread without scarcity, where you will lack for nothing, a land whose stones are iron and from whose hills you may mine copper. You shall

eat your fill and bless the Lord your God for the good land that he has given you (Deut. 8:7–10).

America the beautiful and bountiful has been treated more like a factory than a garden. Its less powerful people have been treated more like spare parts than persons endowed with inalienable rights. Our precious inheritance is being squandered.

C. Dean Freudenberger, international authority on soil and agriculture, cites frightening statistics in 1984 in his book *Food for Tomorrow?*:

- Half our ground water has become polluted;
- Each year in this country, four billion tons of soil are lost because of wind and water erosion—more than was lost in the Dust Bowl disaster of the 1930s;
- In the United States in the past thirty years, almost four million farms and ranches have disappeared, and thirty million people have left the land—the greatest migration in human history.

Freudenberger says that by the year 2000:

- 15 to 20 percent of all the species on the earth may be extinguished;
- 40 percent of the remaining forest cover will be gone;
- One third of the remaining soil will be lost and 5 percent of the earth's surface will remain arable.[3]

God's judgment decreed in Ezekiel 33:28 is coming true: "I [with plenty of human help] will make the land a desolation and a waste, and its proud might shall come to an end."

Our culture has separated people from community, from the land, rather than perceiving them as interdependent. Walter Brueggemann, in *The Land,* asserts: "Land is a central, if not *the central theme* of biblical faith. . . . It will no longer do to talk about Yahweh and his people but we must speak about Yahweh and his people and *his land*."[4] Land is God's gift. Out of the gift grows a community of people. Take away the land and the people become displaced, rootless, and unrelated. Take away community and the people despoil the land. Take away the people and the land becomes fallow at best, barren at worst.

Wendell Berry—farmer, philosopher, poet, and prophet—understands these connections as well as anyone. He sees culture as the glue that holds people, community, and land together.

> If the local culture cannot preserve and improve the local soil, then, as both reason and history inform us, the local community will decay and

perish, and the work of soil-building will be resumed by nature. A human community, then, if it is to last long, must exert a sort of centripetal force, holding soil and local memory in place.[5]

Urban and rural are like male and female, one depends on the other. Yet our language reveals that urban is either prized or taken for granted, while rural is laughed at, enjoyed, and then dismissed. I used *Roget's International Thesaurus* to compare the words *urban, rural, city,* and *country.* The few synonyms for urban and city are neutral terms like *metropolis, municipality, citified,* and *urbane.* But most of the synonyms for *rural* and *country* have a distinctly different sound: the sticks, yokel, hick, hinterland, back country, boondocks, rube, hayseed, clodhopper, uncouth, unrefined, uncultured, one-horse town, jerk-water town, tank town, wide place in the road, and "a little one-eyed, blinking sort o' place." What is not taken seriously is not protected and preserved. The words and ways of our world are established by urban interests.

But there's no surprise in that. The seats of power and influence are on Wall Street, Pennsylvania Avenue, and Capitol Hill. Rural and farm influence and population steadily erode. Power readjustments after each census tip the scales even further, as rural states lose congressional seats and federal money, which are allocated according to population.

Between 1960 and 1990 the percentage of Americans living outside urban areas slipped from 26.5 to 22.9. Some rural areas have grown, most notably the Sunbelt, while others, like the Midwest, continue to erode. The number of people living on farms dropped from 30.2 million in 1940 to 5 million in 1986. Today only two of every one hundred Americans live on a farm. The fact that almost one-third of those leaving rural America are between 18 and 24 years of age and a majority of these have at least some college education makes this rural exodus particularly damaging.

Decreasing rural influence means increasing problems. In 1986, the rural poverty rate was 18 percent, the same as that in America's inner cities. Ninety-one of the nation's one hundred poorest counties are rural. Rural health care, legal services, and other social services lag behind the rest of society.

Rural America's most recent dramatic problem was the farm crisis of the mid 1980s, when over 500,000 American farms failed, the result of several converging factors. Farmers received less money for their crops. Soybean prices dropped from eleven dollars a bushel to six dollars, and corn dropped from six dollars a bushel to one dollar. Land values dropped dramatically. In Iowa the value of land crashed from three thousand dollars an acre to one thousand dollars an acre. Concurrently, midwestern farmers experienced their worst drought in fifty years. Previously, when harvests and crop prices were good, many farmers had borrowed heavily to buy new equipment, more land, additional seed and chemicals, and to make land improvements. Rising interest rates made more borrowing difficult. Farmers were crunched between lower income and higher costs.

When the crash came, many farmers couldn't pay back their loans. Many had to quit farming, farms were sold or foreclosed on, farm families migrated elsewhere in search of employment, farm-related business and industry suffered, and communities were devastated. According to the Department of Labor, at least three nonfarm jobs are lost when a family farm is lost and one business fails for every ten farm failures.[6] Loss of population and tax base results in loss of services and the consolidation of schools. The fruits of the crisis were and are severe emotional stress, suicide, family dysfunction and breakup, unemployment, community distress and despair, and church decline.

The farm families that have survived have done so by working off the farm while still farming, enrolling in unpredictable government programs, going deeper in debt, or farming more land (leased or purchased). The end results are far fewer farmers, far larger farms (often owned and operated by absentee corporations), less sustainable farming practices, depleted soil, weakened communities, and a nation with an even more precarious rural environment. One farmer, trying to lighten his despair with humor, asked another: "What's the difference between a pigeon and a farmer?" Answer: "A pigeon can still make a deposit on a John Deere tractor."

The farm crisis of the 1980s is illustrative of the complexity and gravity of a wide range of critical issues plaguing rural America. But the rural crisis is *more than the farm crisis* and it's more than an American crisis. The rural crisis is a many-pieced puzzle that includes a worldwide environmental crisis, migrant and undocumented farm workers, Appalachian poverty, cyclic famines in Africa, the extinction of black and minority farmers, the destruction of the rain forests in South America, the languishing of native Americans on lands no one else wanted, the decline of the fishing industry along America's coasts, the forces of leisure and retirement development that replace forests and farms with condominiums and ski lifts, water shortages, a collapsed economy that insured the breakup of the Soviet Union, agribusiness interests that care only about profitability, and many other interrelated forces, both local and global.

The Rural Church

Is the situation hopeless? Probably not. But if it's not hopeless, a principal player in the resurrection of rural America will have to be the rural church, with strong, sensitive, and enduring assistance from outside helpers.

Why is the local church so important? It is one of, if not the, only effective, locally operated institution and social service left in rural areas. It has more human, programmatic, and economic resources than it realizes. It has alliances (often ignored) with other religious and voluntary organizations, which, when coordinated, have real influence. More than that, its Christian charter mandates that it care for the whole person—body, mind, and soul—for the whole community, and for the whole creation. Even more, it has biblical and historical roots that provide endurance and power and an energizing theological vision of God's intention for the created order. But is it up to its task?

Carol Bly, who examines the problems and perplexities of rural life from her vantage point in Madison, Minnesota (population 2,242), offers a harsh, but all too often accurate indictment of churches and their pastors:

> The churches in Minnesota have had their part in vitiating the natural energy of people. Most of rural Minnesota go to church regularly, yet nearly never get a sermon on Jesus' turning the tables on the money-changers. . . . The pastors, themselves tottering around in an emotional sleepwalk, don't face the crises of their faith. . . . Since the pastors lack such energy—to think, and feel, and commit themselves—the people are left with no example of Christ's energy. No castle was ever well guarded by sleepwalkers, and certainly no Kingdom of the Spirit can rise up in the hearts of somnambulants.[7]

Bly goes beyond condemnation to possibilities. She writes that humanity (and I would add the church) has "three talents." Our first talent is memory, which makes us poets, philosophers, and historians. Often our churches and communities live in a fog of amnesia, but underneath is a mother lode of memory that tells us where we came from, who we are in the sight of God, to one another, and to ourselves. The fog must be burned away and the mother lode mined for all it's worth.

Our second talent is "being convinced that we have some profound task to do in this universe." Bly says this is what makes people religious. If all humanity has this inbred talent, then we ought to be able to awaken, call forth, and channel a passion in our people to reclaim and re-create our land, community, and culture. Imagine what might happen in our churches and communities if every person left every worship service confirmed in the belief that God is calling her or him to a special ministry that week?

Carol Bly says our third talent is for inventing social structures.[8] Look around. We're surrounded by social structures our ancestors and we ourselves have created—churches, hospitals, schools, civic groups, governmental bodies, social groups. Social structures are the mechanisms by which people build on their memory in the effort to fulfill their task or sense of destiny. Some social structures are working and need our support. Some have lost their sense of direction and commitment and need reviving. Some need a good burial. And some need to be born. The rural church needs to play a key role in supporting, reviving, and (in some cases) burying existing social structures and in birthing new ones.

"Whatever goes around comes around." I don't know who said it, but it's true. Beginning with a Hartford Seminary small church symposium in January 1976, and the book that came out of the symposium, *Small Churches Are Beautiful*, edited by Jackson Carroll, there has been a renewed interest in small and rural churches. Several good books have been written, seminaries now offer courses, denominations are paying more than lip service, grass roots efforts are growing and bearing fruit. But all this attention is not new. Between about 1900 and 1925 there was a vibrant Rural Church Movement in this country. Nine important truths for today's rural pastor and rural church are illustrated by nine timeless statements from that earlier movement's literature.

1. *The church is the natural leader.* In 1913, Charles Otis Gill and Gifford Pinchot wrote:

> It is hardly to be questioned that the church is the natural body to lead in rural social service. It is found everywhere, the doors of every home are open to its ministers, its buildings are the meeting places in which men, women, and children are accustomed to assemble, and its ministers speak to some of the people at least once every week. The country life movement could ill afford to neglect the cooperation of an organization already rooted in the field of country life.[9]

Most rural churches, being unassuming and modest, would never claim this kind of influence. Until rural churches see and accept their important role in their community, they won't play that role. Many small communities don't have any organizations left except the church, and no other organization touches people in so many ways as does the church. Serving as a catalyst, churches can bring together various community groups to learn, coordinate their efforts, and create new structures for addressing community concerns.

2. *As the country goes, so goes the nation.* Gill and Pinchot also affirmed:

> The ability of a nation to maintain the integrity and vigor of its rural population is the real test of its vitality. It was to the decadence of country life, not of city life, that the fall of Rome was due; and it is the rush of the best people of the country to the town that today presents the fundamental question of rural life as affecting the welfare of the whole nation.[10]

It is from the country that the rest of the nation gets its food for the table, fiber for clothing, lumber for building, and resources for manufacturing. Many urban people retreat to the country for rest and recreation and move there when they're able. Rural people have more power over their own destiny than they think, but urban America needs to recognize that its own destiny is inextricably tied to that of the countryside. Rural churches can work with their denominations to raise consciousness about rural issues and to help their urban cousins recognize and value the interdependence that exists between urban and rural areas.

3. *Rural churches can't act wisely until they understand their rural reality.* The facts stated by Edwin Earp in 1914 are close to the facts of today:

A. The phenomenal growth of towns and cities during the last two decades led men to ask why people were leaving the country for the city.
B. The increased cost . . . of the actual food products of the farms, while the farmer and the country folk seemed to be getting relatively poorer.
C. The enormous profits of the middleman, and the monopolies of transportation companies in the marketing of the products of the country.
D. Forest fires, floods, and drought of whole farming regions, due in large measure to the denuding of watersheds by deforestation; also robbing of soil by poor methods of agriculture, resulting in excessive erosion in the open season in certain parts of the country.

E.   Scarcity of farm labor and the resultant *high cost of farming,* or the reduction in produce from the farms in certain regions.[11]

A major theme of Latin American liberation theology has been helping people discover the reality of their lives. Rural leaders have the educational task of helping church and community people understand the realities that are shaping their lives. A rural church could sponsor community forums, bring rural leaders to speak at community gatherings, establish home-study groups, or prepare articles and letters to the editor for the local paper. One excellent resource is a United Methodist six-session study guide called *U.S. Agriculture and Rural Communities in Crisis,* which can be ordered from the National United Methodist Rural Fellowship, P.O. Box 29044, Columbus, Ohio, 43229.

4. Churches need to see themselves not just as conservers, but as changers. Gill and Pinchot summarize the rural church's position:

> At times...the country church...has been the most important agency in promoting civilization in rural life. From being an active uplifting force it has become a conserving influence merely. What the rural church is now doing cannot be measured by positive advance, but only by the amount of deterioration which it helps to prevent. The country church must be restored to its old-time vitality and influence as an indispensable condition of the revival and continuance of a wholesome life in the open country.[12]

This statement in 1913 describes many churches today, churches that have no vision of themselves doing more than conserving the status quo. Preachers need to do some powerful visionary preaching. Churches need to see that they have the ability and vocation to make a difference. They can be led to small, short-term projects in order to build muscle for larger ventures. They can be led to work on issues that are natural for them. For example, a nurse might start a parish nurse program. Two retired teachers might begin a tutoring program. "This Car Stops at All Yard Sales" bumper-sticker people might start a thrift shop. Again I recommend Bill Briggs's book *Faith Through Works* for inspiring imaginative outreach.

5. Find good leadership that will stick around. This is not a new idea. Gill and Pinchot stress:

> The country minister needs a more lasting interest in the country parish. In Windsor and Tompkins counties the average country minister doesn't regard his task as permanent, but rather as a temporary stopping place on the road to a larger church. . . . Under such conditions it is evi-

dent that no continuous policy or sustained plan of work can be followed long enough to produce results proportionate to the effort expended.[13]

One of the most basic questions a rural church should seek to answer is: "How can we find and keep the best possible pastor for our situation?" One of the first questions to ask a candidate is, "How many years will you commit to this church?" Pastor and church need to work together toward a sustaining ministry. Pastoral tenure raises the issue of strong lay leadership. If the pastor starts and does everything, not much that's lasting will happen. When the pastor's goal is to help the church do for itself what it feels called by God to do, important things will happen that last longer than the longest ministry.

6. *Get to know the people and the community.* What is needed is not a generic ministry but an organic one:

> Most country ministers . . . are insufficiently acquainted with their parishes. They are familiar with the roads, and with the people whom they meet, but the essential facts as a rule they have not yet discovered. The country minister needs a deeper and more sympathetic understanding of his community and of the conditions and needs of the people whom he serves.[14]

Gary Farley, associate director of the Rural-Urban Missions Department of the Southern Baptist Home Mission Board, has a remarkable grasp of rural sociology and rural ministry. He has compiled a list of thirty questions to help a pastor understand a community. A pastor who learns the answers to all of the questions will have an organic ministry in that place. Here is Farley's list:

1. How did the community come into being?
2. What are its chief economic functions?
3. What are its magnets—the places, activities, and events that draw people?
4. What are its patterns of movement (how people get places)?
5. What is its symbol, celebration, rhythm?
6. What is its story? How and why has it evolved?
7. What has become of its sons and daughters?
8. Who are the honored/despised of the town?
9. How does it relate to nearby rural areas and towns?
10. How does it relate to larger cities?
11. How do people make a living?
12. How are decisions made? Who are the power-brokers?

13. Where are its sins—its hurts?
14. What seems to be the dream of the future for the town?
15. What are the routines of everyday conversations? What are the taboos?
16. Where and how do people play?
17. What are the barriers dividing people? Are they visible or invisible?
18. Who can make introductions and give credibility by association?
19. What is the people's perception of the place and their awareness of other's perception?
20. Is the town large enough that distinct sub-communities can be identified?
21. Where are the churches located? Who do they reach?
22. How does it assimilate persons?
23. What cultural/ethnic/racial groups are present in the community?
24. What media cover the town? How do these affect the life of the community?
25. How has the town related to this church?
26. What resources does the town provide for helping a pastor in his or her ministry?
27. Who are the unchurched?
28. What are the expectations for the role of a pastor, his or her spouse, and children?
29. How can a pastor get distance from her or his role?
30. Where can a pastor find a friend and confidant.[15]

7. *The rural community needs some fresh air.* In 1911, Kenyon Butterfield pointed to the danger of self-satisfaction and stagnation:

> One grave danger to permanent rural progress is the low level of ideals, determined by community standards. . . . As a consequence the rural community is in constant danger of stagnation—of settling down into the easy chairs of satisfaction. Rural life needs constant stimulus of imported ideas.[16]

One function of the rural leader is to be a conduit for fresh ideas, perspectives, methods, wisdom. A rural colleague of mine said that one thing his church paid him for was to read—and he did. And his church was healthier for it. The rural pastor can gather people to discuss controversial issues, watch and discuss a public television program or a thought-provoking movie on the VCR, or take a cultural trip to a nearby city. Carol Bly suggests having "Enemy Evenings," when a panel of people on opposite sides of an issue are brought together to debate the issue.

8. *The rural pastor will be or become a rural person.* Butterfield points to the need of indigenous leaders: "So the rural clergyman will love the

ways of rural folk. He will enter into their experiences, breathe the same air of simplicity and freedom, respond to the native elements of rural character, understand the rural mind."[17] As noted earlier, the way Steve Burt describes the process, the pastor will "be in character" or in-culturated. This takes time and effort. It means taking people seriously. It means helping plant and harvest. It means spending time in people's homes, barns, shops, fields. An effective pastor understands the ways and issues of his or her people.

9. *All of rural life is spiritual at heart.* In 1923, Edmund deS. Brunner understood that the church cannot divorce itself from any of the matters that affect its people, because it is all part of the fabric of their lives:

> It is suggested . . . that in every parish a community program should be outlined to deal with the more important of such questions as these— better roads; better housing, better living conditions; better schools and agriculture; the care of the sick, the indigent and the feeble-minded; elimination of centers of vice and moral infection. . . . The church should take an interest in everything that is of interest to the people to which it ministers, for *there is nothing which the people do that does not relate itself to their spiritual life*.[18]

There is nothing new about a holistic understanding of the Gospel. Study Jesus' ministry of presence and response to people's need and you'll see the kind of Gospel action that was the heart of the Rural Church Movement. I could provide a list of ideas and strategies, but they probably wouldn't be right for your situation. The harder task is getting in touch with a person's and a community's pain and need. The easier part is finding an appropriate thing to do about it.

Rural America is in trouble. What rural churches do on behalf of rural America will either betray our history and seal an endangered future, or it will fulfill our history and create a sustaining and sustainable future. The truth Jeremiah spoke to the exiles in the city in Babylon is truth for rural churches today: "But seek the welfare of the city [rural area] where I have sent you into exile, and pray to the Lord on its behalf, for in its welfare you will find your welfare" (Jer. 29:7).

The problems seem overwhelming. Taken as a whole, they are. The best way to deal with them is something like how one would eat an elephant. Take one bite at a time.

For Thought and Discussion

1. How do you experience and understand the "rural problem?"
2. If yours is a rural church, how is it important to its community?
3. Which of the statements from the Rural Church Movement seem most important to you and your situation?
4. What could your church do to constructively address the welfare of your rural area?

12. Outside Help: Denomination and Seminary

A young man was driving much too fast in his new sports car on a winding mountain road. Around the bend in the road came another car. Barely in control, this car was skidding from side to side across the road. The sports car driver swerved onto the shoulder to avoid the careening car. As the two cars passed, the woman driving the oncoming car gestured and yelled, *"Pig!"* The young man shook his fist and shouted into the rear view mirror: *"Dizzy Dame!"* Angry, driving even faster, he sped around the curve . . . and crashed head on into an enormous pig wandering down the center of the road.

That's often the way it is between the people of small churches and those in the denomination and seminary who're attempting to assist them. They cruise ahead, intent upon their own business. They happen upon one another, often at the most inopportune time. Their attempts to communicate often don't connect. Failing again to relate, they pass on around the curve . . . often meeting calamity. Seminary leaders feel they're doing all they can to provide competent pastoral leadership for local churches and are dismayed when churches complain that the seminaries aren't preparing good pastors for churches like theirs. Denominational people are frustrated that their efforts to help small churches often go unrequested and unappreciated, and little seems to change. Small churches often feel those outsiders don't care about them or don't understand them.

Robert Kemper, in his *Colleague* newsletter for pastors, describes himself as a white male fifty-five-year-old liberal pastor of a large congregation. He says those five circumstances used to lead to power, but now they lead to alienation. He sees fundamental changes happening in the church and he concludes: "My growing suspicion is that we are living in the last days of the great mainstream Protestant Church *as we have known it.* . . . The dilemma of contemporary pastoral leadership is this: shall we seek to revive, maybe reform, what we have known? Or shall we look for new forms, new understandings, new wineskins?"[1]

I believe we have to do the latter. Old institutions are struggling to adapt. Mainline churches are having hard times, particularly smaller ones. The gulf between denominational office, seminary classroom, and the people in the pews grows wider and deeper. It's difficult to change customary ways of doing things. We, whose job it is to help, need to look for new understandings and new forms that will enable us and our churches to be more faithful and effective. If we will look with fresh eyes for those fresh wineskins, our smaller churches can help us find them.

My present bivocational situation of being both pastor of a small church and area conference minister working with fifty-two mostly small churches in northwest Iowa gives me unique perspective in looking at these relationships. I've also taught for three seminaries, been a Christian education consultant for another state conference, and talked with hundreds of lay people, pastors, and denominational people about small church issues. I've never met any denominational, seminary, or church person who was not conscientious about the life of the church or who sought to be an abusive or ineffective helper or recipient. Yet often small churches feel unhelped by those attempting to help them.

I know from experience that we who are helpers can be very helpful. As an area conference minister with the Iowa Conference of the United Church of Christ, I have three relational tasks with the churches in my jurisdiction. I work in placement—helping churches make the best possible match in their search for a new pastor, pastoral care of pastors and families, and parish relations—brokering the relationship between conference and churches. We have four staff people working out of Des Moines who are very good at providing programming help for our churches. Four full-time programming staff and four half-time area relational people is a cost-effective way for us to make a significant difference in the lives of our 205 churches. Also being a pastor helps me maintain credibility with pastors and lay people, helps me stay honest about life in the parish, and helps me remember that the *primary job* of the denomination is to strengthen local churches. We, who come from the outside, can bring additional wine for still good wineskins and we can help create new wineskins.

No matter how wise and compassionate we are, we also come into churches bringing baggage that may not be our own. When someone says about someone like me, "He's from the conference," it is not necessarily an affirmation. I think I'm a caring and helpful person, but for others I may be a symbol of lack of care and help. When churches and pastors have an accumulated perception of being ignored or poorly served, when they may not approve of what they think the conference or denomination is doing, when they think I'm coming to get money from them or to make them do something "our" way, there is damage to repair and a bridge to build.

Part of the problem grows out of the *times* or *occasions* that we visit. When a church has a budget problem they look to the denominational staff person for help. But it's embarrassing to confess to an outsider that you can't manage your money or pay your bills. Some may expect that we have money to share and are disappointed to discover we probably don't or won't. The outsider will probably either commiserate and be perceived as ineffective or try to lead them in generating more money, which will cost them money. Asking us in can be expensive. It's hard to be helpful when you're perceived either as a Sugar Daddy or Scrooge.

Or churches hear from us when we want them to catch up on or increase their financial support of the denomination. Hearing from us on these matters may make them feel guilty or make them angry because the "denomination always wants more money" and "did you see how much those people in New York make!" It's hard to be helpful when you're perceived as a Big Brother or Fat Cat.

Or they hear from us when we have a new denominational program to sell. We think our new program (a capital funds drive, long-range planning, stewardship, evangelism, caring, and so on) can transform their church. They think our spanking new program will mean going somewhere to another meeting, will cost them money they don't have, will require volunteers they don't have, would only work in a big church, and won't do any more good than the last program we promoted. It's hard to be helpful when you're perceived as a traveling Peddler.

Or we come when there's a church fight. Often we don't get invited until it's too late. Frequently it's too late to prevent people from really being hurt. The pastor thinks we're on the side of his or her antagonists. The church thinks we're trying to protect the pastor. Our coming may open a larger can of worms. Sometimes it's like a domestic squabble in which the hostility is turned on the police officer who's come to break up the fight. Sometimes the denominational person is expected to decide who's right and who's wrong. It's hard to be helpful when you're perceived as Cop or Judge.

Or we come when the pastor is leaving or has left. This is a traumatic time. People may be grieving because the pastor who served and loved them well has left. They may be angry because the pastor they worked hard for and made commitments to has abandoned them. They may be delighted because an ineffective pastor is finally gone. They may be feeling guilty for a variety of reasons. Small churches in particular may be frightened because "no one's going to want to come way out here for what we can pay."

The chances are high that we will disappoint them. If I'm a district superintendent my appointment may be a big disappointment. If ours is a call system, a church is going to be asked to do more assessment and preparation work than they want to, the process will take longer than they think it should, frequently they'll discover they can't afford the kind of pastor they need, we probably can't provide the kind of candidates they expect, and they may conclude we weren't helpful or were too dictatorial. It's hard to be helpful when you're not a Magician.

Often they feel we come to work our agenda rather than to really address theirs. Small churches aren't going to care how much we know until they know how much we care. The following questions may be helpful in examining how we work on their turf or to use in asking them to evaluate *our* helpfulness:

- Have we learned to love small churches? Their small church?
- How have we demonstrated that?
- Is it clear that we've bothered to really learn about their church?
- Do we come talking with a silver tongue or listening with a keen ear?
- Do we come pushing our business agenda or addressing their more relational agenda?
- Do they perceive we're there because we have to be or because we want to be?

- Do we arrive early, not to get ready but to get acquainted?
- Do we bother to learn names and find out how things are with them—in church, home, and community?
- Do we honestly affirm them—again and again and again?
- Are we perceived more as a Cheerleader or Taskmaster?
- Do they perceive that we consider them partners in Christ's ministry?
- Do we defend the denomination or explore with them until we can say and mean, "I understand what you're saying"?
- Do we take time to explore scripture and pray with them?
- Is our number-one question, "How can I help you and your church be the kind of church you and God want it to be?"
- After the meeting do they say to one another, "I think she really cares about us," and "He really helped us"?
- Are we the first to leave or among the last out of the parking lot? Our attitude and approach preaches far more Good News than our finest sermons.

There was a stroke of genius in the Iowa Conference when we area ministers were asked to do only three Ps—placement, pastoral care of pastors, and parish relations. These are the primary tasks in assisting small churches, since their concerns are more relational than programmatic.

Making Matches

Placement. A church may survive, but it won't thrive without quality pastoral leadership. Our Iowa conference spends an inordinate amount of time on placement. There aren't an abundance of pastors wanting to come to Iowa. Our conference minister reads all the profiles that come through the UCC placement system. He writes to each person who looks like an able pastor who might consider placement in Iowa, sends promotional material, and asks if they would consider Iowa. Our whole staff suggests names of people we know who would serve well here. A member of the support staff in Des Moines is our placement coordinator and she works hard helping make interim arrangements, telephoning candidates and search committees, keeping track of profiles, checking references, alerting area ministers to what she's picked up, and encouraging search committees and candidates.

A nearby pastor is appointed to serve as an association counselor for each searching church. He or she provides counsel to the church, keeps an eye on the process, is involved with the development of a profile, helps with a mock interview, sometimes offers his or her church as a neutral pulpit, makes contact when a pastor is called, and shepherds the new pastor through the first year.

As area minister, I'm at the church a minimum of seven times between the time one pastor resigns and the new one is installed. I'm there for an exit interview and to meet with the church's official board; to work with the interim or supply pastor, to help the search committee begin its task, assess their needs, and start preparing their profile; to bring profiles of pastors wishing to be considered by that church and counsel them in the selection process; to participate in one phase of the interviewing; to meet the new pastor when she or he arrives; and to assist with the installation. I'm there to assist when the committee runs into a snag or needs extra assistance. I'm on the phone with the committee, coordinating with our conference office, visiting with candidates. The search process for each church is customized to benefit that church.

The task is more than finding a suitable pastor. This transition time, more than any other, is the time when a church is open to help, open to a change of direction, and willing to reconsider its attitude toward outside help. It's a time when a church can do major self-assessment, a time when new leadership can take hold in the church, when new vision for the church can take root, when a church can make a major shift—like going to a bivocational ministry or a shared ministry with another church. If I work intensively and effectively here, I may not have to pick up the pieces later or help look for a new pastor in a year or two.

The emphasis is on making the right match, not finding the world's best pastor. Our placement staff is more proactive, or giving more counsel and advice, in our work with search committees than we were. The old wisdom was that if we didn't recommend someone during the search, we couldn't be held responsible later. The new wisdom is that we're not dummies, and if we know of a strong candidate or one with problems we should be free to encourage or discourage a search committee.

There are particular qualities I encourage a small church search committee to look for, in addition to what they need for their particular situation. I encourage them to look for a candidate

- Who is faithful (after all, we are a church and faith is what we're about);
- Who understands and loves small churches;
- Who is a relational kind of person—a lover, a care-giver;
- Who listens and learns before teaching and preaching;

- Who is willing to make either a long-term commitment or is willing to come for a specific short-term task;
- Who is not afraid of hard work and a challenge;
- Who knows how important worship and spiritual care are in the life of small churches;
- Whose vision of the church is more than worship and pastoral care (this *alone* can pastor a church to death);
- Who knows how to, or is willing to learn how to, deal with steward-ship and money matters;
- Who knows how to share responsibility and power;
- Who is not a Lone Ranger but willing to work in the community and the wider church;
- Who is excited about the Christian church and enjoys life;
- Who sees ministry not as a job or profession but as a life-style and one of God's greatest callings.

I know this is a utopian list, and we fear people with these qualities are in short supply and come with a hefty price tag. Actually, there *is* a short supply, but the price tag on that kind of person isn't always hefty. There are many gifted pastors who are committed to small church ministry. And there are many pastors who don't fit the stereotype of what a terrific pastor is supposed to be like. I work with two yoked churches and an-other church that found superb pastors because they were willing to call someone with a disability. These two gems were passed over by other wealthier churches.

I urge churches to seriously consider calling a woman. If richer churches act out of prejudice and insist on a man, they will bypass some excellent female candidates who may be available. And I tell small churches that many women have the particular nurturing qualities that are especially helpful in smaller churches. I try to help a church be the kind of church an able pastor might get excited about and take a chance on. Believing that better pastors generate more income for a church, I encourage churches to stretch for the best compensation package they can manage.

I try to help a church that can no longer afford a full-time ordained pastor consider other viable options. I help them imagine having either their own part-time pastor—lay or ordained—or sharing a pastor with one or more churches. They are encouraged not to see this as a second-class ministry—that it doesn't necessarily make them a less effective church. We look at the pros and cons of each possibility and determine which option is right for them.

I've been a *bivocational pastor* for seventeen of my twenty-four years of ministry and am an advocate of this form of ministry. It has a hallowed history. The Apostle Paul supported himself by making tents; hence, "tentmaker" is a synonym for *bivocational*. The Christian church was established throughout the Roman Empire by bivocational pastors. Many churches in America were established by Presbyterian pastors who also worked as school teachers, Baptist farmer-preachers like my great grandfather in North Carolina, and Methodist circuit riders (the ultimate in shared ministries).

An example is Parson Jonathan Fisher in Maine, in early New England, who in addition to being a preacher, also painted, made butter molds, rose conserve, picture frames, a cure for the sore throat of sweetened pine booze, and a tooth powder compounded of pulverized hardwood coal rendered savory by a few drops of oil of lavender. The Reverend Fisher made baskets and buttons, set window sashes, made chests and tables, decorated sleighs, and painted the names on ships and schooners. He built a horse trough for the village, turned out drumsticks at twenty-five cents a pair, and bound books.[2] Today between a quarter and one-third of American pastors are bivocational, that is, they have additional income beyond what their church provides.

Bivocational ministry has allowed me to pastor churches I otherwise couldn't have afforded to pastor, be very involved in helping raise our children, be a student twice, learn counseling and organizational management, write, travel, teach, and consult. The other things I've done have enriched my parish ministry and my life, allowed me to use the full range of my gifts, and helped make these the best and most productive years of my life.

Bivocational ministry can also be good for a church. It forces the laity to assume a greater portion of the responsibility for the ministry of the church. It allows a poorer church to do things other than raising money to pay the pastor—such as developing their spirituality, education, caring for one another, witness, and mission. It allows their pastor to experience the same realities of the world that laity experience. There's evidence to suggest that a bivocational pastor will have a longer tenure in a church than a poorly paid full-time pastor or a shared pastorate with one or more other churches.

It's good theology. It understands ministry to be mutual rather than hierarchical. It affirms that all are gifted and called for ministry, rather than one called to ministry while the others are only responsible for paying for that ministry. Our free-church theology preaches the priesthood of all believers in which everyone is to be a priest for the others. Our creation theology teaches that all of creation is sacred and all work that is true, just, and loving is ordained and sanctioned by God.

Seminaries have treated bivocational ministry as a historical footnote, an anachronism, an aberration, or a stop-gap measure. Seminaries today are full of teachers, nurses, engineers, homemakers, lawyers, retirees, business people who are on a second career track. The seminary should counsel students concerning the growing reality of part-time ministry, the costs and benefits, and help them look at their skills and previous vocational experience as gifts that could be paired with parish ministry in the rich tradition of the Apostle Paul. Every seminary should have a course in bivocational ministry. And they could work with the denomination in developing effective and practical theological education for lay people seeking to prepare for parish ministry in addition to whatever else they're doing with their lives.

We denominational people need to see tentmaking as an honorable and needed ministry, not as a band-aid, headache, or second-class ministry. We need to help churches see the pros and cons of this option and how it could work for them, help them research other employment options for a pastor in the area, and prepare a profile that highlights and defines this possibility. We need to look at our own denominational structures to identify possibilities of combining staff positions with local pastorates, as we've done in Iowa. We need to work with the seminaries and their students in making this a more viable and attractive option. We need to find ways of identifying gifted and committed lay people and calling them to consider lay pastoral ministry. Then we need to see that there is a quality educational program in place for them and a way to place them in appropriate settings when they're ready. We need to work with our national structures to make sure our manuals on the ministry and insurance and pension programs are a help and not a hindrance to developing part-time forms of ministry.

Some form of *shared ministry* between two or more churches is another viable and necessary option for churches that can't afford a full-time ministry. Robert Wilson's book, *The Multi-Church Parish*, is a helpful resource in understanding how these kinds of arrangements can work. Wilson's guess is that probably fifty thousand churches in America share a pastor and that a majority of Protestant pastors will experience such a combination.[3]

There are a several variations. Multiple churches can come under one roof, share a pastor, but maintain separate organizations and call it a *fed-*

eration. This can make economic sense but often has the disadvantages of people dropping out and organizational hassles (separate budgets, membership lists, committees).

Churches can form a partnership, or *yoke,* to share a pastor but do everything else separately. This can often feel polygamous with each church feeling short-changed, and adequately covering Sunday morning responsibilities in two or more places is difficult, if not impossible. It can work when the churches are similar or are continuing a long-standing yoke. I'm helping a church that can't quite afford full-time pastor explore another form of sharing. It would call a pastor almost full-time and share that person with a nearby larger church that would contract with the pastor for specific responsibilities (such as counseling or Christian education or administration).

My former colleague Charlotte Sickbert in southwest Iowa has helped two small churches work out a creative arrangement, which they call a *blended* church, which is somewhere between yoking and merging. They came together and took one name (United Church of Christ of Creston and Orient) and one set of bylaws. They are maintaining two buildings, a worship service and Sunday school in each place, one budget, one treasurer, two financial secretaries, two clerks, one council, seven joint committees (Pastor/Parish, Membership/Fellowship, Worship/ Music, Christian Education, Finance/Stewardship, Building/Grounds, Community/World Outreach), a memorial committee and nominating committee in each site, and one pastor.

Two options being encouraged less often are *merging* churches and *cooperative parishes* (several churches and a staff of pastors). Merged churches tend to result in one church the size of the larger of the former churches. Cooperative parishes have worked beautifully in some places, but they require very strong and enduring leadership, a staff that meshes well, and commonalty in needs and styles among the churches. They tend to break up when the organizing person leaves and the complex organizational structure is often burdensome. People miss having their own pastor.

Shared ministries are easier to arrange and may be more likely to last if they're composed of churches from the same denominational tradition. Shared ministries between churches of different denominations require an ecumenical and trusting spirit between both denominational leaders and local church leaders. The more carefully and thoughtfully spelled out the arrangement, the greater the likelihood of success. The inherited tradition of each church can be carried on more effectively when the churches alternate calling pastors of each denomination. The mainline denominations of Iowa have carefully devised an organizing document to help churches of different denominations develop a shared ministry. An ecumenical shared ministry within a community can be a powerful unifying force in that community.

Finding pastors for smaller and poorer churches and making good and lasting matches between them is more art than science, but it is possible and can work. For the future faithfulness and effectiveness of our churches, the art of placement is our most important work.

Pastoral Care of Pastors

Who is the pastor's pastor and, just as crucial, who's the pastor's family's pastor? A dilemma pastors and denominational staff struggle with is how can a pastor trust someone like me when I'm also involved in their placement. I suspect there will always be tension around that question. I find that being a local church pastor helps me be a better pastor for my peers.

Just as I do in my parish, I pastor my pastors by making pastoral calls on them at least once a year and in crisis times and with a phone ministry. Twice I've arrived to meet the new pastor before the moving van left. In 1985 at the age of 67, Sam Walton, founder of the Wal-Mart chain, was still visiting *every one of his 750 stores every year!* Pastoral calls on pastors are not just social chats but times to do crisis ministry, explore how ministry and life are for them, determine how I can assist their ministry, problem solve and possibility explore, affirm them and their ministry, deal with spiritual matters, and pray together.

Each of our pastors is encouraged to become part of a support group of pastors. In addition to general support groups, it might be helpful to form a group for new pastors with one or two wise and experienced mentors, or a group just for small church pastors. Support groups often are little more than "bitch and brag" sessions, which may feel good but don't help much. Support groups ought to meet at least monthly and include personal and pastoral sharing, a learning component, and some kind of worship.

The support group model that I encourage is the long-standing group I was part of in Vermont. We met monthly for a full day that included small talk and refreshments; a learning time that might be a case study, a presentation, or an outside resource person; going out to lunch together; free time; disciplined sharing in which each person had ten to fifteen minutes to share about his or her life and ministry; worship, usually with communion; happy hour; and dinner together. That group was crucial for me.

Pastoral care of pastors may include counseling, referral to a therapist, involvement with the family, advocacy for the pastor with his or her church(es) or the denomination, phone calls and notes, helping the pastor assess her or his ministry, sharing of resources, encouraging and enabling continuing education, spiritual direction, confrontation, cheerleading, helping pastors connect with one another, and helping the pastor leave when the time has come. Our pastoral care of pastors and their families is the time when we denominational helpers most approximate Jesus' footwashing ministry. A very helpful resource in thinking through these issues is Barbara Gilbert's Alban Institute book, *Who Ministers to Ministers?*[4]

Parish Relations

This is the third *P* in my work for the Iowa Conference. It's a catch-all category. One of the most important things we do with churches is be there for their celebrations. I'm there to help install or ordain new pastors, and whenever possible, for church anniversaries and special occasions. There are joyous times when we can help break ground for or dedicate a building, or burn the mortgage. Celebrating can include baptizing, confirming, marrying, and burying. It can be helping a pastor retire in grand and glorious fashion. It's a time for morale boosting and direction setting. We try to have someone from the conference at a church for a pastor's last service as their pastor—to appreciate what has been, to close that chapter of the pastor's and church's story, and to help the church move into their transition.

There are less celebratory times when we can be helpful. When there has been a tough church fight and we've worked at helping manage or resolve the conflict, we can often minister with a service of penance and reconciliation. When there's been a scandal, we can be present to help interpret, resolve, heal, and start over. Perhaps the least celebratory time is when a church makes the decision to dissolve and we're there to help with a service of closure. At these and similar times a pastor from the denomination is especially helpful. On these occasions we gain credibility with a congregation that will assist our ongoing ministry with them.

Perhaps the most important parish relations work we do is preventive and enabling work with a congregation. Providing stewardship and money management help can prevent financial crisis. Helping create and enable a pastoral relations committee can enable better communication, enrich ministry, and prevent or minimize conflict and a broken ministry. Helping a church build on their history, identify their resources, and plan for their future can build a more self-sufficient church. Using tools such as the morale inventory in this book can help a church assess and increase its self-esteem and morale.

Often difficulties develop in churches over differing expectations between a pastor and people. Numerous times I've used a very simple and helpful process for helping a church and pastor compare and contrast expectations. It works best when an outside helper manages the process. The whole church and the pastor (and spouse, if there is one) participate. Laity are divided into groups of seven or eight. Each group answers the same three questions on three sheets of newsprint:

- What do we expect of the pastor?
- What do we expect of ourselves?
- What do we *think* the pastor expects of us?

The pastor (and spouse) uses three sheets to answer:

- What does the pastor expect of himself or herself?
- What does the pastor expect of the laity?
- What does the pastor *think* the laity expect of the pastor?

The sheets are grouped and hung on the wall. Participants are encouraged to mill around comparing and contrasting what they say. And then the helper leads a discussion of what has surfaced.

One of the most useful guides for helping a congregation look at itself is *Handbook for Congregational Studies,* edited by Jackson Carroll, Carl Dudley, and William McKinney. It is a vast compilation of approaches to helping a church better understand itself and focuses on four areas:

- Identity, or the church's nature as revealed through its history, approach to the world, symbols and rituals, demographic makeup, and character;
- Context, or the social and physical environment in which it lives;
- Process, or the way it gathers information and operates;
- Program, or the activities the church pursues in carrying on its ministry and mission.

The handbook provides a wealth of material that the helper can use in guiding the church toward a clearer perception of itself.[5]

When a conflict is brewing or raging or when a scandal has reared its head are times when we're especially needed. Speed Leas of the Alban Institute offers some of the most helpful material on working with churches in conflict. His manual *Moving Your Church Through Conflict* provides very helpful analysis, theory, and strategies for working with conflicted churches.[6]

There is helpful material to help churches and pastors cope with scandals, particularly ones involving sexual misconduct. Marie Fortune's book *Is Nothing Sacred?* is particularly helpful.[7] Preventive work by the denomination and also the seminary is crucial. Students and pastors need help in understanding all the imperatives and nuances of pastoral ethics. In our denomination, every conference or association is urged to have a team of people trained and ready to immediately intervene when there is a charge of misconduct. Their task is to care for both the one(s) making the accusation and the accused, to investigate thoroughly the charges, to take whatever actions are appropriate, and to assist the church in moving through a difficult and dangerous situation.

The time will come when some churches will no longer be able to maintain a faithful ministry and should dissolve. Tragically, the American landscape is littered with shells of churches that have been closed—usually initiated by the denomination—*before that time came.* I've pastored one church—Warwick—that looked like it ought to close and one—Emmetsburg—that talked about closing. Both churches rebounded to have very vital and faithful ministries. Therefore, I would rather err in doing everything I can to help a church with any hope of faithful living find a way to maintain its life rather than facilitate a premature closure on the grounds of institutional efficiency.

If and when the time comes when a church chooses closure, there is much pastoral, prophetic, administrative, and priestly work to do. People have to be helped to find, and be assimilated into, another church home. Buildings and resources have to be disposed of as faithfully as possible. Legal work has to be done. And the memorial service and burial of a church is just as important as that of one of its human pillars.

We denominational leaders have another difficult piece of work to do on behalf of our small churches—advocacy. In each of our denominational structures there are fallacies, injustices, and inequities concerning small churches that need our passionate attention.

Salary issues need our serious and creative efforts. Do our denominations, especially those that claim to be covenantal, have the courage to develop an equitable salary system? Is there an effective way to subsidize salaries without creating unhealthy dependencies? How about subtle subsidies such as helping with insurance premiums, offering generous continuing education funds for pastors of small churches, and hiring them to do "piece work" at camps and on behalf of the denomination? How about offering program money to small churches as a carrot to move beyond maintenance, which might also provide additional money for the pastor?

We need to see that small church people are present, involved, and listened to at all levels of our denominational structures. When we make awards we need to make sure that small churches aren't competing under rules that are weighted against them. The American Baptists regularly make a national award for excellence and faithfulness to one of their small church pastors.

Pension systems need to be made equitable so that those pastors and spouses who choose to shepherd small flocks are not penalized after retirement. We need to make sure that all of our pastors have good health insurance. Small churches need our prophetic and impassioned voices raised on their behalf. More importantly they need us to see that *their* voices are heard as they speak on their own behalf.

Seminaries

Implicit in much that is written here are implications for seminaries—those institutions responsible for equipping learned, faithful, and effective pastors for our churches. Students need to know that most of them will serve in small churches. They need to know that this type of ministry is important and very different from the kind of ministry they've seen modeled in medium and large churches. They need to be challenged to consider small church ministry and to specifically prepare themselves for it. They need to be counseled to leave a small church alone if they aren't prepared to make a several-year, loving commitment to a small church.

They need specific course work in the dynamics of small churches; rural sociology (for those considering a rural setting); how to make bivocational and shared ministry arrangements work; theology that enables and addresses small churches; how to do worship, education, caring, mission, and administration in size-appropriate ways. Separate courses in these areas are needed, as well as a sensitivity to small church realities in the whole seminary curriculum.

Seminary staff need to be selected and trained with small church realities in mind. Persons with positive small church experience need to be well represented among the faculty. Quality programs need to be created and tailored for lay people preparing for lay pastoral ministry. All of this needs to be done in consultation with those who know small churches best—their pastors and lay people.

Some outside helpers have done more harm than good in small churches. Most of us are doing the best we know how. And our help is desperately needed. When it's offered in sensitive and appropriate ways, ways that are not self-serving and shaped by misconceived notions, our help will be appreciated and useful.

For Thought and Discussion

1. If you've been on the receiving end, when and how have outside helpers been most and least helpful to your church?
2. If you're a helper, when have you felt most and least helpful in your work with small churches?
3. If you were the church doctor, what would be your prescription for how seminaries might better equip pastors to serve in small churches?
4. If you were the church doctor, what would be your prescription for how your denomination might better serve small churches?

13. *Conclusion*

"The Rabbi's Gift" is a poignant story that points to alternative futures for small churches.[1] A monastery flourished in Europe throughout the seventeenth and eighteenth centuries. It had several branch houses and many monks. A wave of secularism swept the land during the nineteenth century and the monastery fell on hard times. One by one, the branch houses closed. One after another, the monks, enamored with other things, dropped away. Finally, five monks were left in the decaying mother house. The abbot and four others, all over seventy years of age, were the remnant. The future seemed hopeless.

There was a little hut deep in the woods surrounding the monastery. It was a hermitage or retreat house used by the rabbi from a nearby village. After many years of prayer and contemplation, the monks had an un-canny sense of when the rabbi was at his hermitage. One monk would whisper to another: "The rabbi is in the woods." As the abbot agonized over the fate of his dying order, it occurred to him that the rabbi might have some wisdom or advice that might help save the monastery.

The abbot found his way to the rabbi's door and was cordially invited in. After an exchange of pleasantries, the abbot shared the sad story of the monastery's decline. The rabbi could only commiserate. "I know how it is," he exclaimed. "The spirit has gone out of the people. It is the same in my town. Almost no one comes to the synagogue anymore. They are too busy with other matters." Then the rabbi and abbot wept together, read from the Torah, and spoke of deep things. When it was time to leave, the abbot thanked the rabbi for the opportunity to meet and visit. At the door, the abbot again asked in desperation: "Don't you have any piece of advice that might help save my dying order?"

The rabbi responded: "No, I'm sorry, I have no useful advice to offer. The only thing I can tell you is that *the Messiah is one of you.*"

When the abbot returned to the monastery, the other four monks gathered around and asked: "Well, what did the rabbi say?"

"He couldn't help," the abbot answered. "We just wept and read the Torah together. The only thing he did say, just as I was leaving—it was something mysterious—was that the Messiah is one of us. I have no idea what that means."

In the days, weeks, and months that followed, the old monks pondered this cryptic message and wondered whether it held any possible significance. The Messiah is one of us? Could he possibly have meant one of us old monks here at the monastery? It seems impossible. But if so, which of us? Could he have meant the abbot? Certainly, if he meant anyone, it would have to be Father Abbot. He's been our leader for so long. On the other hand, he might have meant Brother Thomas. Brother Thomas is certainly a holy man. Everyone knows he is a man of light.

You know he could not have meant Brother Elred! Elred gets crotchety at times. But come to think of it, even though he is a thorn in our side, when you think about it, Elred is virtually always right. Surely he could not have meant Brother Phillip. Phillip is so quiet and passive. But then, without fail, Phillip has a gift for somehow always being there when you need him. He just magically appears at your side. Maybe Phillip is the Messiah. One thing we do know, the rabbi did not mean me! That's certainly not possible. I'm just an ordinary person. But, what if he did mean me? Suppose I am the Messiah?

As they each contemplated in this manner—over weeks and months—the old monks began to treat each other with *extraordinary respect and affection,* on the off chance that one among them might be the Messiah. And on the off, off, off chance that each monk himself might be the Messiah, they began to treat themselves with extraordinary respect and appreciation.

Because the monastery was situated in a beautiful forest, people occasionally came to visit the monastery to picnic on its lawn, to wander along the paths in the surrounding woods, and now and then to meditate in its dilapidated chapel. As they did so, even without being conscious of it, they sensed this *aura of extraordinary respect and affection* that now began to surround the five old monks and seemed to radiate out from them to permeate the atmosphere of the place. There was something strangely attractive, even compelling, about it—something at the monastery that was missing in wider society. People came more and more frequently to the monastery and they brought their friends to picnic, play, and pray. Friends brought other friends.

Some of the younger visitors talked more and more with the old monks. After a while one asked to join the order, then another and another. Within a few years, the monastery was once again a thriving order, radiating faith, respect, and affection for all.

This is a marvelous parable that small churches and those who love and serve them can chew on and hopefully savor. So many of our small churches are remnants like that old, diminished monastery. Hope is gone, morale eroded, mission forgotten. Even respect and affection for one another and ourselves is taken for granted or lost. In a megaworld, we've lost the vision of how to be and why to be a microchurch.

We've not yet believed Carl Dudley:

> In a big world, the small church has remained intimate. In a fast world, the small church has been steady. In an expensive world, the small church has remained plain. In a complex world, the small church has remained simple. In a rational world, the small church has kept feelings. In a mobile world, the small church has been an anchor. In an anonymous world, the small church calls us by name.[2]

We've often tried to be what we are not and forgotten to be what we are. Loren Mead of the Alban Institute has reminded us that although the small church

> is *not* always beautiful, it is enough. Small is enough. It is enough for keeping on. It is enough for faithfulness. It takes only two or three, Jesus said. Most small churches have at least a dozen or two. Small is enough for holding lives and families together and for making a contribution to a community. It is enough for breaking bread and sharing wine, for wrestling with the scriptures, for calling one another to new life. It is enough for praying, for following Jesus. What else do we need?[3]

What else do we need? First, we need to believe what I have been saying throughout this book and for the last ten years, and that is that small churches are the right size to be and do all that God calls a church to be and do—without apology and without excuse. Second, we need to put into practice the size-appropriate strategies found throughout this book and in the other good material that is available.

Oh, and one other thing to remember. It is God who will revive us—if only we will cooperate:

> And the surviving *remnant* of the house of Judah [Iowa, Maine, Alabama, Canada, Oregon, or your place] shall again take root downward [in our biblical faith and history] and bear fruit upward [in faithful ministry and mission]; for out of Jerusalem [the inner-city, suburb, small town, and open country] shall go forth a *remnant*, and out of Mount Zion [out of faithful small churches] a band of survivors. The zeal of the lord will do this (2 Kings 19:30–31).

Amen.

Notes

Chapter 1.

1. William Simbro, "Last Day in the Life of a 132–Year-Old Albia Church," *Des Moines Register,* 1 January 1990, 2A.
2. T. S. Eliot, "Choruses from 'The Rock,'" *The Complete Poems and Plays, 1909–1950* (San Diego: Harcourt Brace Jovanovich, 1950), 101–2.
3. Carl S. Dudley, *Making the Small Church Effective* (Nashville: Abingdon Press, 1978), 48.

Chapter 2.

1. Walker Percy, *The Moviegoer* (New York: Popular Library, 1962), 13, italics added.
2. John Macquarrie, *Principles of Christian Theology* (New York: Charles Scribner's Sons, 1966), vii.
3. e. e. cummings, *95 poems* (New York: Harcourt, Brace & World, 1950), 77.
4. Williams, ibid., book-jacket endorsement.
5. Kurt H. Wolff, *The Sociology of Georg Simmel* (New York: Free Press, 1950), 115.

6. Dietrich Bonhoeffer, *Life Together*, trans. John W. Doberstein (New York: Harper & Row, 1954), 21.

7. Elizabeth O'Connor, *The New Community* (New York: Harper & Row, 1976), 58.

8. Paul D. Hanson, *The People Called* (San Francisco: Harper & Row, 1986), 1, 5–6.

9. Walter Brueggemann, *The Land* (Philadelphia: Fortress Press, 1977), 1.

Chapter 3.

1. Dudley, *Making the Small Church Effective*, 23.

2. Jackson W. Carroll, Carl S. Dudley, and William McKinney eds., *Handbook for Congregational Studies* (Nashville: Abingdon Press, 1986), 7.

3. Lyle E. Schaller, *The Small Church Is Different!* (Nashville: Abingdon Press, 1982), 11.

4. Schaller, "UMC: What's the Future of the Small-Church Denomination?" *Circuit Rider* 11, no. 11, (Dec. 1987–Jan. 1988): 8.

5. *1992 Year Book and Directory of the Christian Churches* (Disciples of Christ), ed. Robert L. Friedly (St. Louis: Christian Board of Publication, 1992), 130, no. 7:39.

6. Dudley, *Making the Small Church Effective*, 23.

7. E. F. Schumacher, *Small Is Beautiful* (New York: Harper & Row, 1973; reprint, Harper Colophon Books, 1975), 63.

8. Winthrop S. Hudson, *Religion in America* (New York: Charles Scribner's Sons, 1965), 411.

9. *Grassroots*, Winter 1978: 7.

10. Kirkpatrick Sale, *Human Scale* (New York: Coward, McCann, & Geoghegan, 1980), 64–65.

11. Ibid., 60.

12. Carl Dudley and Douglas Alan Walrath, *Developing Your Small Church's Potential* (Valley Forge, Pa.: Judson Press, 1988), 11–30.

13. Douglas A. Walrath, "Types of Small Congregations and Their Implications for Planning," in *Small Churches Are Beautiful*, ed. Jackson W. Carroll (San Francisco: Harper & Row, 1977), 42–44.

14. Dudley and Walrath, *Developing Your Small Church's Potential*, 38–45.

15. Lyle E. Schaller, *Looking in the Mirror* (Nashville: Abingdon Press, 1984), .15–23.

16. Arlin Rothauge, *Sizing Up a Congregation for New Member Ministry* (New York: The Episcopal Church Center).

17. Dudley, *Making the Small Church Effective*, 35.

18. Edwin H. Friedman, *Generation to Generation: Family Process in Church and Synagogue* (New York: The Guilford Press, 1985), 195.

19. Anthony G. Pappas, *Entering the World of the Small Church* (Washington,

D.C.: The Alban Institute, 1988), 9.

20. Paul O. Madsen, *The Small Church—Valid, Vital, Victorious* (Valley Forge, Pa.: Judson Press, 1975), 19–27.

21. Theodore H. Erickson, "New Expectations: Denominational Collaboration with Small Churches," in Carroll, *Small Churches Are Beautiful*, 160.

22. A. Paul Hare, *Handbook of Small Group Research* (New York: Free Press, 1962), 16.

23. Carl S. Dudley, "Small Churches Are Special," *JED Share* 8, no. 1 (Spring 1979): 5.

24. Carl S. Dudley, *Unique Dynamics of the Small Church* (Washington, D.C.: The Alban Institute, 1977), 20–21.

Chapter 5.

1. Dudley, *Making the Small Church Effective*, 36–37.

2. Bonhoeffer, *Life Together*, 21.

3. Annie Dillard, *Holy the Firm* (New York: Harper & Row, 1977), 55–59.

4. William H. Willimon and Robert L. Wilson, *Preaching and Worship in the Small Church* (Nashville: Abingdon Press, 1980), 65–66.

5. Gilbert Cope, ed., *Making the Building Serve the Liturgy* (London: A. R. Mowbray, 1962), 5.

6. Quoted in Miriam Therese Winter, *Preparing the Way of the Lord* (Nashville: Abingdon Press, 1978), 78.

7. Bonhoeffer, *Life Together*, 60–61, italics added.

8. Anthony Trollope, *Barchester Towers and the Warden* (New York: Random House, Modern Library, 1950), 252.

9. Henri J. M. Nouwen, *Creative Ministry* (Garden City, N.Y.: Doubleday, 1971; reprint, New York: Image Books, 1978), 35–39.

10. Bonhoeffer, *Life Together*, 62.

11. Ibid.

12. Willimon and Wilson, *Preaching and Worship in the Small Church*, 91.

13. Bonhoeffer, *Life Together*, 82.

14. Dudley, *Making the Small Church Effective*, 44–45.

Chapter 6.

1. Reprinted by permission from Peter L. Benson and Carolyn H. Eklin, *Effective Christian Education: A National Study of Protestant Congregations—A Summary Report on Faith, Loyalty, and Congregational Life.* © 1990 by Search Institute, Minneapolis, Minn.; 1–800–888–7828. All rights reserved.

2. John H. Westerhoff III, *Will Our Children Have Faith?* (New York: Seabury Press, 1976), 11.

3. Ibid., 82.

4. Ibid., 84, italics added.

5. Henri J. M. Nouwen, *Reaching Out* (Garden City, N.Y.: Doubleday, 1975), 46.
6. Westerhoff, *Will Our Children Have Faith?* 126.

Chapter 7.

1. Robert N. Bellah et al., *Habits of the Heart: Individualism and Commitment in American Life* (New York: Harper & Row, 1985), 28. © 1985 by The Regents of the University of California. Used by permission.
2. Ibid., 295.
3. Dudley, *Unique Dynamics of the Small Church*, 8.
4. Margery Williams, *The Velveteen Rabbit* (New York: Avon Books, 1975), 16–32.
5. O'Connor, *The New Community*, 58.
6. Abraham Maslow, "A Theory of Human Motivation," *Psychological Review* 50 (1943): 370–96.
7. Bonhoeffer, *Life Together*, 94, italics added.
8. Elizabeth O'Connor, *Eighth Day of Creation* (Waco, Tex.: Word Books, 1971), 17.
9. Stephen Kliewer, *How to Live with Diversity in the Local Church* (Washington, D.C.: The Alban Institute, 1987), 15f.
10. David L. Ostendorf, "Toward Wholeness and Community: Strategies for Pastoral and Political Response to the American Rural Crisis," *Word & World: Theology for Christian Ministry* 6, no. 1 (Winter 1986): 58.
11. O'Connor, *The New Community*, 9.
12. James C. Fenhagen, *Mutual Ministry* (New York: The Seabury Press, 1977), 14.
13. Henri J. M. Nouwen, *The Wounded Healer* (Garden City, N.Y.: Doubleday, 1972), 94.
14. Fenhagen, *Mutual Ministry*, 9.
15. Elie Wiesel, *Souls on Fire* (New York: Random House, 1972), 257.

Chapter 8.

1. James H. Cone, "The Servant Church," in *The Pastor as Servant*, ed. Earl E. Shelp and Ronald H. Sunderland (New York: The Pilgrim Press, 1986), 63–64. (This poem was circulated at a poor people's rally in New Mexico. The language has been made inclusive by the author.)
2. Dudley, *Making the Small Church Effective*, 85–86.
3. Carroll, Dudley, and McKinney, *Handbook for Congregational Studies*, 29–31. The following discussion of four types of orientation to mission—Activist, Civic, Evangelist, and Sanctuary—is from this book.
4. Kliewer, *How to Live with Diversity in the Local Church*, 21.
5. Carroll, Dudley, and McKinney, *Handbook for Congregational Studies*, 49.

6. Quoted in Edwin L. Earp, *The Rural Church Movement* (New York: Methodist Book Concern, 1914), 88.
7. Bill Briggs, *Faith Through Works* (Franconia, N.H.: Thorn Books, 1983), 28.
8. Ibid., 86.
9. Philip Hallie, *Lest Innocent Blood Be Shed* (New York: Harper & Row, 1979), 57.

Chapter 9.

1. Paul O. Madsen, *The Small Church—Valid, Vital, Victorious* (Valley Forge, Pa.: Judson Press, 1975), 10, 16.
2. Tom Peters and Nancy Austin, *A Passion for Excellence: The Leadership Difference* (New York: Random House, 1985), 232–34.
3. Schaller, *The Small Church Is Different!* 58–61.
4. Ibid., 86.
5. Daniel D. Biles, *Pursuing Excellence in Ministry* (Washington, D.C.: The Alban Institute, 1988), 18.
6. Fred D. Milligan, Jr., "Persevering and Preserving: An Inspired Partnership," *The Christian Ministry,* September-October 1991, 16f.
7. Douglas Alan Walrath, *Leading Churches Through Change* (Nashville: Abingdon Press, 1979).
8. C. Peter Wagner, *Your Church Can Grow* (Ventura, Calif.: Regal Books, 1984), 97.
9. Dudley, *Making the Small Church Effective,* 47.
10. Schaller, *The Small Church Is Different!* 10–12.
11. Lyle E. Schaller, *Growing Plans* (Nashville: Abingdon Press, 1983), 15–49.
12. Godfrey Sperling, Jr., "Reflections from Fritz," in "Washington Letter," *Christian Science Monitor,* 29 December 1980, A8.
13. Speed B. Leas, *Moving Your Church Through Conflict* (Washington, D.C.: The Alban Institute, 1985), 75–77.
14. Ibid., 19–22.
15. G. Douglass Lewis, *Resolving Church Conflicts* (San Francisco: Harper & Row, 1981), 49–69. The following discussion summarizes Lewis's seven principles for managing conflict.
16. Dudley, *Unique Dynamics of the Small Church,* 20.
17. Lyle E. Schaller, *Survival Tactics in the Parish* (Nashville: Abingdon Press, 1977), 157.

Chapter 10.

1. Lyle E. Schaller, *Getting Things Done* (Nashville: Abingdon Press, 1989), 192.
2. Peters and Austin, *A Passion for Excellence,* 289.

3. Steve Burt, *Activating Leadership in the Small Church* (Valley Forge, Pa.: Judson Press, 1988), 28–33.

4. Lyle E. Schaller, Foreword to Robert L. Wilson, *The Multi-Church Parish* (Nashville: Abingdon Press, 1989), 11.

5. Robert W. Lynn and James W. Fraser, "Images of the Small Church in American History," in Carroll, *Small Churches Are Beautiful,* 6–7.

6. Lyle E. Schaller, *Hey, That's Our Church!* (Nashville: Abingdon Press, 1978), 96.

7. Biles, *Pursuing Excellence in Ministry,* 65.

8. Ibid., 53.

9. Ibid., 79–81.

Chapter 11.

1. "New York Garbage Rolls Through Iowa," *Des Moines Register,* 5 June 1990, 1.

2. Quoted in *United Church of Christ A.D. 1980,* May 1980, 30–31. Excerpted from an address given by Chief Seattle in 1854 to an assembly of tribes preparing to sign treaties.

3. C. Dean Freudenberger, *Food for Tomorrow?* (Minneapolis: Augsburg Publishing House, 1984), 15–16, 21, 27, 31.

4. Brueggemann, *The Land,* 3, 6.

5. Wendell Berry, "The Work of Culture," Lecture for the Iowa Humanities Board (1988), 4.

6. Douglas Meeks, "The Farm Crisis and the Rural Economy in the Perspective of God's Economy," *Prism: A Theological Forum for the UCC,* Spring 1987, 80.

7. Carol Bly, *Letters from the Country* (New York: Harper & Row, 1981), 6.

8. Ibid., 153–54.

9. Charles Otis Gill and Gifford Pinchot, *The Country Church* (New York: Macmillan, 1913), 53.

10. Ibid., 3.

11. Earp, *The Rural Church Movement,* 85–86.

12. Gill and Pinchot, *The Country Church,* 4.

13. Ibid., 46–47.

14. Ibid., 48.

15. Gary E. Farley, "Associational Involvement—The Director of Missions and a Field of Churches," in *Field of Churches,* ed. Thomas E. Sykes (Atlanta: Home Mission Board, 1989), 82–90. (The language has been made inclusive by the author.)

16. Kenyon L. Butterfield, *The Country Church and the Rural Problem* (Chicago: University of Chicago Press, 1911), 75.

17. Ibid., 92–93.

18. Edmund deS. Brunner, *Church Life in the Rural South* (New York: George H. Doran, 1923), 10, italics added.

Chapter 12.

1. Robert G. Kemper, "Dilemmas of Pastoral Leadership in the Nineties," *Colleague* (Dec. 1990–Jan. 1991): 4.
2. Mary Ellen Chase, *Jonathan Fisher, Maine Parson, 1768–1847* (New York: Macmillan, 1948), 129.
3. Robert L. Wilson, *The Multi-Church Parish* (Nashville: Abingdon Press, 1989).
4. Barbara G. Gilbert, *Who Ministers to Ministers?* (Washington, D.C.: The Alban Institute, 1987).
5. Carroll, Dudley, and McKinney, *Handbook for Congregational Studies.*
6. Speed B. Leas, *Moving Your Church Through Conflict* (Washington, D.C.: The Alban Institute, 1985).
7. Marie M. Fortune, *Is Nothing Sacred?* (San Francisco: Harper & Row, 1989).

Chapter 13.

1. M. Scott Peck, *The Different Drum: Community Making and Peace* (New York: Simon and Schuster, 1987), 13–15.
2. Dudley, *Making the Small Church Effective,* 176.
3. Loren Mead, "Judicatory Interventions Can Help Small Congregations," in *New Possibilities for Small Churches,* ed. Douglas Alan Walrath (New York: The Pilgrim Press, 1983), 87.

Selected Bibliography

Bellah, Robert N., et al. *Habits of the Heart: Individualism and Commitment in American Life*. New York: Harper & Row, 1985.

Bernanos, Georges. *The Diary of a Country Priest*. New York: Macmillan, 1937.

Berry, Wendell. "The Work of Culture." Lecture for the Iowa Humanities Board, 1988.

Bettleheim, Bruno. *A Home for the Heart*. New York: Knopf, 1974.

Biles, Daniel D. *Pursuing Excellence in Ministry*. Washington, D.C.: The Alban Institute, 1988.

Blunk, Henry A. *Smaller Church Mission Guide*. Philadelphia: Geneva Press, 1978.

Bly, Carol. *Letters from the Country*. New York: Harper & Row, 1981.

Bonhoeffer, Dietrich. *Life Together*. Translated by John W. Doberstein. New York: Harper & Row, 1954.

Briggs, Bill. *Faith Through Works*. Franconia, N.H.: Thorn Books, 1983.

Brueggemann, Walter. *The Land*. Philadelphia: Fortress Press, 1977.

Brunner, Edmund deS. *Church Life in the Rural South*. New York: George H. Doran, 1923.

Burt, Steve. *Activating Leadership in the Small Church*. Valley Forge, Pa.: Judson Press, 1988.

Burt, Steve, and Hazel Roper. *Raising Small Church Esteem*. Washington, D.C.: The Alban Institute, 1992.

Butterfield, Kenyon L. *The Country Church and the Rural Problem*. Chicago: University of Chicago Press, 1911.

Carroll, Jackson W., ed. *Small Churches Are Beautiful*. San Francisco: Harper & Row, 1977.

Carroll, Jackson W., Carl S. Dudley, and William McKinney, eds. *Handbook for Congregational Studies*. Nashville: Abingdon Press, 1986.

Ceynar, Marvin E. *Healing the Heartland: Nonviolent Social Change and the American Rural Crisis of the 1980s and 1990s*. Cedar Falls, Ia.: Heartland Promotions, 1989.

Chase, Mary Ellen. *Jonathan Fisher, Maine Parson, 1768–1847*. New York: Macmillan, 1948.

Cook, Walter L. *Send Us a Minister . . . Any Minister Will Do*. Rockland, Me.: Courier-Gazette, 1978.

Cooley, Charles Horton. *Social Organization*. New York: Charles Scribner's Sons, 1929.

Cope, Gilbert, ed. *Making the Building Serve the Liturgy*. London: A. R. Mowbray, 1962.

Costas, Orlando E. *The Integrity of Mission*. New York: Harper & Row, 1979.

Dillard, Annie. *Holy the Firm*. New York: Harper & Row, 1977.

Dudley, Carl S. *Making the Small Church Effective*. Nashville: Abingdon Press, 1978.

———. *Unique Dynamics of the Small Church*. Washington, D.C.: The Alban Institute, 1977.

Dudley, Carl, and Douglas Alan Walrath. *Developing Your Small Church's Potential*. Valley Forge, Pa.: Judson Press, 1988

Earp, Edwin L. *The Rural Church Movement*. New York: Methodist Book Concern, 1914.

Elliott, John Y. *Our Pastor Has an Outside Job*. Valley Forge, Pa.: Judson Press, 1980.

Fenhagen, James C. *Mutual Ministry*. New York: The Seabury Press, 1977.

Foltz, Nancy T., ed. *Religious Education in the Small Membership Church*. Birmingham, Ala.: Religious Education Press, 1990.

Fortune, Marie M. *Is Nothing Sacred?* San Francisco: Harper & Row, 1989.

Freudenberger, C. Dean. *Food for Tomorrow?* Minneapolis: Augsburg Publishing House, 1984.

Friedman, Edwin H. *Generation to Generation: Family Process in Church and Synagogue*. New York: The Guilford Press, 1985.

Gilbert, Barbara G. *Who Ministers to Ministers?* Washington, D.C.: The Alban Institute, 1987.

Gill, Charles Otis, and Gifford Pinchot. *The Country Church*. New York: Macmillan, 1913.

Griggs, Donald I., and Judy McKay Walther. *Christian Education in the Small Church*. Valley Forge, Pa.: Judson Press, 1988.

Hallie, Philip P. *Lest Innocent Blood Be Shed*. New York: Harper & Row, 1979.

Hanson, Paul D. *The People Called*. San Francisco: Harper & Row, 1986.

Hare, A. Paul. *Handbook of Small Group Research*. New York: Free Press, 1962.

Hassinger, Edward W., John S. Holik, and J. Kenneth Benson. *The Rural Church: Learning from Three Decades of Change*. Nashville: Abingdon Press, 1988.

Hawley, Amos H. *Human Ecology*. New York: Ronald Press, 1950.

Henrichsen, Margaret. *Seven Steeples*. Boston: Houghton Mifflin, 1953.

Hopewell, James F. *Congregation: Stories and Structures*. Philadelphia: Fortress Press, 1987.

Hudson, Winthrop S. *Religion in America*. New York: Charles Scribner's Sons, 1965.

Judy, Marvin T. *From Ivy Tower to Village Spire*. Dallas: Southern Methodist University Printing Office, 1984.

Kliewer, Stephen. *How to Live with Diversity in the Local Church*. Washington, D.C.: The Alban Institute, 1987.

Kraemer, Hendrik. *A Theology of the Laity*. Philadelphia: Westminster Press, 1958.

Learning in the Small Church. Atlanta: John Knox Press, 1976.

Leas, Speed B. *Moving Your Church Through Conflict*. Washington, D.C.: The Alban Institute, 1985.

Leas, Speed, and Paul Kittlaus. *Church Fights*. Philadelphia: Westminster Press, 1973.

Lewis, G. Douglass. *Resolving Church Conflicts*. San Francisco: Harper & Row, 1981.

Lowery, James L., Jr., ed. *Case Histories of Tentmakers*. Wilton, Conn.: Morehouse-Barlow, 1976.

Madsen, Paul O. *The Small Church—Vital, Valid, Victorious*. Valley Forge, Pa.: Judson Press, 1975.

Maslow, Abraham H. "A Theory of Human Motivation," *Psychological Review* 50 (1943): 370–96.

Mathieson, Moira B. *The Shepherds of the Delectable Mountains: The Story of the Washington County Mission Program*. Cincinnati: Forward Movement Publications, 1979.

Meeks, Pauline Palmer. *Ministries with Children in Small Churches*. Philadelphia: Geneva Press, 1975.

Millar, William R., ed. *American Baptist Quarterly* 9 (June 1990).

Nouwen, Henri J. M. *Creative Ministry*. Garden City, N.Y.: Doubleday, 1971. Reprint. New York: Image Books, 1978.

———. *Reaching Out*. Garden City, N.Y.: Doubleday, 1975.

———. *The Wounded Healer*. Garden City, N.Y.: Doubleday, 1972.

O'Connor, Elizabeth. *Eighth Day of Creation.* Waco, Tex.: Word Books, 1971.

———. *The New Community.* New York: Harper & Row, 1976.

Olmstead, Michael S. *The Small Group.* New York: Random House, 1959.

Pappas, Anthony G. *Entering the World of the Small Church.* Washington, D.C.: The Alban Institute, 1988.

———. *Money, Motivation, and Mission in the Small Church.* Valley Forge, Pa.: Judson Press, 1989.

Peck, M. Scott. *The Different Drum: Community Making and Peace.* New York: Simon and Schuster, 1987.

Peters, Tom, and Nancy Austin. *A Passion for Excellence: The Leadership Difference.* New York: Random House, 1985.

Plunkett, Sir Horace. *The Rural Life Problem in the United States.* New York: Macmillan, 1910.

Ray, David R. *Small Churches Are the Right Size.* New York: The Pilgrim Press, 1982.

Rothauge, Arlin. *Sizing Up a Congregation for New Member Ministry.* New York: The Episcopal Church Center.

Sale, Kirkpatrick. *Human Scale.* New York: Coward, McCann, & Geoghegan, 1980.

Schaller, Lyle E. *Getting Things Done.* Nashville: Abingdon Press, 1989.

———. *Growing Plans.* Nashville: Abingdon Press, 1983.

———. *Hey, That's Our Church!* Nashville: Abingdon Press, 1978.

———. *Looking in the Mirror.* Nashville: Abingdon Press, 1984.

———. *The Small Church Is Different!* Nashville: Abingdon Press, 1982.

———. *Survival Tactics in the Parish.* Nashville: Abingdon Press, 1977.

Schirer, Marshall E., and Mary Anne Forehand. *Cooperative Ministries: Hope for Small Churches.* Valley Forge, Pa.: Judson Press, 1984.

Schmidt, Karla. *Renew the Spirit of My People: A Handbook for Ministry in Times of Rural Crisis.* Des Moines: Prairiefire Rural Action, 1987.

Schumacher, E. F. *Small Is Beautiful.* New York: Harper & Row, 1973. Reprint. Harper Colophon Books, 1975.

Shelp, Earl E., and Ronald H. Sunderland. *The Pastor as Servant.* New York: The Pilgrim Press, 1986.

Slattery, Patrick. *Caretakers of Creation: Farmers Reflect on Their Faith and Work.* Minneapolis: Augsburg Publishing House, 1991.

Smith, Rockwell D. *Rural Ministry and the Changing Community.* Nashville: Abingdon Press, 1971.

Sykes, Thomas E., ed. *Field of Churches.* Atlanta: Home Mission Board, 1989.

Vidich, Arthur, and Joseph Bensman. *Small Town in Mass Society.* Princeton: Princeton University Press, 1958.

Wagner, C. Peter. *Your Church Can Grow.* Ventura, Calif.: Regal Books, 1984.

Walrath, Douglas Alan. *Leading Churches Through Change.* Nashville: Abingdon Press, 1979.

————. *New Possibilities for Small Churches.* New York: The Pilgrim Press, 1983.

Westerhoff, John H., III. *Will Our Children Have Faith?* New York: The Seabury Press, 1976.

White, Phyllis C. *The Broadly Graded Group: A Manual for Children in the Church.* Memphis: Board of Christian Education, Cumberland Presbyterian Church, 1981.

Wiesel, Elie. *Souls on Fire.* New York: Random House, 1972.

Williams, Margery. *The Velveteen Rabbit.* New York: Avon Books, 1975.

Willimon, William H., and Robert L. Wilson. *Preaching and Worship in the Small Church.* Nashville: Abingdon Press, 1980.

Wilson, Robert L. *The Multi-Church Parish.* Nashville: Abingdon Press, 1989.

Winter, Miriam Therese. *Preparing the Way of the Lord.* Nashville: Abingdon Press, 1978.

Wolff, Kurt H. *The Sociology of Georg Simmel.* New York: Free Press, 1950.

Subject Index

Scripture Index